# 1980 Summer Emplo
## of the Unite

# 1980
# Summer
# Employment
# Directory
## of the
## United States

### Edited by
### Sally Davidow
### Lynne Lapin
### Leslie Burke Wilson

Distributed in England (£4.95)
by Vacation-Work
9 Park End Street
Oxford, England

Writer's Digest Books
9933 Alliance Road/Cincinnati, Ohio 45242

## Note to Summer Employers:

If you would like to list your business as a summer employer in the 1981 edition of *Summer Employment Directory*, write us a brief note describing the openings you will be having in 1981 and how prospective employees should apply. Annual cost of the listing is $20 (subject to change, however). Send the note to: Summer Employment Directory, New Listing Department, 9933 Alliance Rd., Cincinnati, Ohio 45242. Or call us with your information at 513/984-0717.

Summer Employment Directory is published by
Writer's Digest Books
9933 Alliance Road
Cincinnati, Ohio 45242

Publisher/Editorial Director: Richard Rosenthal

Managing Editor: Douglas Sandhage

Assistant to the Managing Editor: Connie Achabal

International Standard Serial Number 0081-9352
International Standard Book Number 0-89879-005-0 (paperback)
                                    0-89879-006-9 (cloth)
Library of Congress Catalog Card Number 54-33991
Copyright 1979 by Writer's Digest Books

# Preface

Finding a summer job is usually one of the most frustrating undertakings that a person can encounter. Word of job openings usually comes by word of mouth, through newspaper advertisements, or by a notice posted in a public place by the employer. But in all three cases mentioned, the exact details of the job, the payment, and how to go about applying are not usually very clear and thus the prospective employee may not apply. Also, through these sources the prospective employee *only* gets a *local* overview of the job opportunities.

That's why we publish *Summer Employment Directory of the United States (SED)*. Job openings are clearly defined, payment is given, instructions are precise on how to apply, job dates are specified, and facts on housing and transportation are provided. AND, job opportunities are given from all across the country. Each employer who lists in *SED* is told that the book is sold nationwide and that they may receive applicants from all over. So, almost all are looking for the *best possible candidates* regardless of where the person lives.

*SED*—because of the multitude of the types of jobs listed—spells ADVENTURE. There are jobs at fishing lodges; summer theaters; with expedition services—including caving, horseback, and whitewater trips; at resort businesses in the national parks; at camps of all sorts; with amusement parks—including the *best* parks in the country; with dude ranches; and with temporary services located in every state in the union.

*SED* also spells EXPERIENCE, SALARY, AND A GOOD TIME.

Now is the time to start applying for these opportunities. Most of the listings in *SED* indicate a deadline date for receiving applications; some as early as December 1979, most in the spring of 1980. Timing is a very big key to getting a job. A quick read of the few articles in the front of *SED* will help you in putting together your resume and application and, if a personal interview is required, will help you in preparing your presentation. A chart is also included that gives you a roundup of approximately how many jobs are open in each state based on those listings published in *SED*.

Good luck and enjoy your summer.

—Sally Davidow

# Contents

## Job Hunting

Know what you're getting into. This article explains what information you can find in *SED* and lists abbreviations we've used throughout.

Sleeping with a copy of *SED* under your pillow won't get you a job. However, reading this article will help you to write your letter of application, prepare your resume, and tell you how to conduct yourself during an interview if one is required.

Wouldn't you like to know what employers say about job applicants? Summer employers speak out on applicants and employees.

Competition is heavy, but Uncle Sam offers some of the most interesting and well-paying jobs in the U.S. each summer. Find out how to apply for most of them.

Some states or areas have more job openings than others. To get an idea on how many job openings there are in each state—based on the information supplied in the listings in this book—check the map. You'll fine some real surprises (like Wisconsin and Pennsylvania) and some things you probably already knew (like the majority of the summer jobs listed in *SED* are in the far West and the far East).

(1) *Summer Employment Directory* will offer a January 1980 update of the book which will contain approximately 50 more employers looking for summer help. These listings came to us too late to be included in this edition. (2) If you know of an employer not listed in *SED* that you think might like to be, let us know. If the employer lists in the 1981 edition, you get a free book. (3) *SED* pays for short evaluations of your summer work with an employer listed in the 1980 edition. If the evaluation is published, you get $2.

## The Jobs

Almost 900 summer employers from all over the U.S., plus a handful in Canada, Puerto Rico, and the West Indies. We list amusement parks, dude ranches, national parks, summer camps, carnivals, office temporary personnel agencies, summer theaters, and many other employers looking for summer staff.

Businesses and organizations with locations across the country. Even though their headquarters may be far away, these employers could have a job opening around the corner from you.

More job listings but which came in to our office too late (right at presstime) to be included under the state in which they are located.

## Other Opportunities

Find experience related to your course of study or future career plans here.

Many of the employers listed in *SED* will consider hiring you if you live outside of the U.S. But before applying to any of them, read this piece carefully. There are forms you must complete before you get to the States.

# Using Your Summer Employment Directory

*Summer Employment Directory* is divided into three parts. The first part offers articles that give you basic information on how to apply for a job, the second part lists actual job openings in all parts of the United States for the summer of 1980, and the third presents other opportunities for a rewarding summer.

The articles tell you how to write a letter of application, what to put in your resume, and how to prepare for an interview. They also give inside tips from employers on what they look for in an applicant and information on summer jobs in the federal government.

The second and largest part of *SED* contains state-by-state listings of job openings in the U.S.—and some in Canada—in resorts, amusement parks, offices, summer theaters, summer camps, restaurants and many other businesses that need help in the summer. After the listings by state is a U.S.A. section for organizations or firms with nationwide locations.

Within each section, jobs are categorized according to the type of business or organization offering the job. The major categories are Business and Industry; Commercial Attractions; National Parks; Expeditions, Guide Trips; Resorts, Ranches, Restaurants, Lodging; Summer Camps; and Summer Theaters. Don't limit your search to one category. For instance, if you want to cook, you should look at the listings under the subhead Resorts, Ranches, Restaurants, Lodging; but you can also find jobs for cooks under Summer Camps, National Parks and Commercial Attractions.

Under Other Opportunities, the last part of *SED*, are listed internships and work/learn programs that can provide you with important, preprofessional experience.

The information in each listing comes directly from the employers themselves. Look for these details:
- Name of the company, organization or facility, and its location
- Type of positions open; the number of openings often are given also
- Whether college credit may be received for work
- Salaries; many employers also give bonuses to those who stay the entire season
- Whether the employer supplies room and board
- Dates of employment; pay particular attention to end-of-season dates, as they may conflict with other schedules you may have
- Name and address to send application; this may differ from the name and location given at the top of the listing
- How to apply; unless stated otherwise, send a letter and resume
- Skills or degree of education that may be required to fill the job

Buying a copy of *Summer Employment Directory* won't guarantee that you'll get a job. However, we do guarantee that all employers listed have indicated that

The following are some common abbreviations used in the book and also the U.S. Postal Service's two-letter state codes used in the listing addresses:

## Abbreviations

| | | | |
|---|---|---|---|
| ACA | American Camping Association | HI | Hawaii |
| ALS | Advanced Life Saving | IA | Iowa |
| | | ID | Idaho |
| ARC | American Red Cross | IL | Illinois |
| | | IN | Indiana |
| BUNAC | British University North American Club | KS | Kansas |
| | | KY | Kentucky |
| | | LA | Louisiana |
| CAA | Camp Archery Association | MA | Massachusetts |
| | | MD | Maryland |
| CIT | Counselor-in-training | ME | Maine |
| | | MI | Michigan |
| EMT | Emergency Medical Technician | MN | Minnesota |
| | | MO | Missouri |
| LIT | Leader-in-training | MS | Mississippi |
| LPN | Licensed Practical Nurse | MT | Montana |
| | | NC | North Carolina |
| LSC | Life Saving Certificate | ND | North Dakota |
| | | NE | Nebraska |
| NRA | National Riflery Association | NH | New Hampshire |
| | | NJ | New Jersey |
| RN | Registered Nurse | NM | New Mexico |
| SCI | Small Craft Instructor | NV | Nevada |
| | | NY | New York |
| SLS | Senior Life Saving | OH | Ohio |
| WSI | Water Safety Instructor | OK | Oklahoma |
| | | OR | Oregon |
| | | PA | Pennsylvania |
| | | PR | Puerto Rico |

## State Codes

| | | | |
|---|---|---|---|
| | | RI | Rhode Island |
| | | SC | South Carolina |
| AK | Alaska | SD | South Dakota |
| AL | Alabama | TN | Tennessee |
| AR | Arkansas | TX | Texas |
| AZ | Arizona | UT | Utah |
| CA | California | VA | Virginia |
| CO | Colorado | VI | Virgin Islands |
| CT | Connecticut | VT | Vermont |
| DC | District of Columbia | WA | Washington |
| DE | Delaware | WI | Wisconsin |
| FL | Florida | WV | West Virginia |
| GA | Georgia | WY | Wyoming |

they want to be in the book and are thus actively looking for summer/seasonal help. All await your application.

If you obtain a job by using *SED*, we'd appreciate hearing about it. Tell us what approach you used in getting accepted, how you liked or disliked the job, whether or not the listing represented the job accurately, and any advice you might want to offer on making the book better. Send this information to Editor, *Summer Employment Directory*, 9933 Alliance Rd., Cincinnati OH 45242.

Also, if you are aware of seasonal/summer employers who are not listed in *SED*, please let us know. We will then contact the employer with one of our job questionnaires to see if he or she would like to be listed in our 1980 book. (See the special *SED* offer at the end of this book.)

# Applying for a Job

Most of the employers listed in *Summer Employment Directory* require you to write a cover letter and attach a resume to apply for a job. Some also will want to interview you either over the phone or in person. The letter, resume and interview weigh heavily on your chances of being hired. It is important therefore to approach all three in a professional manner.

## The Cover Letter

Introduce yourself to the employer in your cover letter. Remember that the letter you write will be his or her first impression of you and that it must reflect your most positive qualities in a succinct and imaginative way. You must inspire the employer to take special notice of your application and make him want to read your resume to find out more about you.

What information should you include in a letter? First, keep in mind that you're presenting your qualifications, not the story of your life. Do not waste the employer's time with irrelevant biographical data or by repeating all of the information you have presented on your resume. However, if there is any one particular qualification that you think makes you an outstanding candidate, display it prominently on both the letter and resume. For example, if you are applying for a job as a counselor at a tennis camp and you are the current Amateur Athletic Union champ, don't be shy about letting the employer know who you are.

In your letter, you should introduce yourself, explain why you are writing, and invite the employer to consider your qualifications and contact you. Include your name, address and telephone number on the letter as well as on the resume.

The tone of your letter does not have to be stiffly formal; learn to be yourself. Use your imagination to arouse the curiosity of the reader to learn more about you. Be careful with humor, however; it's better to be deadly serious than to try to be funny and fail. Unless you're applying to be a clown, keep your feet on the ground and your jokes to yourself.

Read your letter critically. Do you make yourself sound shy or unsure of yourself? Are you too boastful and brash? How should you present yourself? Remember not to let yourself be defensive, as this person did:

I'd like to apply for the job of cabin counselor I saw listed in

> *SED.* I don't have any experience as a counselor, but I think I could do the job if you gave me a chance. I'm not sure what I'm qualified to do, but if you don't think I would be a good counselor maybe you could give me a job in maintenance or in the kitchen.

Why should the employer trust the care of children to such a sniveling coward? Be positive! Before you write your letter, think carefully about the job you want and consider what qualities the employer might need in an employee. Then, think of the reasons why you would be the *best* person to fill those needs. Convince yourself. Then, sit down at the typewriter and convince the employer:

> I'm writing to apply for the job of cabin counselor I saw listed in *SED.* I love children and, as the oldest of four in our family, have had lifelong experience in caring for them. I have many special interests and abilities, listed on my resume, that I want to share, and I am sure that I could be a good addition to your counseling staff.

Don't use a mass-produced cover letter. Instead, typewrite a separate letter for each job. Use white bond or good quality typing paper (no flowers, toadstools or happy faces, please!) and a standard business-letter format. Keep a carbon of each letter you send so that you will have an accurate record of whom you've contacted. Read your letter over carefully before sending it. Bad grammar and spelling—especially if you misspell the name of the employer or his company—will tell the reader you are careless with details.

## The Resume

There is no one best format for a resume, but all good resumes begin with the applicant's name, address, telephone number and date of birth. The rest of the resume should be divided into at least five other categories: education, work experience, special interests, personal data and references.

*Education:* List your most important educational experiences—best subjects, college major, activities and honors. If you've finished or are nearly done with college, drop any mention of your high school days from your resume unless the information relates directly to the job you want. For example, it is all right to say you were president of the high school ecology club if you're applying to be a scientific aid for the Environmental Protection Agency. You don't have to report grade point averages or class standings if they are not above average.

*Work experience:* This is a problem for those writing a first resume; obviously, they have little work experience to report. In that case, stress your abilities. You can also include volunteer work and major tasks you have tackled at home, such as painting the house. Let the employer know you haven't been idle, even if no one has been paying you for your work.

Persons who have had jobs should list the most recent first. List employers' names, addresses and the dates of your employment, and describe your duties on each job briefly. You may give details about your military experiences here or put them in a separate section.

*Special interests:* Let your individuality show through. List hobbies, favorite leisure and sports activities, and organizations you belong to outside of school.

*References:* List at least three persons not related to you who can testify to your good character and conscientiousness; former employers or coworkers are best. Be sure to get permission from your references before you use their names. List each individual's name, address and phone number so that the employer can easily contact the reference.

*Personal data:* Use your judgment. Employers usually don't need to know your height and weight unless the job you're applying for is unusually physical or requires a slender appearance. Obviously, being slim is an asset if you want to be an exercise instructor at a weight-reducing camp or a canoe guide along a whitewater river. Let the employer know you're in excellent health if the job requires stamina, and also let him know if you have any limitations or handicaps that might interfere with your work.

Your marital status may or may not be important to the employer, but you should mention it. The employer does not need to know your parents' occupations or other personal data about your family. You may include a photo of yourself, if you have a good quality, wallet-size portrait; but it's better to send no photo at all than a snapshot of you romping with the family dog. The employer should not require you to send a photograph, since such a requirement has often been used to discriminate against racial minorities.

If you're applying for more than one job, you don't have to retype your resume every time you apply. A good, *clean* photocopy on standard paper stock is acceptable. Standard paper stock is white and similar to bond or good quality typing paper. Don't use a copier that copies on a waxy or cheap-looking, off-color paper. A copying or duplicating service should be able to give you 20 copies for around $2. Coin-operated copiers generally give you less than quality photocopies and are usually more expensive.

If you need 100 copies or more, consider having your resume printed by an offset process. Your resumes can be printed on any kind of paper, including the highest-quality bond or even a colored paper stock. The copying service will need a clean copy with no obvious corrections typed on white paper (no onionskin) using a new ribbon. Use an electric typewriter if one is available. The copying service will make a photographic plate of your resume and use the plate to print copies in the same way most newspapers and magazines are printed. Cost for the 100 copies should only be $5-8.

When mailing your resume and letter to the employer, it is courteous to enclose a stamped, self-addressed envelope for his reply.

## The Interview

Not every employer listed in this book will want to interview you before hiring you, because of the distance involved in many cases. Those who do require an interview may rely on his or her impression of you in the interview far more than on what you have written in your letter or resume.

Most interviewees have two major questions about the interview process: What should I say, and what should I wear?

Don't go into an interview without preparation, planning *only* to answer the questions the interviewer asks. The interviewer may not have a clear idea of what he wants to say, and silence is deadly during an interview. Find out whatever you can about the organization you may be working for before the interview, and don't be shy about displaying your knowledge: "Your theater's production of 'Under the

# Sample Resume

RESUME

Sinclair Lewis

123 First Avenue                                          telephone 123/456-7890
Cincinnati, Ohio 45299

PERSONAL DATA: Born 10/1/58, single, excellent health.

EDUCATION: Will complete third year of college at State University this spring, majoring in education in biology. Working toward teaching biology in secondary school level. Maintaining a 3.2 grade point average. 80% of tuition paid by athletic scholarship. Lettered in tennis; also member of Alpha Beta Gamma social fraternity and the university's ecology club.

WORK EXPERIENCE: June 6 to August 12, 1978, tennis counselor at Green Woods Summer Camp in Oshkosh, Maine. Responsible for giving tennis lessons to children ranging from 9 to 14 years of age. Also organized and supervised in-camp tennis tournament. Assisted camp athletic director to care for camp's equipment.

September 8, 1977 to May 15, 1978, worked part-time in campus book store. Unpacked new books and kept them in stock on shelves. After first year was made assistant to store manager.

PERSONAL INTERESTS: Enjoy golf and many other sports. Jog three miles a day. Have been active in Sierra Club and other organizations involved in saving natural resources.

REFERENCES:

Ms. Jane Gray, Manager, Campus Bookstore, 111 East West Street, Cincinnati, Ohio 45299; 123/456-7890.

Mr. L. John Silver, Director, Green Woods Summer Camp, Box 1, Oshkosh, Maine 12345; 123/456-7890.

Dr. Clara Barton, Professor of Biology, 123 Taft Hall, State University, Cincinnati, Ohio 45299; 123/456-7890.

Dr. Joseph Blow, Professor of Biology, 456 Taft Hall, State University, Cincinnati, Ohio 45299; 123/456-7890.

# Sample Cover Letter

123 First Avenue
Cincinnati OH 45299
February 15, 1979

Mrs. Mary W. Shelley
Camp Xanadu
Round Pond ME 04566

Dear Ms. Shelley:

I would like to apply for the position of nature specialist
at Camp Xanadu that you list in Summer Employment Directory of
the United States.

I am majoring in education in biology in college, and I
have had experience as a summer camp counselor. I have
several ideas for a summer nature/education program for children
that I would like to discuss with you.

The enclosed resume gives the details of my educational and
employment background. Please call or write me if you have any
questions about my qualifications. Thank you for your consideration of my application.

Sincerely,

Sinclair Lewis
(123)456-7890

Enclosures: resume
photograph
self-addressed, stamped envelope

Yum-Yum Tree' was a big success last year," or "I understand that the Girl Scouts stress work on badges and campcraft skills in their camping program" are comments that tell the employer you've taken an interest in his or her theater or summer camp.

Be carefully prepared to explain why you want the job you're interviewing for. "I want to work for a summer camp because I want to spend the summer outdoors, not cooped up in an office," is a poor response. It doesn't tell the employer what you can do for him, only what you want for yourself. "I'm majoring in art education, and I have some great ideas for a children's summer crafts program, such as . . ." will tell your employer that you're ready to take on the job.

If you're nervous, just remember that the person interviewing you has been in your position himself, and he won't hold sweaty palms and a catch in your voice against you. However, try to avoid fidgeting in your chair, playing with objects on his or her desk, scratching yourself frequently, or any other action that might distract the interviewer from what you are saying to him.

Take the job into consideration when deciding what to wear. It probably won't be necessary to wear a business suit if you're interviewing to be a trail guide, truck driver or camp counselor. The most important part of your appearance when you're interviewing for a job is cleanliness. Author John Molloy, in his nationally syndicated column "Making Good," reported recently that more and more interviewers and job recruiters were seeing applicants who had dressed neatly but who had not bathed, apparently, for some time. Those applicants were not being hired.

For an outdoors job, a simple dress or good pants and blouse would be a good choice for women; men can interview in shirt and slacks, possibly also a sports coat. Women should remember that there are still a few people who are negative toward women wearing pants, however. For an office job, of course, your best businesslike outfit is necessary.

An employer should tell each applicant being considered for a job when to expect a decision. If that date passes and you haven't heard, call the employer to ask about your application. He should understand your anxiety, and your call will serve to show that you're interested in the job. It's also a good idea to write a thank-you letter to an employer after an interview to let him know that you enjoyed speaking to him and that you hope he keeps you in mind for the job. A paragraph or two will suffice.

However, you should not call the employer several times before he has had a chance to decide. Such harrassment usually works against your chances for getting the job.

## To Get More Information

For more tips on getting a job, see *Who's Hiring Who* by Richard Lathrop, published in 1977 by Ten Speed Press; and *Resume Writing: A Comprehensive, How-to-Do-It Guide,* by Burdette E. Bostwick, published in 1976 by John Wiley and Sons. Lathrop's book covers all aspects of getting a job, including seeking out the employers; preparing a resume (Lathrop prefers a "qualifications brief" approach); writing a letter; and interviewing. Although it is about resumes, Bostwick's book also deals with cover letters and gives many good examples of letters and resumes.

With sincerity, hard work and faith in yourself and your skills, you should be able to beat the competition and get a good job this summer. Good luck!

# Inside Tips from Employers

"The process of finding a job can be summed up in 'selling yourself,' " says Edward Grant, president of Temp Force personnel agency, which has offices in several states. Competition for jobs for summer 1980 will be keen, as it is every summer. In order to stand out in that crowd of applicants, you will have to learn to sell yourself to the employer. Since a good salesman learns what his customer wants, it is important that you understand the employers' point of view.

"I look for sincerity, openness and good eye contact," says Bill Chase, Personnel Coordinator for Silver Dollar City, Inc., Missouri. He conducts two weekends of "en masse" interviews each February for the 1880-theme amusement park. "Candidates with good personal appearance stand out. They should have an outgoing personality and show a genuine interest in the particular job they are applying for."

The same interest and attention should be demonstrated if the application is not made in person, but by mail. "Sending a resume never hurts; it looks impressive," offers Resident Director Topher Schlatter, Camp Potawotami, Indiana. "Presentation is critical," said Peter Webster, assistant manager of Bishop's Lodge in New Mexico. "If we get a handwritten letter from someone saying, 'My girlfriend and I want to come to Santa Fe, New Mexico, for the summer,' I know that person isn't serious about working. Thought and consideration should be given to the initial presentation, the letter and resume."

"My pet peeve is bad photographs. Most applications contain photographs, but some of the ones applicants send are really funny. Maybe it's the only photo they have, but if they don't have a good one they shouldn't send one at all. I'd rather not have a picture of a waitress in a bikini, lounging on the beach with a beer in her hand."

Whether you apply in person or by letter, the employer may contact you for more information, or ask you to fill out one of his own application forms. You should always respond as quickly as possible if asked for more information and Bill Chase advises, "Application forms should be filled out completely, especially in the areas of education and experience. Blanks somehow cast a shadow of suspicion."

A major conflict between summer employers and employees is caused by the employee leaving before the season is over to return to school, according to Peter Webster and other summer employers. "We can no longer live with people who leave before the season's over," says Webster. "The first thing I look for in an applicant is what dates they're available. If they can't work through Labor Day, I can't use them. I know that students often need to get back to school the second week of August, or the third week of August, and it's not their fault, but someone ought to lobby the schools about this because it makes it difficult for them to get jobs." Many employers now offer bonuses to those employees who do stay for the entire season.

Even though the jobs are temporary, employers look for the same qualities in a summer worker that they look for in a permanent employee—experience, good speech communication skills, outgoing personality, and skill.

"Summer work is becoming a more sophisticated job market," says Peter Webster. "If a person wants a lucrative position in a luxury resort, he or she should be able to bring a good element of professionalism to the job."

Summer camp directors are also looking for experience and professionalism. Executive Director John R. Emery, Jr. of The Aloha Foundation, New Hampshire says, "Applicants must possess a high degree of skill in their field (arts and crafts, canoeing, sailing, swimming, music, archery, photography and ecology)."

Another important requirement for summer camp work is the ability to relate to the needs of children. "It is hard work, requiring patience and a real interest in and concern for young people," says Don Shellenberger, Director of Camp Becket, Massachusetts.

"We are looking for enthusiastic, mature, intelligent, outgoing people with high energy levels, a love of the out-of-doors, and a love for kids. Previous experience in a camp setting is a plus. Moody and/or defensive personalities need not apply," offers Camp Executive M. Daniel McCain, Fairview Lake YMCA Camp, New Jersey.

Adds Stephen A. Edgerton, Camp Dark Waters, Philadelphia, "They must like children and people in general; must be bright, creative and flexible."

In fact, flexible seems to be a key word. Employers from all areas of the country and from all types of jobs mention the importance of being able to adjust. From Nevada, Don Willar, assistant general manager, Echo Bay Resort says, "You must be able to acclimate to a hot, dry climate. The resort is located in a remote area but it is only 60 miles from Las Vegas."

From the Cripple Creek Resort in Alaska, owner Donald W. Pearson says, "You must be personable and able to live with others harmoniously."

"This is a work situation, seven days a week for eleven weeks in the high backcountry of Glacier National Park with semi-primitive living conditions," says L.R. Luding, Chalet Coordinator for Belton Chalets, Inc., Montana. You must be able to adjust.

Also from Montana, Paul L. Van Cleve, Lazy K Bar Ranch, advises, "The ability to work happily without complaining is necessary. We place great value on our employees' loyalty to us as an employer."

Edward Grant of Temp Force sums it all up by advising applicants to evaluate themselves carefully before applying or interviewing for a job. "Think of yourself as a product," he says. "How should you dress? How should you speak? How aggressive should you be? How strong is your desire for work, and why? Put yourself in the employer's shoes and ask yourself these questions: What would I want to hear? What would I want to see? And, would I hire that person to represent my company if I were interviewing them? Then, act accordingly."

# Working for the Federal Government

The United States federal government offers many summer jobs that involve the use of both brains and brawn, and with educational and skill requirements ranging from none to a Ph.D. However, the first page of a booklet published by the U.S. Civil Service Commission—"Summer Jobs: Opportunities in the Federal Government," hereafter called Announcement No. 414—annually carries this stern warning:

"Opportunities are very limited. There are many more applicants than there are positions available. Therefore, you would be wise not to apply for summer work solely with the federal government."

If you are one of the few employed by Uncle Sam, you can have the opportunity to gain valuable professional experience in your summer months as well as earn a salary. You could be an agricultural or scientific aid for the Department of Agriculture; a computer aid with the Environmental Protection Agency; an engineering aid with the National Aeronautics and Space Administration; or a graphic designer for the Department of the Treasury.

Other positions offer adventure. The Forest Service, for example, has openings in national parks and forests for aids and technicians in such areas as conservation, fire control, surveying, physical and biological science and recreation. Other government departments have openings for legal aids, veterinarian trainees and journalists.

To obtain information—deadline dates, forms needed, positions open—about all government summer jobs, get a copy of Announcement No. 414 from any Federal Job Information Center (FJIC). Copies of No. 414 for summer 1980 should be available by November 1979.

Many federal jobs require applicants to apply in January and to take a written Civil Service test in February. Late applications are never accepted. You may apply directly for jobs in some government agencies, and you can find a list of these in booklet No. 414.

The Civil Service Commission has classified government summer jobs into five groups. Jobs in Group I, which are mostly clerical positions on the level of GS-1 through GS-4, require that persons take the February test before applying. So do most jobs in Group II, which are also in grades GS-1 through GS-4 but which involve technical, nonclerical work. These jobs require some college or experience in specific occupational fields.

Jobs in Group III are in grades GS-5 or above and involve technical, professional and administrative work. Some of these positions require four years of college; others a master's or doctoral degree. In many cases, persons with four years of college must supply proof of acceptance into graduate school to obtain a Group III job.

Group IV positions are for laborers and tradesmen. This group includes such jobs as printing plant worker, animal caretaker and carpenter's helper.

Two special government programs are listed under Group V. The Summer Employment for Needy Youth program provides jobs for young people from low-income families and for youths who need incomes from summer jobs in order to return to school in the fall. To apply, contact the nearest Bureau of State Employment Services. If there is no State Employment Services office in your area, contact the local Civil Service Commission Area Office for information on referral procedures.

A limited number of outstanding undergraduate and graduate students nominated by their colleges are selected annually to participate in the Federal

Summer Intern Program, which offers internships related to administrative, professional or technical career fields. Most internships are located in Washington DC, although a few are in other parts of the country. The grades involved range from GS-4 to GS-11. Students may not file applications directly; if you would like to participate, contact your college placement office. For more information, see Announcement No. 414.

# Where the Summer Jobs Are

Summer Employment Directory editors counted the number of jobs openings in each listing represented in the book. As the following chart shows, there are more summer jobs in the far West and the far East than in the states in-between. The exceptions include states like Ohio, Georgia, North Carolina and Texas.

In all, there are more than 50,000 summer job openings through the employers listed in *SED*. Each listing was read carefully and then the number of jobs in each was recorded. Since employers do not indicate an exact number of openings, an estimate or average was taken into consideration for the chart.

Almost all employers listed in *SED* will consider applicants from any part of the country. Most employers list in *SED* because they like to receive a wide variety of applicants to choose from and/or because they cannot obtain enough or the right kind of local help.

## Number of Jobs in Each State

| | |
|---|---|
| Alabama 250 | Massachusetts 1198 |
| Alaska 347 | Michigan 742 |
| Arizona 1327 | Minnesota 1459 |
| Arkansas 285 | Missouri 494 |
| California 6573 | Mississippi 280 |
| Colorado 1728 | Montana 2122 |
| Connecticut 853 | Nebraska 250 |
| Delaware 274 | Nevada 325 |
| District of Columbia 260 | New Hampshire 861 |
| Florida 1484 | New Jersey 805 |
| Georgia 2910 | New Mexico 888 |
| Hawaii 290 | New York 2827 |
| Idaho 361 | North Carolina 2660 |
| Illinois 638 | North Dakota 418 |
| Indiana 512 | Ohio 3946 |
| Iowa 652 | Oklahoma 272 |
| Kansas 312 | Oregon 478 |
| Kentucky 287 | Pennsylvania 1677 |
| Louisiana 267 | Rhode Island 788 |
| Maine 2788 | South Carolina 292 |
| Maryland 774 | South Dakota 164 |

Tennessee 385
Texas 4554
Utah 478
Vermont 393
Virginia 607
Washington 452

West Virginia 500
Wisconsin 1349
Wyoming 3111
Canada 304
Puerto Rico 250
West Indies 8

# Special Offers

## Missing Employers

If you know of a summer employer not listed in *SED* that you think might like to be, let us know. We'll send the employer one of our questionnaires along with your recommendation. If the employer agrees to list, you—or someone of your choice—gets a free copy of the 1981 *SED* (to be published November 1, 1980).

Employers

Name _____
Address _____
City _____
State _____ Zip _____
Type of Employer _____

Name _____
Address _____
City _____
State _____ Zip _____
Type of Employer _____

Name _____
Address _____
City _____
State _____ Zip _____
Type of Employer _____

Send my book to this address if
you get the employer to list:

Name _____
Address _____
City _____ State _____
Zip _____ Phone _____

14 Summer Employment Directory of the U.S.

Employer Evaluation

Write below—in 50 words or less—your evaluation of your summer job with one of the employers listed in *SED*. Tell us briefly, what your duties were; what you liked and what you didn't like about your job; and whether or not you would return to the employer next season. Your evaluation will be considered for publication as part of that employer's listing next year and thus will help other prospective employees evaluate whether or not they should apply to that employer. We pay $2 for each published evaluation. Send in your evaluation to us after the 1980 season.

_____

_____

_____

_____

_____

_____

_____

_____

_____

_____

_____

_____

_____

_____

_____

*Summer Employment Directory* Update

Since a number of summer employers are not able to let us know of their summer needs by our *SED* publication date, we offer an update of additional listings in January of each year. The 1980 update will be approximately 50 new listings and will have some new information on employers already in the book. Cost is $1 plus 50¢ for postage and handling.

(      )YES, send me the *Summer Employment Directory Update* for 1980 summer jobs. Enclosed is $1.50 to cover the cost of the update and then to have the listings sent to me in January 1980.

Name _____

Address _____

City _____

State _____ Zip _____

Send check or money to:
Summer Employment Directory
1980 Update
9933 Alliance Rd.
Cincinnati, Ohio 45242

# Alabama

## Business and Industry

### Kelly Services, Inc.
More than 450 branches coast to coast, Puerto Rico, Canada, England and France. Temporary work assignments. Offers over 100 job classifications (office, marketing and light industrial assignments) to college students, teachers and other qualified people during summer breaks and year 'round. Kelly Services also has a special referral system that allows you to register at a Kelly office near your school then work near your home during summer recess—or register near your home then work on temporary assignments during the school year. Assignments available include clerks, typists, secretaries, keypunch operators, word processors, bookkeepers and a variety of marketing and light industrial. Offers flexible schedule with "attractive hourly pay rates equal to or higher than the accepted industry standards in most cities." No paycheck deductions except Social Security and income tax. No employment fee for temporary work. See the White Pages for the branch of Kelly Services nearest you. Apply in person or write to: Summer Employment, National Headquarters, Kelly Services, GPO 1179, Detroit MI 48266.

# Alaska

## Expeditions, Guide Trips

### America & Pacific Tours, Inc. (A&P)
Located in Anchorage. Alaskan tour guide service. Openings for college students, teachers and foreign students from June 1 through August 31. Needs 10 Japanese speaking tour guides, $1,000/month plus overtime. "Room and board is not included but we will assist in locating housing in Anchorage with close access to our offices." Includes training on Alaska. "Our groups are all Japanese ranging from age 20 up. We also have specialty groups ranging from commercial filming to government officials. Applicant must speak fluent Japanese, should be outgoing, and willing to work long hours for which they will be properly paid. Our season is short with many groups, so be ready to do hard but enjoyable work." Send resume and letter by April 30. Apply to Keizo Sugimoto, Executive Vice President, Dept. SED, Box 1068, Anchorage AK 99510; tel. 907/272-9401.

## Business and Industry

### Kelly Services, Inc.
More than 450 branches coast to coast, Puerto Rico, Canada, England and

France. Temporary work assignments. Offers over 100 job classifications (office, marketing and light industrial assignments) to college students, teachers and other qualified people during summer breaks and year 'round. Kelly Services also has a special referral system that allows you to register at a Kelly office near your school then work near your home during summer recess—or register near your home then work on temporary assignments during the school year. Assignments available include clerks, typists, secretaries, keypunch operators, word processors, bookkeepers and a variety of marketing and light industrial. Offers flexible schedule with "attractive hourly pay rates equal to or higher than the accepted industry standards in most cities." No paycheck deductions except Social Security and income tax. No employment fee for temporary work. See the White Pages for the branch of Kelly Services nearest you. Apply in person or write to: Summer Employment, National Headquarters, Kelly Services, GPO 1179, Detroit MI 48266.

# Resorts, Ranches, Restaurants, Lodging

### Cripple Creek Resort
Located in Ester. Hotel and restaurant in restored gold camp. Openings for college students, teachers and foreign students from May 15 to Labor Day (except bartenders-waiters work May 1 to September 10). Needs 5 bartender-waiters, $500-700/month plus tips; 4 dining room waiters, $500/month plus tips; 3 office workers and maids, $450/month; 3 kitchen helpers, $500/month. "Applicants may do any or all of the job descriptions, so are trained in all phases at the start." Salaries include room and board, plus transportation one way if contract is completed. Applicants "must be personable and able to live with others harmoniously." Resort is tourist oriented but has a substantial local clientele. Send resume by February. Apply to Donald W. Pearson, Dept. SED, 17 Galloway Drive, Concord CA 94518; tel. 415/676-5894.

### Evergreen Lodge
Located on Lake Louise. Wilderness resort lodge. Needs 1 experienced assistant cook and 2 lodge helpers, $50/week plus tips, room and board; and 2 dock attendants, $50-75/week plus tips, room and board. College students, teachers and high school seniors preferred. Work from June 5 to August 20, possibly to September 20. "Employment at Evergreen Lodge provides a summer of wilderness experience on one of the most beautiful and remote lakes in Alaska. The lodge is accessible by road, 17 miles from a major highway and 45 miles from the nearest small town. We need individuals who work well and pleasantly with people and can forego the luxuries of city life. Employees work hard but also have a lot of fun, are allowed use of lodge boats and a chance to catch 20-pound lake trout, or swim in the icy lake waters." Apply by May to Paul Kuske, Manager, Evergreen Lodge, SRC Box 264, Palmer AK 99645.

### Gwins Lodge
Located at Cooper Landing. Family motel, trailer park, restaurant, liquor store, fishing tackle shop. Openings from May 1 to September 30. Needs 1 dinner, short order cook, $3.50/hour plus room and board; 1 bartender (also to help in kitchen, restaurant and liquor store), $3.50/hour plus tips; 3 waitresses, $350/hour plus tips, room and board. Applicants must be "reliable and conscientious." Send

resume by April to Bob or Louise Dubois, Mile 52, Sterling Highway, Cooper Landing AK 99572; tel. 907/595-1266.

## McKinley KOA Kampground

Located in Healy. Family campground, grocery store, automotive repair shop, propane service and garage (with wrecker service). Openings for college students, teachers and local applicants from May 15 to September 30 (June 1 to September 5 for recreation director and bus driver). Needs 3 store clerks (minimum age 19), $4.25/hour; mechanic helper (with basic knowledge of automotive repair), $6/hour; recreation director and bus driver (willing to learn and narrate about area and McKinley Park, plus work split shift and help in store and campground), $4.50/hour. "We have some on-site housing, but most workers have to provided their own. Applicant must be able to enjoy a rural area and be willing to keep working hours and social hours separate." Send resume by May 1 to Corrine Colrud, Dept. SED, Box 34, Healy AK 99743; tel. 907/683-2379.

## Mt. McKinley Village/North Face Lodge/The Mountain Haus

Located at McKinley Park, at entrance to Mt. McKinley National Park. Small resort facilities. Openings for college students, teachers, and "young" retired couples, May 1 through September 30. Needs 10 waitresses/waiters, 4 drivers/bellhops, 3 kitchen utility/dishwashers, 4 desk clerks, 8 maids/laundry, 2 bartenders, 4 cooks. Salaries are $3.60/hour (Alaska minimum wage); salaries negotiable for skilled positions. Room and board available. An equal opportunity employer. Apply to Mt. McKinley Village Inc., Box 66SED, McKinley Park AK 99755; tel. 907/683-2265.

## Rainbow King Lodge, Inc.

Located on Iliamna Lake. Luxury sport fishing lodge for families, upper class business persons, major corporations. Openings from June 1 to October 1; employees must stay complete season. Needs 6 lodge helpers for serving, cleaning, room make up, kitchen help, etc.; and 6 fishing guides, should be experienced fishermen and boatmen with congenial personalities. Salaries are $550/month, plus tips, room and board. No transportation to lodge provided; served by scheduled airlines. Wants applicants who are "refined, with high morals; we have strict rules and regulations." Apply by April to Ray Loesche, Owner/Manager, Rainbow King Lodge, Inc., Box 3446, Spokane WA 99220.

## Tundra Lodge

Located in Tok. Campground, hotel, restaurant, liquor, sundry grocery, gift shop. Openings from May to September; prepare to work through the fall season. Needs 2 cooks, 3 waitresses, 2 bartenders (for all jobs some experience and willingness to learn and perform duties necessary), salaries depend upon experience and learning ability; 5 maids, $4/hour; gift shop clerk, pays commission; 2 assistant managers (year-round), salary negotiable. "Bonuses will be made. Room and board available at cost of approximately $150-200 out of monthly paycheck. Send in application as early as possible. Heavy clothing needed. Bring your fishing clothes and cameras, heavy hiking boots." Send resume by March 31 to Steve and Penny Johnson, Managers, Box 336, Dept. SED, Tok AK 99780; tel. 907/883-2291 or 883-2292.

# Arizona

## Business and Industry

**Kelly Services, Inc.**
More than 450 branches coast to coast, Puerto Rico, Canada, England and France. Temporary work assignments. Offers over 100 job classifications (office, marketing and light industrial assignments) to college students, teachers and other qualified people during summer breaks and year 'round. Kelly Services also has a special referral system that allows you to register at a Kelly office near your school then work near your home during summer recess—or register near your home then work on temporary assignments during the school year. Assignments available include clerks, typists, secretaries, keypunch operators, word processors, bookkeepers and a variety of marketing and light industrial. Offers flexible schedule with "attractive hourly pay rates equal to or higher than the accepted industry standards in most cities." No paycheck deductions except Social Security and income tax. No employment fee for temporary work. See the White Pages for the branch of Kelly Services nearest you. Apply in person or write to: Summer Employment, National Headquarters, Kelly Services, GPO 1179, Detroit MI 48266.

## National Parks

**Grand Canyon National Park Lodges**
Located on South Rim Grand Canyon National Park in northwest Arizona (7,000 foot elevation). National park with resort hotels, restaurants, and curio shops. Equal opportunity employer. Openings year-round with peak season being Easter through September. Summer staff of 1,000, winter staff of 550; interested in active retirees. All personnel must be able to work for at least 90 days; has opportunity to become full-time/permanent. Needs hotel/restaurant personnel for various lodges, coffee shops, cafeterias, curio shops, all positions front and back of the house, etc. Minibus drivers must be 21. Entry-level jobs start at federal minimum wage; room deduction automatic. Meals available at cost in employee cafeterias; no cooking in rooms. Housing available for couples (no children allowed). Minimum number of trailer spaces available to rent. No beards or goatees; men required to have conventional tapered haircuts not to exceed collar length. Apply to Grand Canyon National Park Lodges, Personnel Dept.—SED, Grand Canyon AZ 86023.

## Resorts, Ranches, Restaurants, Lodging

**Canyon Squire Inn**
Located at Grand Canyon. Motel and restaurant. Openings from April through October. Needs clerks for gift shop and front desk, waiters/waitresses, maids and housemen, recreation attendants, bus people, porters, and kitchen help. Salary open, includes room and board. "Call us." Apply by February or early March to General Office, Canyon Squire Inn, Box 130, Highway 64, Grand Canyon AZ 86023; tel. 602/638-2681, ext. 150.

## Kohl's Ranch
Located in Payson. Ranch resort. Openings for college students, minimum age 19, from Memorial Day through Labor Day. Needs 4 chambermaids, 4 waitresses, 4 yardmen. Salaries are $250, plus room and board. Apply to Michael Mikol, Kohl's Ranch, Payson AZ 85541.

## Wahweap Lodge & Marina, Inc.
Located in the Glen Canyon National Recreational Area in southern Utah/northern Arizona on Lake Powell (180-mile-long lake with 1,900 miles of shoreline). Resort with boat rentals, boat tours, campgrounds, fishing charters, lodging, restaurants, service stations and boat and car repair shops. "Our primary season runs from Easter through mid-October although open year-round, presenting a continuous need for qualified employees." Needs marina mechanics, boat pilots, dockhands, housekeepers, cashiers, food servers, cooks, accounting clerks, office clerks, maintenance people, service station attendents and houseboat maids and instructors. "Employees are housed primarily in mobile homes. Housing for married couples is limited and available only when both partners are willing to accept shift work and work Sundays and holidays. We encourage semi-retired people to work for short periods in spring, summer and/or fall. Living in this beautiful, but remote, desert area provides the opportunity to take advantage of all the water and outdoor activities. Please specify beginning and ending dates of availability." Equal opportunity employer. Also owns Cottonwood Cove Resort & Marina located on Lake Mohave, an hour from Las Vegas, in the Lake Mead National Recreation Area; Callville Bay Resort & Marina located on Lake Mead, near Las Vegas. Send resume to Personnel Office, Del Webb Recreational Properties, Inc., Box 29040, Phoenix AZ 85038.

# Summer Camps

## The Salvation Army Camp
Located in Oracle. Summer camp. Openings from June through the first part of September. Needs 14 counselors, male and female, $60/week, college students preferred; 1 lifeguard, $75/week, college student preferred; 1 nurse (RN), $100/week; 3 cooks, $50-100/week; 3 dishwashers, $30/week, high school seniors preferred; 2 maintenance workers, $35/week, high school seniors preferred; 1 secretary, $75/week, college student preferred; 1 crafts director and 1 wilderness director, $60/week, college students preferred. Apply before May to Captain Ray Peacock, Divisional Youth Secretary, The Salvation Army, Box 13307, Phoenix AZ 85002; tel. 602/258-8085.

## Sky-Y
Located in the Bradshaw Mountains at Prescott. YMCA coed camp for children ages 8-13. Openings for college students and teachers from June 15 to August 15. Needs 18 general counselors, nurse, WSI. Salaries are $400-600/season plus room and board. Apply to Cecil Miller, Camp Director, 350 N. 1st Ave., Phoenix AZ 85003.

# Arkansas

## Business and Industry

### Kelly Services, Inc.
More than 450 branches coast to coast, Puerto Rico, Canada, England and France. Temporary work assignments. Offers over 100 job classifications (office, marketing and light industrial assignments) to college students, teachers and other qualified people during summer breaks and year 'round. Kelly Services also has a special referral system that allows you to register at a Kelly office near your school then work near your home during summer recess—or register near your home then work on temporary assignments during the school year. Assignments available include clerks, typists, secretaries, keypunch operators, word processors, bookkeepers and a variety of marketing and light industrial. Offers flexible schedule with "attractive hourly pay rates equal to or higher than the accepted industry standards in most cities." No paycheck deductions except Social Security and income tax. No employment fee for temporary work. See the White Pages for the branch of Kelly Services nearest you. Apply in person or write to: Summer Employment, National Headquarters, Kelly Services, GPO 1179, Detroit MI 48266.

### Temp Force
Temporary office personnel contractor. Openings for college students, teachers, high school seniors during vacations and holidays. Needs secretaries, typists, stenographers, clericals and accountants. Salaries based upon experience. Apply to Temp Force, 920 University Towers, 12th and University, Little Rock AR 72204; tel. 501/661-9600

## Summer Camps

### Cahinnio
Located near Booneville. Girl Scout camp for girls ages 9-15. Openings from June 8 to July 26 (7-week season). Needs 3 unit leaders and 1 small-craft instructor, $300-400/season, college students or teachers preferred; 10 unit counselors, $200-300/season, college students or high school seniors preferred; 1 waterfront director, $350-450/season, college students or teachers preferred; and 1 nurse, $400-500/season, college students or teachers preferred. Room and board included at nominal cost. Apply by mid-February to Jo Lynn Glasscock, Camp Director, Mt. Magazine Girl Scout Council, Dept. SED, Box 3274, Fort Smith AR 72913; tel. 501/452-1290.

### Noark
Located on 1,039 acres at Huntsville in the Ozark Mountains. Primitive Girl Scout camp for girls ages 7-17. Openings for college students and teachers from June 8 to July 18. Needs 6 unit leaders (minimum age 21), who are mature, able to work with children and supervise unit staff, $55-75/week; 11 unit counselors, minimum age 18, $35-50/week; waterfront director (minimum age 21), WSI or equivalent plus ability to teach children, supervise teaching process, keep records and organize large groups, $55-75/week; and business manager (minimum age

21), experience in business methods, record keeping, buying and inventory control, $55-75/week. Food and lodging provided. "We want people who are imaginative, creative, responsible, and enjoy primitive outdoor life." Send for application and return by May 30 to Elizabeth A. Hastings, Camp Director, Dept. SED, Girl Scout Service Center, Rt. 1, Box 43, Fayetteville AR 72701; tel. 501/442-4507.

# California

## Business and Industry

### Aames Bureau of Employment, Inc.
Located in Beverly Hills. Permanent and temporary employment agency. Needs persons for all temporary positions in offices and specializes in medical personnel in all areas including hospitals, clinics, and physicians' offices. "Review your skills so you can earn highest hourly rate." Apply to Jacob Albert, Vice President, Aames Bureau of Employment, Inc., 5570 Wilshire Blvd., Suite 450, Beverly Hills CA 90212; tel. 213/271-6164.

### Bentley Personnel Services
Located in San Francisco. Needs secretaries, typists, dictaphone operators, receptionists, convention aides, messengers, switchboard and all office positions. Considers college students, teachers and high school seniors. "Brush up on typing, filing and office skills as the rate paid per hour depends upon your office skills and experience. We try to place our summer workers in the kind of office and industry they prefer. We deal with all types of industries and the experience is invaluable." Apply to Brenda Foster, Manager, Bentley Personnel Services, 625 Market St., San Francisco CA 94105.

### Kelly Services, Inc.
More than 450 branches coast to coast, Puerto Rico, Canada, England and France. Temporary work assignments. Offers over 100 job classifications (office, marketing and light industrial assignments) to college students, teachers and other qualified people during summer breaks and year 'round. Kelly Services also has a special referral system that allows you to register at a Kelly office near your school then work near your home during summer recess—or register near your home then work on temporary assignments during the school year. Assignments available include clerks, typists, secretaries, keypunch operators, word processors, bookkeepers and a variety of marketing and light industrial. Offers flexible schedule with "attractive hourly pay rates equal to or higher than the accepted industry standards in most cities." No paycheck deductions except Social Security and income tax. No employment fee for temporary work. See the White Pages for the branch of Kelly Services nearest you. Apply in person or write to: Summer Employment, National Headquarters, Kelly Services, GPO 1179, Detroit MI 48266.

### Mature Temps Inc.
Located in Los Angeles. National temporary employment service. Openings for college students, teachers, high school seniors, local applicants and foreign

students from May to September or year-round. Needs secretaries, clerks, typists, bookkeepers, stenographers, accountants, demonstrators and marketing research persons. High hourly rates based on skills. Apply to Mature Temps Inc., 3660 Wilshire Blvd., Suite 1130, Los Angeles CA 90010, tel. 213/380-6515; 9301 Wilshire Boulevard, Suite 203, Beverly Hills CA 91210, tel. 213/550-4522; 690 Green St., Pasadena CA 91101, tel. 213/796-0363; 44 Montgomery St., Suite 2716, San Francisco CA 94104, tel. 415/986-7787.

**Office Overload**
Located in Los Angeles. Temporary service. Positions available year-round for secretaries, $280/week; typists, $200/week; accounting personnel, $200/week; general office, $140/week. Apply to Service and Assignment, Office Overload, 3435 Wilshire Blvd., Suite 728, Los Angeles CA 90010; tel. 213/385-5276.

**TemPositions, Inc.**
Located in San Francisco. Temporary employment service. Openings from from June 1 to September 15. Needs 20 word processors, $7-10/hour; 125 secretaries, $5-7/hour; 100 typists, $4-6/hour; and 75 clerk/typists and 25 receptionists, $3.50-4.50/hour. College students, teachers, high school seniors or local applicants preferred. "Be flexible. Attitude and willingness to work are as important as skills. Because of US Immigration laws, we cannot accept applications from England or Europe." Apply to Patience Talcott, Vice President, 690 Market St., San Francisco CA 94104; tel. 415/392-5856.

**Tempo Temporary Services**
Located in San Juan Capistrano. Unlimited openings for college students, teachers, high school seniors and foreign students. Needs workers with all skills anywhere in southern California. Salaries vary, based on skills. Top pay and vacation pay plan. Apply to Tempo Temporary Services, 32122 Camino Capistrano, San Juan Capistrano CA 92675.

# Commercial Attractions

**Disneyland**
Located in Anaheim. Hires about 3,500 people (minimum age 18)/year for seasonal positions. Summer is biggest season, but open year-round. Gives preference to persons available through Labor Day. "Orientation and training average 24 hours so it's very important to be available and train before our peak season begins." Needs ticket sellers/takers; merchandise markers; office and clerical workers; and hosts/hostesses for: culinary, custodial, attraction, warehouse, merchandising and wardrobe positions. Starting salary averages $3.25-3.50/hour (somewhat less for tipping positions). "It is necessary when you are cast as a part of 'The Disney Show' you display 'The Disney Look,' a neat and natural look with no extremes. You could expect to work approximately 25-30 hours/week during summer, Christmas and Easter holidays." Provides wardrobe for most positions. Living quarters, rentals, meals and transportation are not furnished, and "rentals are high in this area during the holidays and the summer season." Applications may be requested by mail, but requires personal interview at Disneyland Casting Office. Equal opportunity employer. Apply to Disneyland Casting Office #J.S.P. 1313 Harbor Blvd., Anaheim CA 92803.

**Magic Mountain**
Located in Valencia, 30 miles north of downtown Los Angeles. Amusement park.
Openings for 2,000 college students, high school graduates, teachers, people 18
years of age and older, from Memorial Day weekend through the middle of
September. Needs ride operators, RNs, EMTs, costume seamstresses, food and
beverage counter helpers, cooks, buspersons, merchandise salespersons, ushers,
stage production assistants, cashiers, ticket takers, wardrobe attendants, security
officers, parking lot attendants, tram drivers, games host/hostesses, grounds
quality people, clerical, craftspeople, warehouse. Most positions pay minimum
wage. Slightly higher rates for the more skilled positions including crafts demonstrators. "There is no adequate public transportation to Magic Mountain. All
meals can be taken at the employees' cafeteria at reasonable rates. Employees
are responsible for their own housing. The best arrangement would be to stay
with friends in the San Fernando or Santa Clarita Valleys. We may have a special
International Program for 1980. Plans on this are not final at this time." Write for
an application to the Employment Manager, Magic Mountain, 26101 Magic
Mountain Pkwy., Valencia CA 91355.

# National Parks

### Sequoia and Kings Canyon Hospitality Service
Located in Sequoia and Kings Canyon National Parks. Openings for 350,
minimum age 18. Year-round with peak season May 1 to October 1. Needs maids,
housemen, waitresses, bus boys, cooks, kitchen helpers, pantry workers, service
station attendants, drivers, night watchmen, gift shop clerks, market clerks, night
auditors, maintenance men, mechanics, accounting and personnel clerks,
recreation and management personnel. Pay scale starts at federal minimum wage,
minus room and board. Send application between November 1 and March 31 for
early positions; later for positions after June 1. An equal opportunity employer.
Apply to Director of Personnel, Government Services, Inc., Sequoia National Park
CA 93262.

# Resorts, Ranches, Restaurants, Lodging

### Boulder Lodge Inc
Located at June Lake. Motel and housekeeping apartments. Openings for college
students and teachers, minimum age 19, for any three-month period, year-round.
BUNAC (British University North American Club) full-time students with social
security number are most welcome to apply. Needs 6 maids for cleaning. Salaries
to start at $3.25/hour; room with kitchen at $15/week rent. Bonus for full term
through September 9. Enclose stamped return envelope for application. Apply by
June 1 to D.M. Oldfield, Boulder Lodge Inc., Dept. SED, Box 68, June Lake CA
93529.

# Summer Camps

### Bearskin Meadow
Located in Kings Canyon National Park. Coed camp for children, ages 6-18, full
program with diabetes care and education. Openings for college students and

teachers from July to August, four 2-week sessions. Needs 10 specialty counselors for music, drama, woodwork, field sports, ceramics, leather craft; 5 cabin counselors. Some types of medical and nursing experience accredited. Apply by April to Diabetic Youth Foundation, 1128 Irving St., San Francisco CA 94122.

## Boys' Club of Hollywood—Camp 365

Located at Running Springs. Camp and conference center. Openings for college students and teachers from June 11 to September 2. Needs 12 counselors, $400-600; 2 crafts directors, 2 aquatics directors, $600-700; 2 naturalists, nurse (RN), $500-700. Apply to John Yingling, Boys' Club of Hollywood, Box 751, Running Springs CA 92382.

## Cielo

Located at San Marcos Pass, Santa Barbara. Camp Fire resident camp for children ages 6-18. Openings from July to mid-August. Needs assistant camp director/program director, minimum age 21, (SLS, CPR, and First Aid preferred); unit director, minimum age 21; general counselor, minimum age 18; leadership training director, waterfront director, (must have CPR, First Aid, and WSI); waterfront assistant (WSI, CPR and First Aid required); handcraft specialist; archery specialist; outdoor specialist; horseback riding specialist; business manager (Class II license required); nurse (licensed in California); head cook; assistant cook; kitchen assistants; foods and equipment supervisor. Salaries $250-600/season, plus room and board, depending on position and experience. Apply to Judy S. Hoskins, Executive Director, Camp Fire, Inc., Box 5363, Oxnard CA 93031; tel. 805/485-3417 or 659-2642.

## Double E Ranch

Located at Yorkville in Mendocino County. Camp for mentally and physically handicapped people ages 14 and older. Openings for 41 persons for 12 weeks during the summer. Needs unit leaders (2 male, 2 female), arts and crafts directors (1 male, 1 female experienced in nature classes), water safety director (WSI, 1 male, 1 female), food director (experienced in menu planning and outdoor cooking), minimum age 21, 3 years college, some camping experience, $600-700/season; cabin counselors (6 male, 6 female, experienced), minimum age 18, $500/season; counselors assistant (6 male, 6 female, must have extreme willingness to learn), minimum age 16, $300-400/season; 4 food assistants (experienced or extreme willingness to learn), minimum age 16, $300-400/season; 2 groundskeepers/maintenance persons, minimum age 18, $500/season; nurse (RN, preferably with experience), $1,000-1,200/season; nursing assistant, minimum age 18, $500/season. Salaries include room and board, laundry facilities. "There is scheduled time off and recreational sessions during working date. Special interests all staffers should have include camping, outdoor cooking, recreation, sports, hiking, nature lore, plus related activities." Send resume and send for application. Apply to Lois Eaquinto, Director, Double E Ranch, Box 215, Dept. SED, Yorkville CA 95494; tel. 707/894-5415.

## Golden Valley Girl Scout Council

Located at Dinkey Creek. Girl scout camp. Openings from June 23 to August 23. Needs 6 unit leaders, $750-800/season, college students or teachers preferred; 13 assistant unit leaders, $500-550/season, college students preferred; and 1 horse-riding director, $800-850/season, college students or teachers preferred.

"Experience in working with children is essential. Please send a letter of inquiry; we will send an application to you." Apply by March 31 to Mary Bevins, Camp Administration Director, Dept. SED, 5665 E. Westover, Fresno CA 93727, tel. 209/291-9181.

## Harmon Easter Seal
Located near Boulder Creek. Camp for physically and mentally handicapped children and adults, ages 8-60, in separate sessions. ACA accreditation. Openings for college students and teachers from June 17 to August 23, orientation June 13 to June 15. Needs unit directors (minimum age 21, 3 years college), program directors (minimum age 21, 3 years college): pool/water safety, arts and crafts, lodge/special and evening programs, nature/waterfront/boating and fishing, animal farm, campfire/drama; counselors (minimum age 19, 1 year college), head cook (minimum age 25), assistant cook (minimum age 21), supplementary staff (minimum age 19), kitchen aides, kitchen maintenance, maintenance, laundress. Room and board provided. Apply to Kathryn Parodi, Executive Director, Easter Seal Society of Santa Cruz County, Box 626, Santa Cruz CA 95061.

## Mariastella
Located at Wrightwood, in the San Gabriel Mountains. Camp for girls, ages 8-16; coed deaf, ages 7-14; coed EMR, ages 10-40. Openings for college students, teachers and high school seniors from mid-June to end of August. Needs 25 cabin counselors, $225-425/season; 4 program specialists: arts and crafts, waterfront, nature, $300-450/season; nurse (RN), $100/week. Apply by April to Sister Patricia McGowan, Director, Camp Mariastella, 1120 Westchester Pl., Los Angeles CA 90019.

## Mendocino
Located in Fort Bragg. San Francisco Boy's Club; resident camp for boys ages 6-14; approximately 250 campers every two weeks. Openings from June 14 to August 27. Needs 24 cabin leaders, college students, teachers, foreign students, $600/season; 1 chef ($1,200/season), 1 first cook (800/season), 1 second cook ($600/season) must know how to cook for 400; 1 horse corral manager. College student or teacher preferred, $800/season; 1 lifeguard (WSI), $800/season; 1 RN, $1,000/season. Apply to Les Andersen, Executive Director, San Francisco Boy's Club Camp Mendocino, 1950 Page St., San Francisco CA 94117; tel. 415/221-0790.

## Mountain Meadows
Located in the southern Sierra Mountains. Openings for unit leaders, unit assistants, nurse, cook, cook's assistant, specialists—unit leaders in backpacking, rock climbing, photography, theater, and horse wrangler. Salaries in accordance with the California minimum wage laws. Apply by March to Director, Camp Mountain Meadows, Box 2164, Bakersfield CA 93303.

## Murrieta for Girls
## Del Mar for Boys
Located in Washington, California, Texas, Wisconsin and Ohio. Weight loss, nutrition education, and sports fitness camps for people ages 8-21. Needs college-age counselors, $500 and up; nutritionist, $1,000 and up; sports specialists;

administrative personnel. *Qualified applicants must be able to interview in state where camp is located.* Send for application c/o Dave Kempton, Camp Murrieta/Camp Del Mar, Dept. SED, 8245 Ronson Rd., Suite D, San Diego CA 92111.

## Nawakwa

Located in Angelus Oaks. Camp Fire summer resident camp for girls ages 6-17, and boys ages 8-14. Openings mid-June to end of August. Needs 1 program director, minimum age 21, camping and counseling experience preferably in leadership or administrative capacity, $900-1,000/season; 6 unit directors, minimum age 21, $600-850/season; 18 counselors, minimum age 19 with 1 year of college or equivalent, $350-500/season; program specialists, minimum age 19, for arts and crafts, campcraft, environmental interpretation, waterfront/aquatics, $600-850/season; 2 cooks, $1,000-1,200/season; 2 water safety instructors, $600-850/season; 8 program aides, minimum age 18 or high school graduate, (assistant counselor/kitchen aide), $600-700/season. Room and board deducted at $50/week. "Send carefully thought-out application with any pertinent supplemental information. Interview at Camp Fire office in Claremont if at all possible. Three written references required." Apply by April 30 to Jan Matson, Camp Director, Camp Fire Girls-Mt. San Antonio Council, 951 W. Foothill Blvd., Claremont CA 91711; tel. 714/624-5076, 213/339-6086.

## Okizu

Located in Nevada City. Coed Camp Fire camp for children ages 6-17. Openings for college students and teachers from mid-June to August. Needs assistant camp director, 6 waterfront/boating (WSI, ARC, small craft), program director; 5 program specialists: nature, campcraft, archery, crafts, backpacking; 22 unit counselors, 6 unit directors, male and female. Apply to Camp Okizu, 2745 Downer, Richmond CA 94804; tel. 415/232-8765.

## Osito Rancho
## White's Landing

Girl Scout resident camp for girls ages 7-17. Openings available from mid-June to August. Needs assistant directors (experienced in camp programing and camp administration), minimum age 21, $125-175/week; 2 waterfront specialists (WSI and waterfront experience), minimum age 21, $100-$150/week; 4 program specialists in crafts, horseback, nature (camp experience), minimum age 21, $100-150/week; 15 unit leaders, $65-75/week; 30 counselors, $55-65/week. Salaries include room and board. "Camp Osito-Rancho is a mountain camp, whose program includes backpacking, swimming, horseback riding, crafts and nature. Camp White's Landing is an ocean-front camp located on Santa Catalina Island whose program includes backpacking, swimming, skin diving, sailing, canoeing, waterskiing, crafts and nature." Send resume or send for application to Mary Lawson, Adult Services Director, Angeles Girl Scout Council, Dept. SED, Box 57967 Foy Station, Los Angeles CA 90057; tel. 213/388-9471.

## San Domenico Summer Adventure

Located in San Anselmo. Camp for girls ages 8-14; operated by Dominican Sisters. Openings for college students and teachers from June 23 to July 27. Needs waterfront director (minimum age 21, WSI) and counselor/instructors with teaching skills in 2 of the following areas: swimming and water safety (WSI), tennis, gymnastics, arts and crafts, creative stitchery, macrame, guitar, drama, nature study, team sports, dance (modern, interpretive, folk). Salaries are $250 up plus room and board. Personal interview required. Apply by February (may accept some applications in March) to Director, San Domenico Summer Adventure, Dept. SED, 1500 Butterfield Rd., San Anselmo CA 94960.

## Shadowland Ranch for Girls

Located in Campo. Camp for girls ages 8 up. Openings for college students and teachers from July 5 to August 17. Needs instructors for riding (hunt seat) and swimming (WSI and RC). Salaries are $525 plus room and board, laundry, insurance. Apply to Shadowland Ranch for Girls, Dept. SED, RFD 1, Box 584, Campo CA 92006; tel. 714/478-5737.

## Unalayee

Located near Callahan (Trinity Alps). Wilderness residential camp for children ages 10-17. Openings for 18 counselors, 18 years or older, college students, teachers, local applicants and foreign students from mid-June through August. Needs arts and crafts director, local teacher preferred; truck driver, 25 years or older; work crew supervisor; program director; office person. Salary is $540/2-month season. Room and board available. "Contact camp office for staff application. Personal interviews will be conducted in the spring. Experience with youth and wilderness skills needed." Apply by April 1 to Director, Camp Unalayee, 1176 Emerson St., Palo Alto CA 94301; tel. 415/328-1513.

## Wilshire Boulevard Temple Camps

Located in Malibu, California. Two resident camps serving Reform Jewish children, ages 9-16. Openings from June 17 to September 2. Needs 20 general counselors, college students preferred, $52/week and up; 2 waterfront specialists, college students or teachers preferred, $90/week and up; 2 assistant cooks, $150/week and up; 8 kitchen aides, college students, high school seniors or foreign students preferred, $100/week and up; 3 secretaries, college students preferred, $80/week and up; and 2 nurses, college or graduate students preferred, $100/week and up. Room and board provided. "General counselors should have Jewish background." Write for application. Apply by April to Steve Breuer, Director, 3663 Wilshire Blvd., Los Angeles CA 90010; tel. 213/388-2401.

## Wintaka

Located at Running Springs. Rustic camp, primarily for girls ages 7-17. Openings for college students (teachers and local applicants also for assistant director and cooks) from mid-June to mid-August. Needs assistant director, $150-200/week; head cook and assistant cook, $120-150/week; nurse (RN), $130/week; 20 unit counselors, $55-65/week; waterfront director and waterfront assistant, $65-95/week; riding director and riding assistant, $65-95/week; crafts specialist, $65-85/week; nature specialist, $65-85/week. Room and board provided. Send for application. Apply until season starts to Patty Berry, Camp Director, Dept. SED, 7070 E. Carson St., Long Beach CA 90803; tel. 213/421-2725.

## Youth Outreach

Located at Lake Tahoe. Camp ministry with Christian emphasis. Openings from June to August 31. Needs 6 food service workers, college and high school seniors preferred, pay varies. Also needs volunteers for these positions: 4 housekeepers (college and high school seniors preferred); 16 counselors, 1 nurse, 1 recreation director, 1 nature studies director, 1 waterfront director, 5 craft director and workers, college students preferred; and 6 maintenance workers, college students or high school seniors preferred. "We are a Christian organization with a Bible emphasis and desire applicants who are interested in such an emphasis. Our work is with underpriviledged children from the San Jose area." Apply by May 31 to Chuck Starnes, Director, Youth Outreach, Box 143, San Jose CA 95103; tel. 408/998-7400.

## Summer Theaters

### Summer Repertory
Located in Santa Rosa. Openings from June-August with 1 conference in February and 1 in April; California teachers preferred. Presents 5 plays, June-August. Needs 5 stage directors, $1,500/show; 3 scenic designers, $1,100/show; 3 costume designers, $1,100/show; 1 lighting designer, $2,500/season; 1 makeup designer, $2,000/season; 1 technical director, $3,500/season; 1 choreographer, $1,500/season; 1 musical-vocal director/conductor, $3,000 season; 1 box office/promotions manager, $2,500/season; 1 costumer, $2,500/season; 1 prop master, $1,500/season. Note: Stage directors, designers, choreographer and prop master are released after their shows open. Send full resume and/or portfolio. All applicants must have a master's degree or higher or be enrolled in an accredited program. Apply by December 1 to Frank Zwolinski, General Director, Summer Repertory Theatre, c/o Santa Rosa Junior College, 1501 Mendocino Ave., Santa Rosa CA 95401.

# ——— Colorado ———

## Business and Industry

### ADIA
Located in Denver. Temporary help service. Needs 10-25 secretaries, $4-6/hour; 25-50 typists, $3.50-5/hour; 10-20 PBX, $3.75-4.50; 50-100 clerks (accounting, file, 10-key, general), $3.50-4; 25-50 receptionists, $3.25-4; 50-100 warehouse personnel, $3.25-3.75; and 25-50 data processing, open. Salaries are hourly. College students, teachers, high school seniors, foreign students and local applicants all acceptable. "It would be extremely helpful if transportation is available." Apply to Office Manager, ADIA, 820 16th St., No. 630, Denver CO 80202; tel. 303/572-3499.

### Kelly Services, Inc.
More than 450 branches coast to coast, Puerto Rico, Canada, England and France. Temporary work assignments. Offers over 100 job classifications (office, marketing and light industrial assignments) to college students, teachers and other qualified people during summer breaks and year 'round. Kelly Services also has a special referral system that allows you to register at a Kelly office near your school

then work near your home during summer recess—or register near your home then work on temporary assignments during the school year. Assignments available include clerks, typists, secretaries, keypunch operators, word processors, bookkeepers and a variety of marketing and light industrial. Offers flexible schedule with "attractive hourly pay rates equal to or higher than the accepted industry standards in most cities." No paycheck deductions except Social Security and income tax. No employment fee for temporary work. See the White Pages for the branch of Kelly Services nearest you. Apply in person or write to: Summer Employment, National Headquarters, Kelly Services, GPO 1179, Detroit MI 48266.

# Commercial Attractions

### Santa's Workshop
Located in North Pole. Openings for 55 college students, teachers and high school seniors from mid-May to December 25, but mostly during summer. Needs salesclerks, cashiers, office help, ride operators, parking lot attendants, warehouse workers. Salary is $2.40/hour plus bonus to those on contract; some higher without bonus. Apartments available in Colorado Springs. Apply by April 15 to Personnel Manager, Santa's Workshop, North Pole CO 80809.

# Expeditions, Guide Trips

### Four Corners Expeditions
Located in Buena Vista. River rafting. Needs 10 whitewater river guides, $1,500-2,000/season, prefers college students, teachers and high school seniors; 1 bus driver, $1,000-1,300, June 1 to August 31, college students, teachers and local applicants preferred. Possibly some work in May. "Housing in area not too expensive, but availability is limited. All applicants must have taken a Red Cross First Aid course and have a current First Aid card. Applicants must send resume which includes height, weight and photograph to be considered. One week training course in late May or early June is required at applicants expense." Also needs 2 photographers. "Must be willing to work long hours for low pay and do other odd jobs." Apply to Reed Dils, Owner, Four Corners Expeditions, Dept. SED, Box 1032, Buena Vista CO 81211; tel. 303/395-8949.

# National Parks

### Rocky Mountain Park Company
Located at Estes Park. National park concessioner. Openings for college students from Memorial Day to October 15. Needs 25 food service, 5 stockkeeping, 50 sales. Salaries are $400/month less room and board. Apply by May 1 to Rocky Mountain Park Company, Dept. SED, Box 1020, Estes Park CO 80517.

# Resorts, Ranches, Restaurants, Lodging

### Ah! Wilderness Guest Ranch
Located in Durango. Resort. Openings for college students, teachers and couples

from the US only, from May 24 to September 28. Must stay through August. Needs cabin maid, waitress, laundress, kitchen assistant, dishwasher, child supervisor, $150; general ranch hands, office worker, wranglers, $150. Room and board, shared tips, bonus, laundry and entertainment provided. Needs experienced cooks and older couples interested in 2-3 months work. Salary open. Enclose long, stamped return envelope when making application. Apply by June 1 to Ah! Wilderness Guest Ranch, Box 997, Durango CO 81301.

## Aspen Lodge & Guest Ranch
Located at Estes Park. Guest ranch. Openings from June 1 to September 10 for US high school and college students to 20 years of age. Needs 6 waiters, 5 cabin attendants, 3 kitchen helpers, 2 dishwashers, 1 host or hostess, 1 lifeguard and 1 housekeeper. Salaries plus room and board; equal-split tips. Apply by June 1 to Peggy Adams, Aspen Lodge & Guest Ranch, Long's Peak Route, Estes Park CO 80517; tel. 303/586-4241.

## Aspen Meadows
Located in Aspen. Resort hotel. Openings for college students and teachers from June 15 to September 1. Needs 3 restaurant cashiers, $4.50/hour; 2-4 waiter/waitresses, $1.75/hour plus tips; 2 switchboard operators, $500/month; 1 restaurant bookkeeper, $800/month. "Employees also receive free meals, tennis discount and the opportunity to meet our unusual guests who are participants in the Aspen Institute for Humanistic studies programs. Applicants must find own housing, costs range from $100-250/month depending upon accommodation and number of persons."Apply by April 1 in writing to S. MacMichael, Manager, Aspen Meadows, Box 220, Aspen CO 81611; tel. 303/925-3426.

## Bar Lazy J Guest Ranch
Located in Parshall. Openings for college students and high school seniors from May 1 to September 30. Needs waitresses, counselors, cabin maids, relief employee, laundress, dishwashers, yard worker, wranglers, cook's helpers. Salaries dependent on age and experience. Room, board, tips and bonus provided. Laundry done weekly for free; towels and linens furnished. Attitude and willingness to work and learn are more important than experience. Apply by June 15 to Chuck Broady, Bar Lazy J Guest Ranch, Box NDS, Parshall CO 80468.

## Beavers Ski Chalet and Guest Ranch
Located in Winter Park. Family ranch in summer; family/skiiers chalet in winter. Openings from June 1 to September 15, summer; or November 18 to April 22, winter. Needs 10 wranglers, 20 room attendants, 8 waiter/waitresses, 6 kitchen helpers, 8 counselors, 4 office persons, $200-250/month, college students preferred. Includes room and board. Send resume or write for application. Apply 2-3 months in advance of openings to Employment Department, Beavers Ski Chalet and Guest Ranch, Box 43, Dept. SED, Winter Park CO 80482; tel. 303/726-5741.

## Canyon Motel & Restaurant
Located at Hot Sulphur Springs. Openings for college students and high school seniors. Needs 2 waitresses, kitchen help, 2 maids. Salary is $175/month; room,

board, and tips provided. Apply to Mrs. William Cappello, Box 109, Hot Sulphur Springs CO 80451.

### Coffee Bar Restaurant
Located at Estes Park. Openings for 36 college students, teachers, high school seniors and foreign students, minimum age 18, from May 1 to October 15. Must be able to stay through Labor Day. Needs waitresses, hostesses, bus boys, kitchen helpers, dishwashers, fry cooks. Salaries are hourly. Arrangements for living quarters available. Write for additional information; enclose stamped return envelope. Apply by May 15 to Manager, Coffee Bar Restaurant, Dept. SED, Box 2210, Estes Park CO 80517.

### Daven Haven Lodge
Located at Grand Lake. Lodging, restaurant, lounge. Openings for college students, teachers and high school seniors from mid-May to mid-September. Needs 15 waitresses, 2 cocktail waitresses, $150-200; 8 bus boys, 10 maids, $125-300; 2 bartenders, $225-375; 10 kitchen help, $150-325; entertainer (piano), salary open. Salaries include room and board. Enclose stamped return envelope when writing for application. Apply by February to Daven Haven Lodge, Box 528, Grand Lake CO 80447.

### Drowsy Water Ranch
Located in Granby. Openings from May 15 to September 10. Needs 3 maids, 3 waitresses, 2 yard-maintenance, 1 children's counselor, 2 dishwashers, college students and high school seniors preferred, $125 and up/month; 4 wranglers, college students preferred; 1 cook, college student or teacher preferred. Room, board plus tips provided. Apply to Randy Sue Fosha, Owner, Drowsy Water Ranch, Box 147 J, Granby CO 80446; tel. 303/725-3456.

### Imperial Hotel and Imperial Players
Located at Cripple Creek. Hotel, restaurant, theater. Openings for 45 college students, teachers and high school seniors, minimum age 18, from mid-May through mid-September. Needs actors, actresses, $100/week; young pianist, $150/week and up; hotel maids, pantry and kitchen personnel, desk clerks, full room and board plus salary and end-of-season bonus; busboys, bartenders, waiters, waitresses, full room and board, salary and excellent tip opportunity for competent personnel, plus end-of-season bonuses. Enclose stamped return envelope when writing for application. Apply by May 15 to Wayne S. Mackin, Imperial Hotel and Imperial Players, 123 3rd St., Cripple Creek CO 80813.

### Lazy H Ranch
Located in Allenspark. Guest ranch. Openings from May 1 to September 30. Needs 5 wranglers, $200-250/month; 2 cooks, $250/month; 2 waiters/waitresses, 2 housekeepers, 2 dishwashers, 1-2 counselors, 1-2 maintenance persons, $150/month. Room, board and tips provided. "Applicants should be prepared to work hard, long hours, live with those they work with, be outgoing, enjoy meeting and being with people, plan to stay as long as you stipulate." Apply to Bill Halligan, Manager, Lazy H Ranch, Box 2489, Allenspark CO 80510; tel. 303/747-2532.

## Longs Peak Inn and Guest Ranch

Located at Estes Park. Dude ranch. Openings for 40 college students, teachers, high school seniors and foreign students, minimum age 18, from late May to October 1. Must be able to stay at least through Labor Day. Needs waitresses/waiters, hostess, desk clerk/secretary, maintenance workers, dishwashers, cooks, kitchen helpers, maids, children's counselor, bartender, entertainer, wrangler. Salaries are plus room and board. Write for additional information and application form; enclose stamped return envelope. Apply by May 15 to Bob Akins, Dept. SED, Longs Peak Inn, Longs Peak Route 3, Estes Park CO 80517.

## Mt. Princeton Hot Springs

Located in Nathrop. Resort. Openings for college students, teachers and high school seniors from June 1 through Labor Day. Needs 6 waitresses, 4 cleaning maids, $125 per month; 4 bus boys-maintenance, $150; 3 lifeguards, office girl, receptionist, $200. Room, board plus bonus provided. Enclose long, stamped return envelope with application. Apply to Dennis L. Osborn, Mt. Princeton Hot Springs, Nathrop CO 81236.

## Peaceful Valley Lodge and Guest Ranch

Located in Lyons. Openings for 45 college students, teachers and high school seniors from mid-May through September. Needs waitresses, office assistants, secretary, counselors, driver-mechanics, wranglers, stable hands, general ranch hand-maintenance, housekeepers, gardener, cooks, cook's helpers, dishwashers. Salaries open. Room, board, tips and bonus provided. During the winter season, needs persons capable of and certified in instructing cross-country ski touring; person or persons to man snow-making equipment. Apply to Karl E. Boehm, Peaceful Valley Lodge and Guest Ranch, Dept. SED, Star Route, Lyons CO 80540.

## Sun Valley Guest Ranch

Located at Grand Lake. Openings from May 15 to October 1. Needs 3 kitchen helpers, cabin maids, laundry worker, wranglers, general ranch hand-maintenance, hay hands. Salaries are dependent on age and experience. Room, board and tips provided. Apply to Ken Bruton, Sun Valley Guest Ranch, Box 470, Grand Lake CO 80447.

## Tamarron Inn and Golf Club

Located 18 miles north of Durango. Resort hotel, condominiums and convention center. Openings from April 1 to October 30, November 1 to March 30. Needs personnel in the following areas: housekeeping (training program); kitchen crew (clean up); kitchen staff (chefs, cooks, sauciers, broilermen, pastry chefs, pantry workers, and stewards; must have previous experience in large kitchen, restaurant or hotel); desk clerks (light typing and some computer knowledge helpful); cashiers (typing and 10-key adding machine knowledge, previous background experience in handling money); general office (secretaries, clerk-typists, file clerks, payroll clerks, accounting clerks, stenographers, all require previous experience and skills); hostess and waitress (must be 21, 1 year previous experience); waiters (must be 21, 1 year previous experience); bus persons (must be over 16, 1 year previous experience); maintenance (assist plumbers, electricians, carpenters, etc., knowledge essential); grounds and golf course maintenance (driver's license, minimum age 18, previous experience). Other positions available: recreation leaders and assistants, auditors, mail clerks, activity desk clerks, babysitters, convention set-up crew, banquet waiters and waitresses, bartenders, PBX operators, security guards, bellmen, drivers, spa attendants, golf and tennis clerks, stable wranglers, shipping and receiving clerks. No housing provided; housing lists are available in personnel department. Pay varies with position and experience. Write for application form to Adelle Stephenson, Director of Personnel, Drawer 3131, Durango CO 81301; tel. 303/247-8801.

### Tumbling River Ranch

Located in Grant. Guest ranch serving families. Openings in summer for college students (minimum age 19) and teachers from mid-May through September; winter help needed October through March or mid-April; also needs year-round help. Needs 30 people in summer as waitresses, cabin girls, cooks, assistant cooks, secretary, childrens' counselors, drivers, mechanics, wranglers, general maintenance persons, groundskeepers. Needs 10-12 people in winter as cooks, cabin girls, waitresses, mechanics, general maintenance. Payment is monthly (plus tips). Room and board provided. Can room in bunk houses, individual buildings or in main ranch houses (2 persons/room; 4/bath). Application must be in by March for summer, by September 1 for winter; "state season you are applying for." Apply to Jim and Mary Dale Gordon, Tumbling River Ranch, Grant CO 80448; tel. 303/838-5981.

### Vail Associates

Located in Vail. Ski mountain and summer resort serving young adults and middle aged persons, including many Latin Americans and Europeans. Openings for college students and local applicants from November 15 to April 15 or June 1 to September 15; seasonal openings may lead to year-round employment. Needs for winter: cashiers, cooks, waiters/waitresses, dishwashers, buspersons, food handlers, snow removal, parking attendants, janitors, ticket sellers, nursery attendants, ski rental/repair persons, lift operators and ticket checkers. Needs for summer: laborers, general and grounds maintenance, cashiers, food handlers, and conventional help. "Local housing situation consists of condominiums, duplex and home rentals. Monthly rentals start at $300/month for a studio and run to over $1,200/month for 3-4 bedroom places. As we have limited summer openings, our main employment emphasis is on winter seasonal employees. Candidates interested in winter employment should secure local housing early in September." Apply to Vail Associates, Inc., Box 7, Vail CO 81657; tel. 303/476-5601.

### Wilderness Trails Ranch

Located in Bayfield. Guest ranch. Openings from May 20 to September 12; can start as late as June 1 and leave as early as September 4. Needs 6 wrangler-trail guides and 2 youth wranglers, college students preferred, $180/month or more; 10 kitchen and cabin maids, 1 babysitter and 1 laundry person, high school seniors or college students preferred, $180/month or more; 1 kitchen supervisor, college students preferred, $250/month or more; 1 foreman, college students or teachers preferred, $450/month; and 1 girl's supervisor, college students or teachers preferred, $400/month. "Do not apply if your moral standards are not high, if you have ever used drugs, if you are not a friendly person with an above-average personality, or if you are not willing to work very hard and give our guests the best vacation they've ever had. Do not apply if you will not be 18 by the time you begin work. Our main objective is the well-being and happiness of our guests. Their consideration comes before all others. If you are not willing to strive for this goal, you wouldn't be happy at Wilderness Trails." Apply by March 1 to Gene and Jan Roberts, 776 County Rd. 300, Durango CO 81301; tel. 303/247-0722.

### YMCA of The Rockies
Located at Estes Park Center and Snow Mountain Ranch. Family and conference center. Openings for college students, teachers, retired teachers and foreign students from June 1 to Labor Day. Earlier and later if possible; camps open year-round. Needs 60 business office, shops, fountain persons; 80 program; 80 housekeeping; 40 buildings and grounds maintenance; 90 food service workers. Salaries are $240/month plus room and board. Apply by June to E. Eugene Garris, Resident Director, YMCA of the Rockies, Estes Park Center, Association Camp CO 80511.

# Summer Camps

### Bear Pole Ranch
Located in Steamboat Springs. Coed camp. Openings for college students and high school seniors from June 6 to August 16. Separate programs by age: discovery, 9-13; expedition, 13-15; adventure bound, 15-18. Needs 15 senior counselors, 10 assistant counselors, cook, assistant cooks, nurse, wrangler, assistant wranglers, secretary, ranch hand. Apply to Dr. and Mrs. Glenn N. Poulter, Bear Pole Ranch Camp, Steamboat Springs CO 80477.

### Cheley Colorado Camps, Inc.
Located in Estes Park. Four boys' camps, 4 girls' camps. Openings from June 11 to August 11 for 100 teachers and college students, minimum age 19 and completed sophomore college year; prefers applicants from Colorado, Texas, Arkansas, Oklahoma, Nebraska, Iowa, Illinois, Indiana, Missouri and Kansas. Needs nurses (RN), secretaries, cooks and kitchen helpers; instructors for archery, fencing, tennis, Western riding and horsemanship, mountain hiking, out camping, backpacking, woodcraft, nature lore, riflery (NRA), handcrafts, group singing, land sports (no water sports offered); bus drivers, property maintenance. Staff employed only with personal interviews which are conducted during January and February in Midwest and South Central states; California interviews in December; interviews in Denver office until May 30. Salaries are $550 and up for season, based on experience. Meals, lodging, insurance and travel allowance are provided. "We do most all of our hiring during the months of January and February for the upcoming summer." Apply to D.S. Cheley, Dept. SED, Box 6525, Denver CO 80206.

### Colorado Outward Bound School
Located in Denver. Experiential education school. Needs 16 assistant instructors (to start), $350/month plus food check and basecamp, 32 instructors (after one season as assistant), $575-750/month, college students (over 21) and teachers preferred. Employment June, July, August (limited). "Applicants must meet some mountaineering skills criteria, plus have first aid card, experience at lead rock climbing, teaching experience in some capacity." Apply to Program Director, Colorado Outward Bound School, 945 Pennsylvania St., Denver CO 80203; tel. 303/837-0880.

## Colvig Silver Camps

Located near Durango. Coed. Openings for college students, teachers, high school seniors and foreign students for 9 weeks from mid-June to mid-August. Needs 26 head counselors, $450 up; 10 assistant counselors, $400; wrangler, salary open; nurse (RN), $700; 3 cooks, $750 up. Room, board and health insurance provided. Room, board and health insurance provided. Expedition trips to four states require special emphasis on outdoor living skills: woodsmanship, mountaineering, nature, archaeology and geology, crafts, horsemanship, backpacking, river rafting, riflery (NRA), swimming (WSI), archery, land sports. Apply by April 1 to Craig Colvig, 9665 Florida Rd., Durango CO 81301.

## Earthrider

Located in the southern Rockies at Powderhorn. Private camp for boys and girls, ages 7-17. Openings from approximately June 10 to August 12. Needs 2 program directors ($80-100/week), 15 program and bunkhouse counselors ($40-60/week), college students and teachers preferred; 5 junior counselors ($30-40/week), high school seniors preferred; 2 cooks, 1 nurse, salary depends on experience. "We're a small camp, limiting enrollment to 50 per session. Applicants need to be multitalented to fill in in more than one area. Staff is relatively small and thus each one needs to be flexible. Need people in following areas: horseback riding, archery, riflery, arts and crafts, wilderness skills, WSI, biking, advanced mountaineering, rockclimbing, overnight camping, campcraft skills, nature." Apply to Allen and Nancy Orcutt, Directors, Earthrider, Dept. SED, Box 1436 Gunnison CO 81230; tel. 303/641-4370.

## Easter Seal

Camp for physically and mentally handicapped children and young adults. Openings for college students, teachers and high school seniors from early June through late August. Needs cabin counselors, cooks, kitchen help, maintenance and maintenance helpers, nurse and specialty counselors for riding, swimming, crafts. Room and board provided. Apply by May to Easter Seal Society of Colorado, Dept. SED, 609 W. Littleton Blvd., Room 300, Littleton CO 80120.

## Elephant Rock

Located on Palmer Lake, 50 miles south of Denver. Coed camp for youth, ages 8-12 and seniors. Openings for college students from June 20 to August 30. Needs program director; cook, up to $750; lifeguard, up to $500; 8 counselors, up to $450; maintenance, up to $350; nurse, up to $750; assistant cook, up to $600. Room and board provided. Apply before March 15 to Divisional Youth Director, The Salvation Army, Box 2369, Denver CO 80201.

---

**Be sure to mention that you saw their ad in** *Summer Employment Directory* **when contacting any of the employers listed here.**

## Flying G Ranch
## Tomahawk Ranch
Located near Deckers (Flying G Ranch) and Bailey (Tomahawk Ranch). Girl Scout camps for girls ages 8-17. Openings from June to August. Needs camp director, May to August; 36 troop counselors, $300-450/season; 12 troop leaders, $450-750/season; 8 Western riding staff, $300-800/season; 2 health supervisors, $640-925/season; 8 kitchen staff, $600-1,200/season; 8 administrators with knowledge of camping, Girl Scout program or office skills, $500-1,250/season. Salaries subject to change. "A very rewarding learning experience for resourceful individuals who enjoy working with children and living outdoors in a semi-primitive setting." Request application, February through May, from Sue Boyd, Camp Director, Dept. SED, Girl Scouts Mile Hi Council, 2727 Bryant St., Denver CO 80211.

## Geneva Glen Camps
Located at Indian Hills, 20 miles southwest of Denver. Coed camp for children ages 8-16. ACA accredited; 47th year of operation. Openings for 50 college students from June 13 to August 13. Needs counselors with experience working with children; skills in counseling and leading children and a love of children essential. Skills in swimming, archery, horsemanship, music, crafts and riflery are helpful but not required. Counselors earn $300-400/season; room and board, health and accident insurance, travel allowance for out-of-staters provided, along with tremendous leadership program for staff. "Leadership and personal growth of the staff are a part of the camp philosophy." Other staff needs are nurse, $600/summer; 5 cooks, $400-600, based on experience; 5 maintenance crew persons, $200 and up; director of maintenance, salary based on experience and skills. Apply by May 15 to Robert and Carol Duvall, Directors, Geneva Glen Camps, Inc., Box 248, Indian Hills CO 80454.

## Kotami
Located at Foxton in the Rocky Mountains. Resident coed camp for children ages 8-17. Openings for both males and females from June 8 to August 25. Needs assistant director, $90-100/week; nurse (LPN, RN, or GN), $80-90/week; cook and assistant cook, $75-100/week; handyman, $60-75/week; 5 wranglers, specialists in archery, rock climbing, nature, arts & crafts, 10 unit counselors, $50/week; 7-10 junior counselor/kitchen aides, $30/week. "Applicants do not necessarily have to be college students or teachers, however they are preferred. I am most impressed by a good healthy attitude toward children, the out-of-doors and new learning experiences. A strongly independent, co-operative (team oriented), positive, enthusiastic person has a better chance at the job than one with much experience and a blase attitude. Sell yourself!" Send for application or send resume. Apply by April 30 to Nevada Brown, Outdoor Program Director, Camp Fire Girls, Inc., Dep.. SED, 2901 W. 19th Ave., Denver CO 80204.

## Lazy Acres
Located in Rye. Girl Scout camp. Openings for college students and teachers from mid-June to early August. Needs 4 unit leaders, 7 counselors, assistant camp director, CIT director (minimum age 21), program specialist, handyman, kitchen personnel, nurse (RN). Apply to Camp Lazy Acres, Columbine Girl Scout Council, 21 Montebello, Pueblo CO 81001.

## Sanborn Western Camps

Located 35 miles west of Colorado Springs. Two private western ranch camps, Big Spring Ranch for Boys and High Trails Ranch for Girls, ages 8-16. Openings available for qualified men and women from June 7 to August 24. Minimum requirements are 20 years of age and two years of college. Needs 2 nurses (RN); 4 cooks, $700; 50 counselors in out-camping, riding, nature, fishing, hiking, campcraft, all sports, fly-tying, geology, tennis, riflery, archery, $500 and up. Room, board and laundry provided. Please state qualifications and experience in inquiry. Apply by May to Roger A. Sanborn, Florissant CO 80816.

## Sky High Ranch

Located in Woodland Park. Girl Scout camp for girls ages 6-17. Openings for 28 college students and teachers from June 14 to August 10. Needs riding director, 7 unit leaders, business manager, waterfront director, $93-120/week; 12 unit assistants, assistant cook, 2 riding assistants, trading post manager, $69-89/week. Apply to Gail H. Gurney, Wagon Wheel Girl Scouts, 518 N. Nevada, Colorado Springs CO 80903.

# ——————— Connecticut ———————

## Business and Industry

### Electrolux Corporation

Located in Stamford. Unlimited openings in direct selling for college students, teachers and high school seniors during the summer and year-round. Pays commission plus sales prizes and cash bonuses of $1,500, $1,000, $750 and $500 to qualified *collegiate* sales-makers. Apply to Norma Leitner, Electrolux College Program, 2777 Summer St., Stamford CT 06905.

### Kelly Services, Inc.

More than 450 branches coast to coast, Puerto Rico, Canada, England and France. Temporary work assignments. Offers over 100 job classifications (office, marketing and light industrial assignments) to college students, teachers and other qualified people during summer breaks and year 'round. Kelly Services also has a special referral system that allows you to register at a Kelly office near your school then work near your home during summer recess—or register near your home then work on temporary assignments during the school year. Assignments available include clerks, typists, secretaries, keypunch operators, word processors, bookkeepers and a variety of marketing and light industrial. Offers flexible schedule with "attractive hourly pay rates equal to or higher than the accepted industry standards in most cities." No paycheck deductions except Social Security and income tax. No employment fee for temporary work. See the White Pages for the branch of Kelly Services nearest you. Apply in person or write to: Summer Employment, National Headquarters, Kelly Services, GPO 1179, Detroit MI 48266.

### Temp Force

Temporary office personnel contractor. Openings for college students, teachers, high school seniors during vacations and holidays. Needs secretaries, typists, stenographers, clericals and accountants. Salaries based upon experience. Apply to Temp Force, 459 Summer St., Stamford CT 06901; tel. 203/348-5600.

## Aubrey Thomas Inc.
Located in Stamford. Temporary and permanent personnel agency. Works with over 100 major corporations in the lower Fairfield County area. Openings for full-time and part-time help from May 1 to September 15. Needs 250 typists, $4-5/hour; 250 secretaries, $4.50-5.25/hour; 200 gal/man Fridays, $4-5/hour, 100 receptionists, $3.50-4/hour; 100 clerk-typists, $3.50-4/hour. Never a fee charged to applicants. Apply in person at 777 Summer St., Stamford CT 06902; tel. 203/357-0808; 167 East Ave., Norwalk CT; tel. 203/866-5556.

## Overseas Custom-Maid Agency, Inc.
Located in Stamford. Employment Agency. Places college students from April/May/June through September. 500 openings for "Mother's Helpers" with families in Metropolitan New York and New England. Some with families traveling to resort areas. Duties are mainly child care and light housekeeping. Swimming and driving ability helpful. Salaries are $100-110/week plus room and board; premium wage for cooks. Employer pays airfare to the job. Employee responsible for own transportation home at end of assignment. There is no fee of any kind for any applicant to pay. Write in January or February enclosing stamped return envelope. Apply to Mrs. Henrietta E. Burnett, Overseas Custom-Maid Agency, Inc., 300 Bedford St., Stamford CT 06901; tel. 203/324-9575.

# Summer Camps

## Association of Independent Camps
Camps located in New England and Middle Atlantic States. Openings at 100 children's summer camps. Needs head counselors, group leaders, general and all specialty counselors. Room and board provided. Apply by July to Association of Independent Camps, Dept. SED, 55 W. 42nd St., New York NY 10036; tel. 212/695-2656.

## Awosting for Boys
## Chinqueka for Girls
Awosting is located at Bantam Lake; Chinqueka, Mt. Tom Lake. Independent camps for children ages 6-16. ACA, Connecticut accredited. Openings from June 26 to August 26. Needs counselors: 12 waterfront (WSI certified, includes instructors in rowing, canoeing, waterskiing, and scuba—must be qualified to teach swimming and 1 other specialty), 8 athletic, 2 riflery (NRA), 2 pioneering, 2 dramatic, 2 newspaper, 2 go-carting, 2 mini bike, 4 tennis, 1 modern dance, 2 archery (certified), 2 arts and crafts (fine arts), 2 shop work (woodwork, plastics), 2 gymnastics, 2 trampoline. College students age 19 plus and school teachers preferred. $475-750/season plus room, board, laundry and tips. "If possible send resume, refrences, etc. We are seeking well-qualified counselors who like children and enjoy camp life. We welcome applicants from any place in the United States. We are also international camps. Knowledge of Spanish, German, French an added asset." Also needs 8 kitchen workers (college students, teachers and high school seniors preferred), $400/season plus room, board, and laundry; 2 assistant cooks, $900/season plus room, board, and laundry; 2 cooks, $1,800/season; 2

nurses (RN and LPN), $800/season. Salaries include room, board, laundry and tips. "Preference given to experienced employees." For quick reply send stamped, addressed envelope. Apply to Mr. and Mrs. Oscar Ebner, Directors, Awosting and Chinqueka, Dept. SED, Route 202, Bantam CT 06750; tel. 203/567-9678.

## Birchwood

Located in West Goshen, Connecticut. Private, coed. Openings for college students and teachers for 8 weeks, starting about July 1. Needs 75 general counselors (minimum age 19), $150-300 plus tips; specialty counselors: 4 waterfront, $300-1,000; athletic, arts and crafts, ceramics, nature, etc. Write for application. Apply to Laury Greenberg, Camp Birchwood, 140 Ash Dr., Roslyn NY 11576.

## Buck's Rock

Located at New Milford, Connecticut. Creative work, coed, ages 12-16. Openings for graduate students, artists, teachers, craftsmen, minimum age 21, from late June to late August. Needs instructors for fine arts, crafts, commercial art, printing, performing arts, stage design and construction, folk music, folk dancing, science lab, sports, gymnastics, waterfront, electronics; guidance counselors. Also openings for kitchen, dining room, and maintenance staff (suitable for college students). Salaries are open; room and board provided. Apply to Lou and Sybil Simon, Dept. SED, 140 Riverside Dr., New York NY 10024; tel. 212/362-2702.

## Channel 3 Times Farm Camp

Located in Andover. Coed camp for underprivileged children. Openings for college students from June 15 to August 16. Needs 20 counselors with camping skills and group work experience. Counselors work with a group of six campers, $500-700; pool director (WSI, minimum age 21), $750; assistant pool director (WSI), $550. Nonsmokers only. Apply by May 1 to Edward F. Turn, Camp Director, Channel 3 Times Farm Camp, RR1, Box 341, Andover CT 06232.

## Connri

Located at Ashford. Salvation Army, coed residential youth camp. Openings for college students, teachers and high school seniors from June to August. Needs junior and senior counselors, program director, specialty counselors (crafts, nature, waterfront, recreation), maintenance workers, kitchen help, laundry and housekeeping workers, nurse and relief nurse. Salaries are $250-750 and appropriate professional salaries. Apply by June 1 to Divisional Youth Secretary, The Salvation Army, 855 Asylum Ave., Hartford CT 06101.

## Hadar

Located in Clinton. Private coed Jewish camp. Openings for 75 college students and teachers from June 26 to August 24. Needs counselors with specialties in sailing, canoeing, nature, archery, WSI, music, fencing, tennis; general counselors. Salares are $200-800. Room, board and laundry provided. Apply by May 1 to Hal Watman, Camp Hadar, 435 Brooklawn Ave., Fairfield CT 06432.

## Jewell

Located in Colebrook. Regular camp, outdoor adventure-ranch camp, teen trail camp. Openings for male and female applicants to work June 22 to August 25. Needs waterfront, crafts, ranch, physical education, outdoor adventure directors, college students and teachers preferred, $600-1,000/season; junior counselors, counselors, $200-450/season; nurse, $800-1,000/season; bike, canoe, backpack, sailing trip leaders, $400-800/season, college students, teachers, foreign students all acceptable. Year-round outdoor education and conference programs. Interns and field work students encouraged year-round. An equal opportunity employer. Apply by February 28 to William J. Devlin, Executive Director, Camp Jewell, 160 Jewell St., Colebrook CT 06021; tel. 203/379-2782.

### Ken-Mont
### Ken-Wood
Located in Kent, Connecticut. Brother-sister camps. Located in the Berkshire Mountains in New England. Openings for college seniors and teachers, minimum age 21, from approximately June 21 to August 20. Additional week's work available to staff members selected as faculty for University Family Camp. Needs 180 counselors, group leaders, waterfront instructors (ARC or YMCA), specialty counselors, athletic counselors in all land and water sports, bus drivers, secretaries, bookkeeping assistants, 2 physicians, 6 nurses (RN). Top salaries plus full maintenance; no tipping permitted. Apply by June 1 to Mr. Lloyd Albin, Director, Ken-Mont and Ken-Wood Camps, 2 Spencer Place, Scarsdale NY 10583.

### Laurelwood
Located in North Madison, 100 miles from New York City. Kosher (under Rabbinical supervision) coed camp for children ages 7-12 and teenagers ages 13-14. Needs counselors for a staff of 150. Apply to Norman J. Feitelson, Camp Laurelwood, 1156 Chapel St., New Haven CT 06511; tel. 203/624-2589.

### Lenox Hill
Located in Bantam. Social camp serving children from New York City, ages 6-13. Openings from June 24 to August 30; 10 week season. Needs 2 program directors (teachers, college students), $1,400-1,900/season; nurse (RN, LPN or graduate nurse, must have CPR), $1,000/season; 22 general counselors (college student), $400-750/season; nature counselor (college student), $400-750/season; arts and crafts counselor (college student), $400-750/season; 2 waterfront specialists (college students with WSI), $500-800/season. Salaries include room and board. Send for application or call by June 24 to Walter Thompson, Director, Box 400, Bantam CT 06750; tel. 203/567-9760.

### New England Camping Association, Inc. (ACA)
Located in Connecticut. Camp Counselor Referral Service, for children ages 8-16. Openings for college students and teachers, minimum age 19, for 8 weeks. Needs specialty counselors for advanced lifesaving, archery, arts and crafts, bicycling, boating, campcraft, canoeing, drama, golf, guitar, gymnastics, horseback riding, land sports, music, nature-ecology, photography, piano, radio-electronics, riflery, sailing (SCI), scuba, tennis, waterskiing, WSI; trip leader, unit leader, administrative, chef, baker, kitchen workers, clerical, maintenance, doctors, nurses (RN). Salaries start at $400 and are commensurate with age, education, camp experience and type of position. $2 application fee. Apply to New England Camping Association, Inc., Room 410, 29 Commonwealth Ave., Boston MA 02116.

## Sloane

Located in Lakeville, Connecticut. YMCA, coed. "A camp that uses human relations skills to help staff and campers be winners in life." Openings for college students and teachers from June 22 to September 1. Needs 48 general counselors with activity skills, $500-550; 10 unit supervisors, 10 activity directors (college graduates, teachers), $600-900; WSI, naturalists, performing arts, sailing, clerical, nurse (RN), food service. Apply by May 15 to Dept. SED, YMCA Camp Sloane, 235 Mamaroneck Ave., White Plains NY 10605.

## United Cerebral Palsy Association of Greater Hartford

Located on the Connecticut shore. Summer residential camp for physically disabled kids and adults. Openings for 8 weeks, June to August. Needs approximately 10 counselors, $75-100/week. College students, teachers, foreign students or local applicants preferred. "Must be 18 years of age or older, mature and responsible and have a genuine interest in people. Experience in working with handicapped people would be nice, but is not necessary. Counselors are first and foremost responsible for their campers. They are to see that campers are always comfortable, involved in the activities and happy. They must also make sure that all of the needs of all of the campers are constantly met. This may include dressing, feeding, toilet needs, etc." Needs 1 assistant director, $920/season. College students or local applicants preferred. Must be presently attending or having already completed college with a future vocation in working with the physically disabled. "The assistant director is responsible for implementing and coordinating daily activities and for planning evening programs. He or she provides direct leadership to counselors and campers, maintains the program efficiency and insures safety and happiness of each camper. Also must have a bus driver's license." Also needs 1 director; $1,400/season. Must have a B.S. degree in recreation or physical education with at least 2 years of experience working with the physically disabled, and 3 years in camp settings. "Responsibilities include developing and directing a summer camping program for physically disabled children, teenagers and adults afflicted with cerebral palsy and other multiply disabling conditions, supervising of a staff of 16 counselors, assistant director and a nurse. Assisted by the Program Director, Camp Coordinator and Recreation Director, hires seasonal staff." Additional Advice: "We must always have at least 3 people who are able to drive a bus. In Connecticut a Public Service Operator's license is required. We must also have at least 2 people with their Water Safety Instructor's license." Apply by April 1 to Bev Jackson, Camp Coordinator, 80 Whitney St., Hartford CT 06105; tel. 203/236-6201.

## Yankee Trails

Stafford Springs, Connecticut 06076Girl Scout camp, ages 7 to 17. Openings for college students and teachers from June 22 to August 10; includes pre-camp and closing. Needs 6 troop leaders, $400-650; 14 assistant troop leaders, craft consultant, $350-400; waterfront director, $500-800; small-craft director, $400-550; waterfront assistants, $300-400; assistant cook, $400-600; nurse, $600-800; business manager, $400-650. Salaries are for season. Apply to Carmen Nielsen, Connecticut Yankee Girl Scout Council, Box 504, 504 Main St., Farmington CT 06032.

## YMCA of Greater Bridgeport

Camp Mohawk (for girls) located in Cornwall, Connecticut; Camp Hi-Rock (for boys) located in Mt. Washington, Massachusetts, close to the Connecticut borner in southwest Massachusetts. Camp for children ages 8-15. Openings for teachers and college students, minimum age 18, from June 24 to August 25. Needs cabin counselor/instructors in gymnastics, swimming (ARC or 'Y' SLS), sailing, canoeing, kayaking, birling, landsports (including tennis), riflery, archery, nature lore; specialists in waterfront management, arts and crafts, horseback riding (English), photography, waterskiing, music; CIT director; unit directors; clerical workers; maintenance people; kitchen helpers; nurse (RN). Minimum salaries: $800. Additional salary is available for preseason maintenance from May 15. Room and board provided with all positions. Apply by May 1 to Tom Q. Moore, Executive Director, YMCA Camps, Box 397, Litchfield CT 06759.

### YMCA Northern Branch Day Camp
Located in Hamden. 90-acre day camp for children; Discovery Program, ages 5-6; Boys' and Girls' Unit, ages 7-11; Young Teen Program, ages 12-13. Openings for college students and teachers from June 30 to August 22, plus several training classes during the week of June 23; Maintenance worker must work April/May to August 19. Needs 24 counselors, 3 unit counselors, $300-600/season; CIT director, tennis specialist, young teens specialist, field games director, $600-800/season; tennis assistant, young teens assistant, $400-600/season; maintenance worker, $100-140/week. "Staff must provide own housing. Bus transportation is provided by the camp. Applicant must enjoy children and working with them, and be highly motivated." Send resume by April. Apply to David R. Makowicki, Youth Program Director, Dept. SED, Northern Branch YMCA, 1605 Sherman Ave., Hamden CT 06514; tel. 203/248-6361.

## Summer Theaters

### Westport Country Playhouse/Connecticut Theatre FDTN, Inc.
Located in Westport. Openings for college students and teachers from June 13 to September 10. Needs 12 apprentices, no salary; 8 box office staff, $100; box office treasurer, house manager, $150. Salaries are weekly; room and board found in private homes for an average of $80/week. Apply by May 15 to Westport Country Playhouse, Box 629, Westport CT 06880.

# Delaware

## Business and Industry

### Kelly Services, Inc.
More than 450 branches coast to coast, Puerto Rico, Canada, England and France. Temporary work assignments. Offers over 100 job classifications (office, marketing and light industrial assignments) to college students, teachers and other qualified people during summer breaks and year 'round. Kelly Services also has a special referral system that allows you to register at a Kelly office near your school then work near your home during summer recess—or register near your home then work on temporary assignments during the school year. Assignments available include clerks, typists, secretaries, keypunch operators, word processors,

bookkeepers and a variety of marketing and light industrial. Offers flexible schedule with "attractive hourly pay rates equal to or higher than the accepted industry standards in most cities." No paycheck deductions except Social Security and income tax. No employment fee for temporary work. See the White Pages for the branch of Kelly Services nearest you. Apply in person or write to: Summer Employment, National Headquarters, Kelly Services, GPO 1179, Detroit MI 48266.

## Resorts, Ranches, Restaurants, Lodging

### Nomad Village, Inc.
Tower Shores, Bethany Beach, Delaware. Motel, apartments, bars, package stores at a gay seashore resort. Openings for males only (no foreign students), 20-30 years of age, who are unprejudiced to homosexuals, from June 15 through Labor Day; some from May 15 through September 15. Clientele is gay (homophile) who are extremely discrete. No drag, hippy, S&M, militant or other offensive types tolerated. Needs 4 switchboard operators/desk clerks, 2 lifeguards (pool only—must have Senior Lifesaving Certificate), 6 room stewards; 4 package store clerks, 8 bartenders, $100 up/week. "An apartment on the premises is available for single, male employees only at a nominal charge ($20/week). Employees sharing the apartment share the cost of food. There is no other charge for linens, utilities, etc." Apply by March 15 to Nomad Village, Inc., 2404 NE 13th St., Ft. Lauderdale FL 33304.

# —— District of Columbia ——

## Business and Industry

### Kelly Services, Inc.
More than 450 branches coast to coast, Puerto Rico, Canada, England and France. Temporary work assignments. Offers over 100 job classifications (office, marketing and light industrial assignments) to college students, teachers and other qualified people during summer breaks and year 'round. Kelly Services also has a special referral system that allows you to register at a Kelly office near your school then work near your home during summer recess—or register near your home then work on temporary assignments during the school year. Assignments available include clerks, typists, secretaries, keypunch operators, word processors, bookkeepers and a variety of marketing and light industrial. Offers flexible schedule with "attractive hourly pay rates equal to or higher than the accepted industry standards in most cities." No paycheck deductions except Social Security and income tax. No employment fee for temporary work. See the White Pages for the branch of Kelly Services nearest you. Apply in person or write to: Summer Employment, National Headquarters, Kelly Services, GPO 1179, Detroit MI 48266.

### Mature Temps Inc.
National temporary employment service. Openings for college students, teachers, high school seniors, local applicants and foreign students from May to September or year-round. Needs secretaries, clerks, typists, bookkeepers, stenographers, accountants, demonstrators and marketing research persons. High hourly rates

based on skills. Apply to Mature Temps Inc., 1899 L St. NW, Suite 507, Washington DC 20036; tel. 202/833-8888.

### Tele Sec Temporary Services
See telephone directory for suburban offices in Hyattsville and Rockville, Maryland; Falls Church, Virginia. Many openings year-round and summers. Needs secretaries (60 w.p.m. typing, 80 shorthand), $4.75-5.75; typists (60 w.p.m.), $3.75-5.25; typists (50 w.p.m.), $3.75-4.55; keypunchers, input operators, accounting clerks and others. There is no fee to applicants. Apply to Tele Sec Temporary Personnel Inc., 1725 K St. NW, Room 1002, Washington DC 20006.

### Temp Force
Temporary office personnel contractor. Openings for college students, teachers, high school seniors during vacations and holidays. Needs secretaries, typists, stenographers, clericals and accountants. Salaries based upon experience. Apply to Temp Force, 1701 K St. NW, Washington DC 20006; tel. 202/331-1064.

### Temporary Staffing, Inc.
Temporary help service. Openings for college students and teachers. Needs 30 typists (60 w.p.m.), $4.50-5.50/hour; 20 secretaries (70 w.p.m. typing, 80 w.p.m. shorthand), $6-6.50/hour. There is no fee to applicants. Apply to Temporary Staffing, Inc., 919—18th St. NW, Washington DC 20006; tel. 202/659-3474.

# Florida

## Business and Industry

### Kelly Services, Inc.
More than 450 branches coast to coast, Puerto Rico, Canada, England and France. Temporary work assignments. Offers over 100 job classifications (office, marketing and light industrial assignments) to college students, teachers and other qualified people during summer breaks and year 'round. Kelly Services also has a special referral system that allows you to register at a Kelly office near your school then work near your home during summer recess—or register near your home then work on temporary assignments during the school year. Assignments available include clerks, typists, secretaries, keypunch operators, word processors, bookkeepers and a variety of marketing and light industrial. Offers flexible schedule with "attractive hourly pay rates equal to or higher than the accepted industry standards in most cities." No paycheck deductions except Social Security and income tax. No employment fee for temporary work. See the White Pages for the branch of Kelly Services nearest you. Apply in person or write to: Summer Employment, National Headquarters, Kelly Services, GPO 1179, Detroit MI 48266.

## Commercial Attractions

### Walt Disney World Vacation Kingdom.
Located 16 miles southwest of Orlando. Openings from the first week of June

through Labor Day for 500 persons age 16 and older. Needs persons to work in shops, food locations, custodial department and attractions. Also needs hosts and hostesses. Starting salary is generally $3.30/hour. Salary somewhat less for positions with tipping. Shifts vary greatly and may change often during the season. All applicants must provide their own transportation and their own housing; housing not available on Walt Disney World property. Most employees average 30-35 hours/week. Personal interview is required at the Walt Disney World Employment Center. Do not send resume or request application. Obtain employment information by visiting the Employment Center Monday through Friday throughout the year; appointments not scheduled in advance. Final selection made within 1 month of the holiday season. An equal opportunity employer.

# Expeditions, Guide Trips

### Flint School Aboard Te Vega and Te Quest
Located in Sarasota. Academic school ships in the Mediterranean and Europe. Openings for college students, minimum age 19. Needs 6 crew in training program aboard 156 foot and 173 foot sailing schooners; should have ARC life saving certificate, serve as working maintenance crew (painting, varnishing, sail mending, rust removal, engine cleaning, laundry, galley and food service, ship housekeeping) during travel program; teaching interns for academic or ship staff career appointments. Shore leave schedule when in foreign ports. Only those interested for a minimum of one full school year should apply. Write for application forms to Captain Stoll, 4Rs Academic Method, Inc., Box 5809, Sarasota FL 33579.

# National Parks

### Flamingo Resort
Located at Flamingo, in Everglades National Park, overlooking Florida Bay. Resort serving national park visitors and families; facilities include lodge, cottages, restaurant, cafeteria, lounge, gift shop, boat cruises, tram trains, marina, service station and grocery story. Openings year-round, "with most positions available between November 1-April 15. For lodge, needs 5 desk clerks, $500-600/month; 3 clerical, $400-500/month; 2 housemen to handle hotel maintenance, $400-500/month. For restaurant, needs 10 cooks, $500-600/month; 25 waiters/waitresses $160/month plus tips; 14 utility persons, $400-500/month; 4 bartenders, $250/month plus tips; 6 cashiers, $400-500/month; 3 supervisors, $500-600/month. For marina, needs 7 dock workers to handle boating activities, $400-500/month; 7 grocery store clerks, $400-500/month; 5 naturalists to lead sightseeing activities, $500-600. Room and board provided at cost of $15.60/week per person. Send for application and informational material to Gregory A. Martel, Assistant General Manager, Dept. SED, Flamingo Resort, Flamingo FL 33030; tel. 305/253-2241.

# Resorts, Ranches, Restaurants, Lodging

### South Seas Plantation
Located at Captiva Island. Island resort hotel. Openings for college students,

teachers and high school seniors on a seasonal or year 'round basis. Various positions available, mostly in the restaurant and housekeeping operations. Salaries average $500/month less inexpensive room and board. Three month *minimum* length of employment acceptable. Apply to Roy Collom, Personnel Manager, South Seas Plantation, Captiva Island FL 33924.

# Summer Camps

### Challenge
Located in Sorrento. Easter Seal camp for physically handicapped persons ages 6 to adult; one autistic children's session. Openings for college students, teachers and foreign students from June 8 to August 23. Needs 15 male counselors, 15 female counselors, 5 specialists (crafts, WSI, games), $40/week; 2 head counselors (1 male, 1 female), $50/week; and program director, $60/week; nurse (RN), $200/week. Salaries include room, board, and hospital and accident insurance. Apply to Scott Brockmann, Camp Challenge, Rt. 1, Box 350, Sorrento FL 32776.

### Circle F Dude Ranch
Located at Lake Wales. Private coed camp, ages 6-16. Openings for college students and teachers, minimum age 18, nonsmokers and nondrinkers, from mid-June to mid-August. Needs head counselors (minimum age 25), bunk and specialty counselors for riding, swimming, waterskiing, tripping, tennis, crafts, archery, nature lore, art; song leader, evening program director, nurse (RN). Salaries are $500 and up. Room, board and laundry provided. Apply by April to George F. Fischbach, Circle F Dude Ranch Camp, Lake Wales FL 33853.

### Harder Hall Golf and Tennis Camp for Teens
Located in Sebring. Coed camp. Needs area representatives to recruit campers. Commission paid. "You can earn money all during the winter and spring." Also needs general counselors, college golf and tennis team members preferred; experienced evening activity director to plan and carry out teenage socials, games, dramatics, etc; dining room supervisor; dramatic coach; nurse (RN); waterskiing and sailing instructors, lifeguards (WSI); and mature night security counselors. Considers mature couples in all areas. Camper workers 16 or over, pay part tuition. Write to Harder Hall Golf and Tennis Camp for Teens, Sebring FL 33870.

### Kadima
St. Petersburg, Florida.Jewish oriented day camp for boys and girls ages 2-15. Openings approximately June 18 to August 10. Needs 10 counselors, local college students and teachers preferred, $350-650/season; 10 junior counselors, high school seniors preferred, $300/season; aquatics director and assistant aquatics director, college students and teachers preferred, $600-800/season; 1 supervisor each for arts and crafts, music, tennis, college students and teachers preferred, $600-800/season. Housing should be worked out in area. Apply by May to Fred Margolis, Director, Camp Kadima, The Jewish Community Center of Pinellas County, 8167 Elbow Lane, St. Petersburg FL 33710; tel. 813/344-5795.

### Seacamp
Located in Big Pine Key. Private nonprofit camp for teenagers, ages 12-17;

emphasis on marine science and scuba. ACA accredited. Openings for college students and teachers from June 1 to August 25. Needs 10 marine science staff/counselors preferably with degrees in related science; instructors; 2 sailing (ARC), outboard boating (ARC), first aid (ARC), 5 scuba (PADI, NAUI, YMCA), campcraft; 20 specialty counselors for arts and crafts, photography, journalism, music, WSI, fishing, canoeing; secretary, 2 assistant cooks, nurse (RN), dining hall manager. Apply by May 15 to Personnel Director, Seacamp, Dept SED, Route 3, Box 170, Big Pine Key FL 33043.

### Sparta
Located in Sebring. Private, coed. Openings for college students and qualified high school graduates, mid-June to mid-August. Needs general and specialty counselors for riding, waterfront (WSI), swimming, lifesaving, waterskiing, diving, sailing, canoeing, gymnastics, arts and crafts, archery, tennis, cheerleading, basketball, softball, soccer, all land and water sports. Salaries are $500 and up. Room and board provided. Sparta is modern in every respect. Apply early to F.A. Schwarb, Camp Sparta, Sebring FL 33870.

### Welaka
Located in Jupiter. Girl Scout camp for ages 5-17. Openings for college students, teachers and foreign students from June 8 to July 26. Needs 3 waterfront assistants (WSI), $350-500/season; unit assistant/dramatics specialist, unit assistant/arts and crafts specialist, unit assistant/gymnastics specialist, unit assistant/sports specialist, unit assistant/environmental specialist, unit assistant/canoeing specialist, $450-550/season; 4 unit leaders, $500-600/season; 7 unit assistants, $350-450/season; 3 cooks, $700-1,000/season; program directors, $800-1,000/season; CIT director, $650-850/season; nurse (RN or LPN), $500-800/season. Apply to Lynn Thames, Dept. SED, Camp Welaka, 2728 Lake Worth Rd., Lake Worth FL 33461.

# Georgia

## Business and Industry

### Kelly Services, Inc.
More than 450 branches coast to coast, Puerto Rico, Canada, England and France. Temporary work assignments. Offers over 100 job classifications (office, marketing and light industrial assignments) to college students, teachers and other qualified people during summer breaks and year 'round. Kelly Services also has a special referral system that allows you to register at a Kelly office near your school then work near your home during summer recess—or register near your home then work on temporary assignments during the school year. Assignments available include clerks, typists, secretaries, keypunch operators, word processors, bookkeepers and a variety of marketing and light industrial. Offers flexible schedule with "attractive hourly pay rates equal to or higher than the accepted industry standards in most cities." No paycheck deductions except Social Security and income tax. No employment fee for temporary work. See the White Pages for the branch of Kelly Services nearest you. Apply in person or write to: Summer

Employment, National Headquarters, Kelly Services, GPO 1179, Detroit MI 48266.

## Commercial Attractions

### Six Flags Over Georgia

Located in Atlanta. Theme amusement park. Openings for 2,600 college students, foreign students with work visas, high school seniors and local applicants to work weekends March-May, daily June-August, and weekends September-November. Positions available in rides, food service, games, grounds, parking lot, merchandise, warehouse, wardrobe, cash control, security and first aid. Starting pay is $3/hour and up. Wardrobe furnished and cleaned daily. Many special activities throughout the summer. Housing not provided to employees but apartment complexes are in the area. All applicants must apply in person at the Personnel Office which is located on Six Flags Road. When you are applying, mention that you saw this notice in SED. Beginning in January, the office will be open Monday through Saturday, 9 a.m. to 5 p.m. No appointment is necessary. Applicant must be at least 16 years old and have Social Security number to be employed. Equal opportunity employer. For more information write S. Sims, Personnel Staff Assistant, Six Flags Over Georgia, Box 43187, Atlanta GA 30336; tel. 404/948-9290.

# Hawaii

## Business and Industry

### Kelly Services, Inc.

More than 450 branches coast to coast, Puerto Rico, Canada, England and France. Temporary work assignments. Offers over 100 job classifications (office, marketing and light industrial assignments) to college students, teachers and other qualified people during summer breaks and year 'round. Kelly Services also has a special referral system that allows you to register at a Kelly office near your school then work near your home during summer recess—or register near your home then work on temporary assignments during the school year. Assignments available include clerks, typists, secretaries, keypunch operators, word processors, bookkeepers and a variety of marketing and light industrial. Offers flexible schedule with "attractive hourly pay rates equal to or higher than the accepted industry standards in most cities." No paycheck deductions except Social Security and income tax. No employment fee for temporary work. See the White Pages for the branch of Kelly Services nearest you. Apply in person or write to: Summer Employment, National Headquarters, Kelly Services, GPO 1179, Detroit MI 48266.

### Labor Services Inc.

Located in Honolulu. Temporary help. Jobs available: secretarial, $3-10/hour; industrial, $2.90-8/hour; airline catering, $2.90-3/hour. Applicants accepted from US only. Apply to Bill Guss, President, Labor Services Inc., 505 Ward Ave., Honolulu HI 90814; tel. 808/524-4533.

# Summer Camps

### Mokuleia

Located in Waialua, on the north shore of Oahu. Episcopal Church camp for children ages 8-14. Openings for 14 persons, minimum age 18, from June 11 to August 4; one day off, one night off a week with pay. Needs 6 senior counselors, $575; 6 junior counselors, $400; truck driver, $500; nurse, $550; prefers WSI certification for counselors. Salaries are for season. Applications available December 1. Apply by February 1 to Camp Director, Camp Mokuleia, Dept. SED, 68-729 Ferrington Hwy, Waialua HI 96791.

### Paumalu

Located in Oahu, Hawaii, above Sunset Beach on the Island's north shore. Girl Scout camp for girls ages 8-17. Openings for college students and teachers from June 20 to August 17. Needs assistant camp director, $600-800/season; waterfront director, $500-700/season; 8 unit counselors, $325-400/season; business manager, $400-600/season; 4 unit directors, $425-500/season; nurse (RN), $500-750/season; cook, $650-850/season; kitchen assistant, $400-500/season. Apply to Camp Paumalu Director, Girl Scout Council of the Pacific, Inc., 2103 Nuuanu Ave., Honolulu, HI 96817.

### YWCA

Located in Honolulu. Day camp for children ages 4-12. Openings for college students and teachers from June 10 to August 22. Also requires counselor orientation program week prior to June 10, beginning June 2. No cost for orientation program. Needs 8 counselors, $400/season. Provides room only. Certification in outdoor activities, WSI, sailing, canoeing and strong background in arts and crafts, drama and dance. Apply by May 15 to Noel Fishman or Donna Fouts, Kokokahi YWCA, 45-035 Kaneohe Bay Dr., Kaneohe HI 96744.

# Idaho

# Business and Industry

### Kelly Services, Inc.

More than 450 branches coast to coast, Puerto Rico, Canada, England and France. Temporary work assignments. Offers over 100 job classifications (office, marketing and light industrial assignments) to college students, teachers and other qualified people during summer breaks and year 'round. Kelly Services also has a special referral system that allows you to register at a Kelly office near your school then work near your home during summer recess—or register near your home then work on temporary assignments during the school year. Assignments available include clerks, typists, secretaries, keypunch operators, word processors, bookkeepers and a variety of marketing and light industrial. Offers flexible schedule with "attractive hourly pay rates equal to or higher than the accepted industry standards in most cities." No paycheck deductions except Social Security and income tax. No employment fee for temporary work. See the White Pages for the branch of Kelly Services nearest you. Apply in person or write to: Summer

Employment, National Headquarters, Kelly Services, GPO 1179, Detroit MI 48266.

# Resorts, Ranches, Restaurants, Lodging

### Sun Valley Company
Located in Sun Valley. Resort. Openings for college students and teachers from June 1 to September 15. Needs maids, housemen, and dishwashers. Salaries start at $3.10/hour. Equal opportunity employer. Apply to Personnel Office, Sun Valley Company, Sun Valley ID 83353.

## Summer Camps

### Pine Creek Ranch
### Alice Pittenger
### Ta-Man-A-Wis
Located in Shoup, McCall and Palisades. Girl Scout waterfront camps, for girls ages 6-17. Openings for college students and teachers from June to August. Needs 2 camp directors, $125-143/week; 2 assistant camp directors, $86-100/week; 30 counselors, $62-74/week; 7 waterfront and riding staffers, $62-74/week; 6 cooks and maintenance workers, $62-74/week; 2 nurses/first aiders, $62-74/week. Room and board included. Send for application by June 1. Apply to Silver Sage Girl Scout Council, Camp Staff, Dept. SED, 1410 Etheridge Lane, Boise ID 83704; tel. 208/377-2011.

## Summer Theaters

### Coeur d'Alene Summer Theatre
Coeur d' Alene, Idaho. Musical repertory summer stock. Openings for professional theater aspirants, college students, teachers and high school seniors from mid-June to Labor Day. Needs 32 actors and actresses, dancers, musicians, stage manager, lighting designer-operator, $30/week; 2 stage directors, $40/week; set designer, costumer. Room provided. Apply to Robert E. Moe, Coeur d' Alene Summer Theatre, Box 622, Coeur d' Alene ID 83814.

### Summer Theatre
Located at the University of Idaho, Moscow. Openings for 20 teachers and college students as actors and technicians. Work from mid-June to early August. Pays $300-600. "Local apartments available at fairly inexpensive rates." Apply by April 1 to Frederick L. Chapman, Chairman, Summer Theatre, Department of Theatre Arts, University of Idaho, Moscow ID 83843.

# Illinois

## Business and Industry

### Accountants Temporary Personnel, Inc.

Located in Arlington Heights, Illinois. Temporary help in accounting and data processing. Almost all accounting and data processing positions available. Salary depends on experience; usually $3.50-5.00/hour. Some knowledge of accounting or data processing necessary. Employment anytime. Apply to Helen Becker, Manager, Accountants Temporary Personnel, Inc., 247 E. Ontario, Chicago IL 60611; tel. 312/649-0755. Other offices: Jill Hocker, Manager, 314 N. Broadway, Suite 1163, St. Louis MO 63102, tel. 314/621-4880; Carl Vanhemelrk, Manager, 740 N. Plankinton, Milwaukee WI 53203, tel. 414/276-6515; Stan Frost, Manager, 15 S. 5th St., Suite 1146, Minneapolis MN 55402, tel. 612/339-6923; Larry Brown, Manager, Randhurst Shopping Center, Suite 23A, Mt. Prospect IL 60056, tel. 312/392-2708; and Tom Kane, Manager, 110 Schiller, Elmhurst IL 60126, tel. 312/279-0113; John Littwin, Manager, 2256A Landmier Rd., Elk Grove Village IL 60007, tel. 312/640-8275; Gene Munkirs, 1102 Grand Ave., Kansas City MO 64106, tel. 816/471-2867; Sid Dyer, 910 16th St., Denver CO 80202, tel. 303/534-6163.

### Kelly Services, Inc.

More than 450 branches coast to coast, Puerto Rico, Canada, England and France. Temporary work assignments. Offers over 100 job classifications (office, marketing and light industrial assignments) to college students, teachers and other qualified people during summer breaks and year 'round. Kelly Services also has a special referral system that allows you to register at a Kelly office near your school then work near your home during summer recess—or register near your home then work on temporary assignments during the school year. Assignments available include clerks, typists, secretaries, keypunch operators, word processors, bookkeepers and a variety of marketing and light industrial. Offers flexible schedule with "attractive hourly pay rates equal to or higher than the accepted industry standards in most cities." No paycheck deductions except Social Security and income tax. No employment fee for temporary work. See the White Pages for the branch of Kelly Services nearest you. Apply in person or write to: Summer Employment, National Headquarters, Kelly Services, GPO 1179, Detroit MI 48266.

### Mature Temps Inc.

Located in Chicago. National temporary employment service. Openings for college students, teachers, high school seniors, local applicants and foreign students from May to September or year-round. Needs secretaries, clerks, typists, bookkeepers, stenographers, accountants, demonstrators and marketing research persons. High hourly rates based on skills. Apply to Mature Temps Inc., 180 N. LaSalle St., Suite 1822, Chicago IL 60601; tel. 312/368-0266.

# Commercial Attractions

### Dispensa's Kiddie Kingdom

Located in Elmhurst. Family amusement park catering to children 12 and under. Openings for college students, teachers and local applicants from May to October. Needs 30 ride operators, 8 food service employees, and 10 game operators. Pays $3.25/hour. Applicant "must be clean, courteous, and work well with children. Tardiness or absenteeism will not be tolerated." Send resume and recent picture by May to Nick Dispensa, Secretary Treasurer, 1-S-151 Rt. 83, Elmhurst IL 60126; tel. 312/832-7763.

# Summer Camps

### American Camping Association/Illinois Section

Located in Illinois and surrounding states including Wisconsin, Indiana, Michigan and Minnesota. The American Camping Association/Illinois Section is an association of persons involved with camps operated by social agencies, and private camp owners. More than 100 camps in Association. Openings for college students, teachers, foreign students and local applicants from late June to late August. Needs persons over 18 years of age who possess a variety of camp leadership skills for positions such as counselors, cooks, waterfront staff, camping and athletic skills teachers, nurses and program directors. Salaries are $500-1,000 for eight weeks or more. Room and board provided. Apply by writing or calling the American Camping Association/Illinois Section, 19 S. LaSalle St., Room 1024, Chicago IL 60603; tel. 312/332-0833.

### Camp Dean

Located on Route 1, Big Rock. Girl Scout camp for girls ages 8-14. Openings for college students and teachers from June 14 to August 1. Needs camp director, minimum age 25, $900-1,200/season; assistant camp director, minimum age 21, $600-800/season; 3 unit leaders, minimum age 21, $460-600/season; 7 unit assistants, minimum age 18, $385-500/season; waterfront director, minimum age 21, $600-800/season. Salaries include room and board. Send for application to Gail E. Duchscherer, Camp Advisor, Fox Valley Girl Scout Council, 901 N. Lake St. Aurora IL 60506; tel. 312/897-9193.

### Henry Horner

Located at Round Lake. Camp for children ages 9-15. Openings for college students and special education teachers from June 15 to August 15. Needs instructors: music-drama, archery, pioneer-survival, nature-ecology, $600-800; arts and crafts, waterfront instructors, WSI, $400-800; counselors, $350-600; maintenance, $500-800; driver (maintenance, minimum age 21), $600. Apply to Daniel Farinella, Director of Camping Services, Camp Henry Horner, Box 232, Round Lake IL 60073; tel. 312/546-4435.

### Mayer Kaplan Jewish Community Center

Located in Skokie. Day camp for children ages 3-13. Openings for college students, teachers and high school seniors from June 15 to August 13. Needs 100 counselors. Salaries are $608 and up for season. Apply by March to Mayer Kaplan Jewish Community Center, 5050 W. Church St., Skokie IL 60076.

## Peacock Camp for Crippled Children
Located at Lake Villa. Physically handicapped. Openings for college students, teachers and foreign students from mid-June to mid-August. Needs specialty counselors: 4 waterfront, arts and crafts, 4 land sports (recreation); waterfront director, assistant director; nurse (RN or graduate nurse), 2 cooks. Salaries for beginning counselors, $550-600; others open. Apply by May 15 to Dave Bogenschutz, Peacock Camp for Crippled Children, 509 Deep Lake Rd., Lake Villa IL 60046.

## Pleasant Valley Outdoor Center
Located in Woodstock. Farm and environmental camp for preschool children to seniors. Openings for college students, teachers and foreign students from June 24 to August 31. Needs 4 lifeguards, 2 crafts persons, 2 naturalists, 15 tent camp counselors and 5 maintenance workers. Salaries average $560/season. Apply by April to Fred Jackson, Director, Pleasant Valley Outdoor Center, Dept. SED, 13315 Pleasant Valley Rd., Woodstock IL 60098; tel. 815/338-5080.

## Shady Oaks Cerebral Palsy Camp
Located in Lockport. Employs 75 high school seniors, college students and teachers. Seeks general counselors, head dorm counselors, specialty counselors in arts and crafts, athletics and nature lore, WSI, program director, secretary, nurse, and cook. Season: late June to August. Apply to Camp Director, Shady Oaks Camp, 159th St. and Parker Rd., Lockport IL 60441.

## Sherwood Youth Camp
Located in Dahinda. Resident camp for underprivileged boys ages 10-13. Openings for college students, teachers and high school seniors from first part of June to mid-August. Needs 13 senior counselors, craft-evening program director, $650-800; waterfront director (WSI), assistant director, $800-1,000; 2 junior counselors, $350-500; 2 kitchen helpers, $350-500. Room, board and laundry provided. Apply by May 1 to Mike Robson, 1101 Hawkinson Ave., Apt. 4, Galesburg IL 61401.

## Tapawingo
Located at Metamora. Girl Scout camp for girls ages 7-17. Openings for college students and teachers from June 9 to August 8. Needs lake front arts director and nature consultant, $720-840/season; 6 unit leaders, 12 unit counselors, $520-720/season. Apply to Jeanne Buysee, Kickapoo Council of Girl Scouts, 1103 W. Lake, Peoria IL 61614.

## Waupaca For Boys, Inc.
Located in Lincolnwood. Recreational camp for boys ages 9-14. Openings for college students and teachers from June 20 to August 17. Needs 15 general counselors (to instruct in sports), crafts instructor, nurse (RN), caretaker (minor repairs and general maintenance). Salaries open. Room and board provided. Apply to M. Desnet, Director, 6850 N. Crawford Ave., Lincolnwood IL 60646; tel. 312/676-0911.

## Yomechas
Located in Elmhurst. Openings for college students, teachers and foreign students

from June 16 to August 11. Needs 13 senior counselors, $600-700; assistant director, $1,000-1,200. Apply to Gregory F. Hatch, YMCA, 211 W. 1st St., Elmhurst IL 60126.

# Indiana

## Business and Industry

### Kelly Services, Inc.
More than 450 branches coast to coast, Puerto Rico, Canada, England and France. Temporary work assignments. Offers over 100 job classifications (office, marketing and light industrial assignments) to college students, teachers and other qualified people during summer breaks and year 'round. Kelly Services also has a special referral system that allows you to register at a Kelly office near your school then work near your home during summer recess—or register near your home then work on temporary assignments during the school year. Assignments available include clerks, typists, secretaries, keypunch operators, word processors, bookkeepers and a variety of marketing and light industrial. Offers flexible schedule with "attractive hourly pay rates equal to or higher than the accepted industry standards in most cities." No paycheck deductions except Social Security and income tax. No employment fee for temporary work. See the White Pages for the branch of Kelly Services nearest you. Apply in person or write to: Summer Employment, National Headquarters, Kelly Services, GPO 1179, Detroit MI 48266.

### Temp Force
Temporary office personnel contractor. Openings for college students, teachers, high school seniors during vacations and holidays. Needs secretaries, typists, stenographers, clericals and accountants. Salaries based upon experience. Apply to Temp Force, Twin Towers, Suite 306 S., 1000 E. 80th Place, Merrillville IN; tel. 219/769-3448 (Direct Dial Line Valparaiso, Indiana, 219/465-1187.)

## Resorts, Ranches, Restaurants, Lodging

### French Lick Sheraton Hotel
Located at French Lick. Resort hotel and restaurant. Openings for college students, teachers and high school seniors from April 1 to November 1. Needs 10 housekeeping aides, 10 dishwashers, 3 lifeguards, 6 bus help, 2 desk clerks, 2 cook's helpers, 30 waiters/waitresses. Limited housing available on first come, first serve basis at a nominal fee. An equal opportunity employer. Apply to Dorothy J. Clements, Personnel Manager, French Lick Sheraton Hotel, French Lick IN 47432.

## Summer Camp

### American Camping Association/Illinois Section
Located in Illinois and surrounding states including Wisconsin, Indiana, Michigan and Minnesota. The American Camping Association/Illinois Section is an associ-

ation of persons involved with camps operated by social agencies, and private camp owners. More than 100 camps in Association. Openings for college students, teachers, foreign students and local applicants from late June to late August. Needs persons over 18 years of age who possess a variety of camp leadership skills for positions such as counselors, cooks, waterfront staff, camping and athletic skills teachers, nurses and program directors. Salaries are $500-1,000 for eight weeks or more. Room and board provided. Apply by writing or calling the American Camping Association/Illinois Section, 19 S. LaSalle St., Room 1024, Chicago IL 60603; tel. 312/332-0833.

## Culver Summer School Camps

Located at Lake Maxinkuckee in Culver. Openings for 35 college students and teachers from June 17 to August 2. Needs male and female counselors for both junior high and elementary school age children, $500-800, depending on degree and experience. "Counselors should be skilled in some camp activity area. Certification desirable." Send for application and return by April 1 to Frederick D. Lane, Director, Dept. SED, Culver Summer Schools, Culver IN 46511; tel. 219/842-3311, ext. 207.

## Dudley Gallahue Valley Camp

Located in Morgantown on 569 acres of wooded hills in Brown County. Girl Scout resident camp for girls ages 9-17. Openings for college students, teachers, high school seniors, foreign students and local applicants from June 8 to August 17. Needs director (experience and knowledge of Girl Scouts required, college degree preferred), $1,000-1,400/season; assistant director (college degree preferred), $900-1,200; business manager (typing, bookkeeping, office practice experience preferred), $650-$750/season; health supervisor (physician, physician's assistant, RN, LPN, paramedic, Camp Health Director, EMT, or state licence required, also Red Cross Advanced First Aid and Emergency Care and/or Cardiopulmonary Resuscitation certificates preferred), $900-1,200/season; trip director (work experience with children as teacher or counselor required), $600-700/season; horseback director (work experience with children as teacher or counselor required), $650-750/season; food supervisor (minimum 2 years training in institutional management specializing in food service or experience); 4 cooks, $700-750/season; unit leaders: 1 waterfront, 2 general program, 3 horseback, 1 wrangler, 1 wilderness, 1 general barn (experienced as girl leader, camper or teacher, and supervision, first aid and lifesaving preferred), $600-700/season; assistant unit leaders: 2 waterfront, 6 general program, 2 horseback, 1 wrangler, 1 general barn, 1 wilderness (experience as camper or youth leader preferred), $450-550/season; waterfront director, canoe/sailing trip leader, smallcraft instructor (WSI, ALS, and Cardiopulmonary Resuscitation, or YMCA Aquatic Leader Examiner, or Boy Scouts of America National Aquatic Instructor certificate,

**The best time to apply to any of the jobs listed in SED is EARLY. Many employers close their acceptance of applications as early as February and March of each year.**

experience necessary), $600-750/season; waterfront assistant, canoe/sailing assistant (basic swimming instructor certificate from Red Cross, YMCA, or Boy Scouts of America, experience preferred), $450-550/season. Salaries include room and board. Send for application. Apply by March 1 to Deborah A. Smith, Director of Camping Services, Hoosier Capital Girl Scout Council, Dept. SED, 615 N. Alabama Street, Room 235, Indianapolis IN 46204.

## Happy Hollow Children's Camp, Inc.
Located in Nashville. Coed resident camp. Openings from June to August 8. Needs 16 general male and female cabin counselors, college students preferred, $60/week; 1 waterfront director, college students or teachers preferred, $90/week; 1 small craft director, college students or teachers preferred, $70/week; and 1 program director for boys and 1 for girls, teachers preferred, $90/week. Interested in nonsmokers and nondrinkers. Board and lodging provided. "Have some experience in working with children. Get certified in skill needed (life saving, first aid, etc.). Prepare to be on call 24 hours a day. Prepare to give of yourself. Have your personal life in order so you can advise youngsters." Personal interview given in Indiana only. Apply by March to Don Woodworth, Director, 615 N. Alabama St. #421, Indianapolis IN 46204; tel. 317/638-3849.

## Howe Military School Summer Camp
Located in Howe. Recreational and academic. Openings for college students from July 3 to August 13. Needs counselors, $450-800 plus room and board. Apply to R. Kelly, Superintendent, Howe Military School, Howe IN 46746.

## Julia Jameson Health Camp For Children, Inc.
Located in Indianapolis. Resident coed camp for ages 7-12. Openings from early June through mid-August. Needs assistant camp director, teacher or graduate student preferred, $950/season; nurse (RN), salary open; 10 general counselors, 1 swimming counselor (WSI), 1 arts and crafts counselor, 1 nature counselor, college students or teachers (minimum age 19) preferred, $450-500/season; 3 cooks (experienced), salary open; 1 custodian, local high school senior preferred, salary open. Send resume and application request to Ann Andreson, Dept. SED, Executive Director, Julia Jameson Health Camp for Children, Inc., 1100 W. 42nd St., Indianapolis IN 46208; tel. 317/923-3925.

## Kiwanis Twin Lakes
Located in Plymouth, Indiana. Camp for physically handicapped children ages 7-11, 11-18, 18-30. Openings for 28 college students, teachers and high school seniors from mid-June to mid-August. Needs 4 directors: waterfront, nature study, programs, arts and crafts, $500; 18 senior counselors, $450; 6 junior counselors, $300. Salaries quoted are beginning rates, additions allowed for experience. Meals and lodging provided. Apply to M.C. Kirby, Kiwanis Twin Lakes Camp, 2312 W. Medill, Chicago IL 60647.

## Henry F. Koch
Located in Cannelton. Girl Scout camp for girls ages 8-17. Openings for college students, teachers and foreign students from approximately mid-June to mid-August. Needs 15 assistant troop leaders, 5 troop leaders (minimum age 21), waterfront director, boating instructor, 4 waterfront staff, 3 cooks. Room and board

provided. Apply by May 1 to Camp Director, Raintree Girl Scout Council, Box 3357, Dept. SED, Evansville IN 47732.

### Ella J. Logan
Located in Syracuse. Girl Scout camp for ages 6-17. Needs assistant camp director, $111-200, business manager $86-151; health supervisor (RN or LPN) $86-151; waterfront director (WSI, SCI) $101-191; assistant waterfront director, small craft instructor $81-133; waterfront assistants $61-81 (WSI preferred); unit leaders $73-98; unit assistants $61-81; head cook $81-101; kitchen help $61-93; waterskiing instructor (salary depending on qualifications and experience). Room and board provided. An equal opportunity employer. Apply by May 1 to Limberlost Girl Scout Council Inc., Camping Services Director, "C.E.J.L.," Dept. SED, 1820 N. Wells St., Fort Wayne IN 46808.

### Wapi-Kamigi
Located in Hagerstown. Girl Scout camp. Openings for college students and teachers from early June to early August. Staff positions include 4 unit leaders, 7 unit counselors, waterfront director (WSI), 2 waterfront assistants, naturalists, nurse (RN), business manager and 2 cooks. Salaries are $400-700/7-week season; varies according to position and experience. Camp program includes canoe trips, bike trips, ACA Campcrafter, outdoor cooking, crafts, nature, fitness session, tent living and international staff. Apply after January 1 to Pat Mayer, Treaty Line Council of Girl Scouts, 42 S. 9th St., Richmond IN 47374.

### Windigo
Located in Upland. Girl Scout camp. Openings for college students, teachers and foreign students from mid-June to mid-August. Needs camp director, $120/week; 11 assistant unit leaders, 3 assistant waterfront directors, 4 unit leaders, $45-85/week; 2 waterfront directors, program director, $75-100/week; business manager, $80-100/week. Salaries will vary, depending upon experience. Apply to Phyllis Chezem, Wapehani Girl Scout Council, Box 587, Daleville IN 47334.

### YMCA Camp Potawotami
Located at Blackman Lake, South Milford. Coed lakefront camp for children ages 8-15. Openings from June 1 to July 31, 8 week season. Needs 9 counselors (3 girls and 6 boys), age 21 or 1 year of college or 3 years as CIT for tennis, archery, riflery, canoeing, sailing, $500-650/season; waterfront director (WSI), $500-600/season; craft director, $500-600/season; kitchen manager, $100-175/week; cook, $100-175/week. Room and board provided. Send resume or write for application. Apply to Topher Schlatter, Resident Director, Dept. SED, 226 E. Washington Blvd., Fort Wayne IN 46802; tel. 219/422-6486.

# Iowa

## Business and Industry

### Kelly Services, Inc.
More than 450 branches coast to coast, Puerto Rico, Canada, England and

France. Temporary work assignments. Offers over 100 job classifications (office, marketing and light industrial assignments) to college students, teachers and other qualified people during summer breaks and year 'round. Kelly Services also has a special referral system that allows you to register at a Kelly office near your school then work near your home during summer recess—or register near your home then work on temporary assignments during the school year. Assignments available include clerks, typists, secretaries, keypunch operators, word processors, bookkeepers and a variety of marketing and light industrial. Offers flexible schedule with "attractive hourly pay rates equal to or higher than the accepted industry standards in most cities." No paycheck deductions except Social Security and income tax. No employment fee for temporary work. See the White Pages for the branch of Kelly Services nearest you. Apply in person or write to: Summer Employment, National Headquarters, Kelly Services, GPO 1179, Detroit MI 48266.

# Summer Camps

### Foster
Located on East Lake Okoboji, Spirit Lake. YMCA coed camp for children ages 8-16. Openings for college students and teachers (some high school students) from approximately June 2 to August 17. All staff must have minimum one year of college except for junior staff who must be leaving grades 10, 11 or 12 depending on position. Needs about 18 general counselors, approximately $525/season; 1 waterfront director (WSI, age 21), $625/season; 2 pool directors (WSI, age 19 and 21), $525-625/season; 3 waterski instructors, $525 plus/season; 6 cooks, $550-650/season; 2 ranch directors, $525 plus/season; 1 camp nurse (RN), $850 plus/season; tripping director (experienced), $625 plus/season. Also seeking office, store, maintenance, day camp and campground staff; 20 junior staff, junior counselors and dish/support staff. "Apply early. A staff growth experience results, staff role models are of utmost importance." Apply to Ken Lockard or Mike "Chief" Olson, Directors, Camp Foster YMCA, Box 296, Spirit Lake IA 51360; tel. 712/336-3272.

### Hantesa
Located in Boone. Camp Fire camp for boys and girls ages 6-18. Openings from June to August (8 weeks of camp and 1 week of training) for college students, teachers, foreign students, local applicants. Needs 8 unit directors with interest in children, supervising counselors and programs, $440-600/season; 4 water safety instructors to supervise and instruct pool, canoe, sail, row boats, $400-600/season; 6 food service staff to prepare for 150-225 people/meal, $400-600/season; 1 nurse (RN), $400-600/season; 18 general counselors, $400-600/season. "Write for application before the end of March, prefer during the months of January and February." Apply to Susan Welch, Director, Camp Hantesa, Dept. SED, RR 1, Boone IA 50036; tel. 515/432-6325.

### Hitaga
Located in Walker. Camp Fire Girls camp for girls ages 7-17. Openings for college students, teachers and foreign students from June 8 to August 10. Needs 40 counselors for riding, swimming, canoeing, nature, campcraft, hand crafts, archery, photography, $450-600/season; 3 cooks, $450-800/season. Apply to Joan Wimme, Camp Hitaga, 712 3rd Ave. SE, Cedar Rapids IA 52401.

**Abe Lincoln**
Located in Blue Grass. Family Y camp—resident, day and trip—for children ages 7-16. Openings from June 8 to August 16. Needs 12 cabin leaders ($190-710/season), 15 program counselors ($440-770/season), 4 goundskeepers-repairmen ($440-1,200/season), 6 program counselors-lifeguards ($490-820/season), college students, teachers, high school seniors preferred; 1 aquatic director ($490-820/season), 1 wrangler ($440-770/season), college students and teachers preferred; 1 camp nurse, RN or LPN ($700-1,200/season). "Traditional program, personal interviews required. Interviews arranged from Chicago to Quad Cities to Omaha. Salary based on age and experience. YMCA standards, conservative in behavior, progressive in programming." Apply by May 1 to Jack P. Zahn, Camp Director, Camp Abe Lincoln, Dept. SED, 606 W. 2nd St., Davenport IA 52801; tel. 319/322-7171.

**Little Cloud**
Located in Dubuque, Iowa. Girl Scout camp. Openings for college students, teachers and high school seniors for 7-week season. Needs specialists: 6 unit leaders, 2 horseback riding, 6 WSI waterfront, nurse, naturalist, canoe instructor, arts and crafts, dancing and folklore, photography, $400-900. Salaries are commensurate with qualifications and experience. Room, board and training for job provided. Can arrange for college credit. Enclose stamped return envelope. Apply to Joan Geisler, 3250 Dodge St., Dubuque IA 52001.

**Lutheran Lakeside**
Located at Spirit Lake. Coed LCA camp for children ages 9-18, families and mentally retarded persons. Openings for college students and teachers from early June to mid-August. Needs 10 general counselors, 2 WSI, nurse/secretary, program director, head cook, 3 kitchen assistants, 2 maintenance persons, 2 backpack leaders. Salaries are $650-900/season. Room, board and insurance provided. Apply early to Pastor Roy Miltner, 3125 Cottage Grove, Des Moines IA 50311.

**Mississippi Valley Girl Scout Council**
Located in Bettendorf. Two summer camps in Iowa, one in Illinois. Openings for 45 college students, teachers and foreign students from early June through mid-August. Needs 7 unit leaders, 15 unit assistants, 2 pool directors (WSI), 5 pool assistants, 6 canoeing instructors (WSI, SCI), 6 specialized program staff including primitive, backpacking, and canoe tripping, 3 horseback riding staff, 2 nurses (RN, LPN), 3 cooks, 1 handyperson. Salaries are $500-1,000. Room, board and laundry provided. Apply by June 1 to Mississippi Valley Girl Scout Council, Dept. SED, 2388 Cumberland Sq., Box 1051, Bettendorf IA 52722.

**Moingona Girl Scout Council Resident Camps**
**Sacajawea**
**Strother**
Located in southern and central Iowa. Ages 7 to 17. Openings for college students, teachers, high school seniors and foreign students from early June to mid-August. Needs 40 counselors for sports, arts, campcraft, $55-70/week; 6 waterfront and small-craft instructors, $55-80/week; 2 nurses (RN, EMT or LPN), $100-140/week; head cook, 7 kitchen assistants, $85-160/week. Apply to Camping Services

Director, Moingona Girl Scout Council Resident Camps, 10715 Hickman Rd., Des Moines IA 50322.

### Sunnyside
Located in Des Moines. Easter Seal Society residential camp for physically handicapped children and adults. Openings for college graduates, college students, high school juniors and seniors, and foreign students from the beginning of June to August, 11-12 weeks. Needs 12 unit counselors, $80-95/week; 24 cabin counselors, $60-75/week; 12 counselors in training, $40-55/week; 14 activity specialists (arts and crafts, sports and games, water safety instructor, nature, and boating), $60-95/week; 3 program directors, $100-115/week; 2 assistant nurses (RN or LPN with pharmacology course or graduate nurse), $90-200/week; Challenge Camping Program personnel experienced in outdoor camping, camp craft skills, nature and canoeing, swimming (current WSI or SLS required) and sports; program director, $95-110/week; 5 counselors, $70-95/week. Apply by March 31 (may accept applications as late as May 23 depending upon qualifications) to Ed Stracke, Camp Sunnyside, Box 4002, Dept. SED, Des Moines IA 50333.

# Kansas

## Business and Industry

### Kelly Services, Inc.
More than 450 branches coast to coast, Puerto Rico, Canada, England and France. Temporary work assignments. Offers over 100 job classifications (office, marketing and light industrial assignments) to college students, teachers and other qualified people during summer breaks and year 'round. Kelly Services also has a special referral system that allows you to register at a Kelly office near your school then work near your home during summer recess—or register near your home then work on temporary assignments during the school year. Assignments available include clerks, typists, secretaries, keypunch operators, word processors, bookkeepers and a variety of marketing and light industrial. Offers flexible schedule with "attractive hourly pay rates equal to or higher than the accepted industry standards in most cities." No paycheck deductions except Social Security and income tax. No employment fee for temporary work. See the White Pages for the branch of Kelly Services nearest you. Apply in person or write to: Summer Employment, National Headquarters, Kelly Services, GPO 1179, Detroit MI 48266.

## Summer Camps

### Aldrich
Located in Claflin. Modern Girl Scout camp for girls ages 8-18. Openings for college students, teachers and local applicants (teachers and local applicants only for camp director and nurse) during June. Needs camp director, minimum age 25, $800-1,200; program director, $500-700; nurse (RN, EMT, LPN, First Aider), $400-600; 12 counselors, $250-400; 2 cook's assistants, $400-600. Room and

board provided. Send resume or write for application to Lynette Wolfe, Executive Director, 113 W. Sherman, Hutchinson KS 67501; tel. 316/662-5485.

## Wiedemann

Located 45 miles east of Wichita. Girl Scout camp for girls ages 4-12; 220 acres with facilities including tennis courts, swimming pool, darkroom, potters wheel/kiln, infirmary, horse program. Openings from May 25 to July 30. Needs assistant camp director (minimum age 25, experienced in program activities, supervision, record keeping, purchasing, menu planning), $800/season; program director (preferably experienced in campcraft, art, drama, etc.—please indicate), $650/season; CIT director (ability to train teen-age girls in leadership, campcraft, arts, nature and tripping), $650/season; nurse (RN, graduate nurse or public school nurse with current knowledge of Red Cross first aid), $700/season; trading post/pack-out counselor (minimum age 18, ability to handle trading post items and records, prepare packouts for cookouts), $300/season for resident camp, $25 bonus for core camp; head cook (minimum age 21, experienced in quantity cooking, ability to keep accurate food inventory and to supervise, current Food Handlers Permit required), $700/season for resident camp, $25 bonus for core camp; 3 assistant cooks (minimum age 18, prefers experience in quantity cooking, ability to take charge of camp packouts for cookouts, current Food Handlers Permit required), $500/season for resident camp, $25 bonus for core camp; 3 kitchen/general helpers (washing kitchen utensils, operating electric dishwasher, keeping dining room and kitchen clean, current Food Handlers Permit required), $300/season; 4 western riding personnel, director and assistants (direct or assist in riding program, care for horses and equipment, experienced in teaching western riding); waterfront director (WSI, minimum age 21, experienced in teaching swimming, ability to coordinate all waterfront activites, supervise and keep accurate records, small-craft instructor desirable, knowledge of most waterfront activities such as canoeing, diving, water games, synchronized and competitive swimming), $600/season for resident camp, $35 bonus for core camp; assistant waterfront director (WSI, experience and/or ability to teach swimming, ability to supervise and keep accurate records, knowledge of most waterfront activites listed above, small craft instructor preferred), $450/season; 3 waterfront counselors, (WSI, experience and/or ability to teach swimmng, ability to supervise and keep accurate records, knowledge of most waterfront activites listed above), $350 for resident and core camp; 6 unit leaders (minimum age 21, ability to coordinate, supervise, keep accurate records, special talents in arts, drama, music, nature, campcraft, bicycling, canoeing, sports, must like children), $600/season; 6 assistant unit leaders (minimum age 18, ability to promote good out-of-doors program, prefers some experience working with groups, special talents as listed above, must like children), $450/season; 12 unit leaders (minimum age 18, with ability to promote good out-of-doors program, prefers some experience working with groups, special talents as listed above, completion of CIT not required but one year of college helpful, must like children), $350/season. Salaries are beginning salaries. Room and board provided. Send for application. Apply to Karen Cahow, Camping Services Director, Dept. SED, Wichita Area Girl Scout Council, Inc., 2009 North Woodlawn, Wichita KS 67208; tel. 316/684-6531.

# Kentucky

## Business and Industry

### Davis & Associates

Business opportunity in sales management and marketing. Openings for college undergraduates, graduates, teachers, retirees, couples or singles during the summer, year-round, full time or part time. Needs salespersons for 250 consumer goods (home care, food supplements, household, farm and commercial size items including smoke alarms, mail order items and cosmetics) with opportunity to develop into area management. No experience necessary. In Kentucky, apply to: Joe Davis, 2449 Williams, Cincinnati OH 45212. Other area coordinators: (Indiana) C. Magee, Keyway Associates, 3530 Redwood Lane, Anderson IN 46012; (Illinois) J. Nethero, 7162 Juniper View, Cincinnati OH 45243; (Ohio) R. Teigen, 6648 Michael Dr., Cincinnati OH 45243.

### Kelly Services, Inc.

More than 450 branches coast to coast, Puerto Rico, Canada, England and France. Temporary work assignments. Offers over 100 job classifications (office, marketing and light industrial assignments) to college students, teachers and other qualified people during summer breaks and year 'round. Kelly Services also has a special referral system that allows you to register at a Kelly office near your school then work near your home during summer recess—or register near your home then work on temporary assignments during the school year. Assignments available include clerks, typists, secretaries, keypunch operators, word processors, bookkeepers and a variety of marketing and light industrial. Offers flexible schedule with "attractive hourly pay rates equal to or higher than the accepted industry standards in most cities." No paycheck deductions except Social Security and income tax. No employment fee for temporary work. See the White Pages for the branch of Kelly Services nearest you. Apply in person or write to: Summer Employment, National Headquarters, Kelly Services, GPO 1179, Detroit MI 48266.

## Summer Camps

### Midway-Longview Riding Camp

Located at Midway, near Lexington. Private coed camp, formerly called Longview Riding Camp. For children ages 8-15. Openings for 30 male and female college students from June 8 to August 2. Needs specialty counselors for riflery, tennis, swimming (WSI), archery, arts and crafts, campcrafts, drama, general sports, horseback riding and jumping. Salaries are $450-700 for counselors; and salary open for kitchen helpers. Room, board and laundry provided. Submit resume and photo. Apply to Ron Boyle, Midway-Longview Riding Camp, Dept. SED, Midway College, Midway KY 40347, tel. 606/846-4421.

### Old Kentucky Home Council, Boy Scouts of America

Located in Leitchfield at Prospect and Rough River. Summer camp. Openings for college students and teachers from June 15 to August 19. Needs camp director, $150-175/week; program director, $110-125/week; health lodge director, nurse preferred, $90-115/week; nature director, $90-115/week; aquatics director, $90-115/week; cook, $75-100/week; rifle range director, $75-100/week. "Apply early, list qualifications and any Scouting background. We prefer to hear by Christmas break but will consider later applications." Send resume to Charles E. Cicchella, Director of Support Services, Old Kentucky Home Council, Boy Scouts of America, Box 21068, Louisville KY 40221; tel. 502/361-2624.

# Louisiana

## Business and Industry

### Kelly Services, Inc.
More than 450 branches coast to coast, Puerto Rico, Canada, England and France. Temporary work assignments. Offers over 100 job classifications (office, marketing and light industrial assignments) to college students, teachers and other qualified people during summer breaks and year 'round. Kelly Services also has a special referral system that allows you to register at a Kelly office near your school then work near your home during summer recess—or register near your home then work on temporary assignments during the school year. Assignments available include clerks, typists, secretaries, keypunch operators, word processors, bookkeepers and a variety of marketing and light industrial. Offers flexible schedule with "attractive hourly pay rates equal to or higher than the accepted industry standards in most cities." No paycheck deductions except Social Security and income tax. No employment fee for temporary work. See the White Pages for the branch of Kelly Services nearest you. Apply in person or write to: Summer Employment, National Headquarters, Kelly Services, GPO 1179, Detroit MI 48266.

## Summer Camps

### Wi Ta Wentin
Located in Moss Bluff, near Lake Charles. Camp Fire day camp for girls grades 1-6 and boys in grades 1-4; resident camp for girls grades 2-12 and boys in grades 2-4. Openings in June and July, both day and residence. Needs camp director, minimum age 25; business manager, CIT director, waterfront director, riding director, minimum age 21; 4 waterfront counselors, 8 general counselors for horseback riding, crafts, campcraft, archery/riflery, photography, minimum age 18. During 3 weeks of resident camp, room and board is provided; during 3 weeks of day camp, counselors bring sack lunch and may ride camp bus if desired. Arrangements can be made for counselors from out-of-town during day camp sessions. Apply by one week prior to each 5-day session to Caroline S. Hollins, Executive Director, Sowela Area Council of Camp Fire, Dept. SED, 2126 Oak Park Blvd., Lake Charles LA 70601.

# Maine

## Business and Industry

### Kelly Services, Inc.
More than 450 branches coast to coast, Puerto Rico, Canada, England and France. Temporary work assignments. Offers over 100 job classifications (office, marketing and light industrial assignments) to college students, teachers and other qualified people during summer breaks and year 'round. Kelly Services also has a special referral system that allows you to register at a Kelly office near your school then work near your home during summer recess—or register near your home then work on temporary assignments during the school year. Assignments available include clerks, typists, secretaries, keypunch operators, word processors, bookkeepers and a variety of marketing and light industrial. Offers flexible schedule with "attractive hourly pay rates equal to or higher than the accepted industry standards in most cities." No paycheck deductions except Social Security and income tax. No employment fee for temporary work. See the White Pages for the branch of Kelly Services nearest you. Apply in person or write to: Summer Employment, National Headquarters, Kelly Services, GPO 1179, Detroit MI 48266.

## Commercial Attractions

### Funorama
Located at York Beach. Arcade. Openings from May to mid-September. Needs cashiers (college students or teachers with some experience); floor or ticket people (college students or teachers); electronic engineer (electronic and mechanical machine experience necessary). Pays minimum wage commensurate with ability. "There is plenty of housing nearby." Housing information available with application. Write or call for personal interview at business address. Apply by June 15 to Mr. Dugrenier, Box 306, York Beach ME 03910; tel. 207/363-4421.

## National Parks

### Acadia Corporation
Located in Bar Harbor, in Acadia National Park. Concessionaire. Openings for college students, teachers, foreign students and nonstudents, minimum age 18, from May 15 to October 15; August 1 to 31 minimum. Needs 25 waiters and waitresses, $74/week plus tips; 20 kitchen helpers, 20 shop clerks, $124-156/week. Employees must find own housing. Apply by March 15 to Acadia Corporation, Dept. SED, 85 Main St., Bar Harbor ME 04609.

## Resorts, Ranches, Restaurants, Lodging

### Farrington's Resort
Located in Center Lovell. Summer resort. Openings from June 30 to September 3 (some longer, some shorter). Needs 5 waitresses, college freshmen, high school

seniors, foreign students acceptable, minimum $750/season; 2 waterfront (skiing and boats), college freshman and high school seniors preferred, $820/season; 4 kitchen (dishes and pots), high school students and foreign students acceptable, $700-800/season. Room and board provided. "Because of the nature of our establishment, all applicants must be attractive and clean. Drinking (illegal in Maine if under 20) and any use of drugs is basis for dismissal. A number of employees take part in physical fitness program designed especially for high school and college athletes. It is our policy to hire persons 17-20 years of age." Apply by March 1 to Manager, Farrington's Resort, Center Lovell, Maine 04016; tel. 207/925-2500.

## Linekin Bay Resort
Located in Boothbay Harbor, Maine. Resort for active, sailing couples. Openings for college students, college graduates and high school seniors from June 18 to September 2. Needs 7 chambermaids, 11 waitresses, $1,000/season; schooner captain, activities director, chef's assistant, pastry and salad assistants, salaries depend on training and experience; 4 sailing instructors, 5 kitchen assistants, $100-120/week. Room and board provided. Personal interview required. Apply by April 1 in Massachusetts, by May 1 in Maine, to Linekin Bay Resort, 61 Meadow St., Florence MA 01060.

## Oakland House
Located in Sargentville. Resort. Openings from June 16 to September 10. Needs secretary-receptionist ($80-115/week), hostess ($45/week plus tips), college student or teacher preferred; 6 waiter/waitresses ($35-40/week plus tips), 4 kitchen helpers and assistant cooks ($70-115/week), 2-3 maintenance workers and groundskeepers ($80-115/week), college students, foreign students both acceptable; 3 housekeepers ($35-45/week plus tips), college students, teachers, foreign students all acceptable. Room and board provided. Apply to James Littlefield, Manager, Dept. SED, Oakland House, Sargentville ME 04673.

## Quisisana Lodge
Located in Center Lovell, on Lake Kezar. Resort hotel. Openings for college students from early June to September 2. Needs 16 dining room waitresses and busboys, $1,000 plus tips averaging $400 additional; 5 bellhops, $1,000 plus tips averaging $300 additional; 8 chambermaids, $875 plus tips averaging $300 additional; 6 groundsmen, $900 plus tips averaging $250 additional; 8 kitchen helpers, $1,000. Staff participates in some musical evenings, both classical and popular. Room and board provided. No application forms will be sent unless a large stamped return envelope is enclosed with inquiry. Apply to Quisisana Lodge, Box 25068, Fort Lauderdale FL 33320.

## Spruce Point Inn
Located at Boothbay Harbor. Resort hotel. Openings for college students and college graduates from mid-June to mid-October; students after summer school to mid-October. Needs dining room busboys and waitresses, kitchen help, bellhops, desk clerk, swimming pool attendants, night auditor. Apply to John Druce, Manager, Spruce Point Inn, Boothbay Harbor ME 04538.

# Summer Camps

### Alford Lake
Located in Union. Private camp for girls, ages 8-15. Openings for college students and teachers from about June 16 to August 16. Needs 10 specialists for tennis, art, swimming, nature, dramatics, riding, sailing, canoeing, campcraft, dance. Salaries are $375-500/season plus room, board and laundry. Apply by May 1 to Mrs. Andrew N. McMullan, 17 Pilot Point Rd., Cape Elizabeth ME 04107.

### Androscoggin Jr.-Sr.
Located in Wayne. Boys camp. Openings for college students and teachers from end of June through end of August (8½ weeks). Needs specialty counselors: archery, arts and crafts, pottery, dramatics, bicycling, tripping, 5 canoe, 2 waterskiing, 3 baseball, 7 tennis, 6 swimming (WSI), 2 riflery, 3 sailing; 2 trip leaders, 2 radio broadcasters. Salaries are $400 and up, depending on age and experience. Room, board, laundry and travel allowance provided. "We have an extensive wilderness tripping program. If you like kids, teaching your particular activity, and the outdoors, you should have a great time at camp. Both our staff and campers have a high return rate." Apply to Stanley L. Hirsch, 4 Spruce Dr., White Plains NY 10605.

### Arundel
Located in Rangley, Maine. Coed, academic and recreational, ages 7 to 18. Openings for college students and teachers from July 1 to August 19. Needs instructors for mathematics, language, arts, ecology, $600; English and western riding instructor, waterfront director, $500; riding supervisor-trail master, $450; counselors: 3 water and sports, 2 environmental, $300. Room and board provided. Apply to Joseph R. Manella, Camp Arundel, 299 Central St., Milford MA 01757.

### Association of Independent Camps
Openings at 100 children's (ages 6-16) summer camps located in New England and Middle Atlantic States. Needs head counselors, group leaders, general and all specialty counselors. Room and board provided. Apply by July to Association of Independent Camps, Dept. SED, 55 W. 42nd St., New York NY 10036; tel. 212/695-2656.

### Cedar
Located in Casco, Maine. Camp for boys, ages 8-15. Openings for 57 counselors, minimum age 18, from approximately June 21 to August 22. "We are looking for people who like to work with boys, have teaching skills and are willing to work hard. Specialists needed in all camp activities, including: swimming (WSI), boating, sailing, waterskiing and boat drivers, scuba, arts and crafts, soccer, tennis, baseball, football, lacrosse, riflery, archery, photography, golf, campcraft, backpacking, judo, ham radio, music, drama, wrestling, track, and other skills. We also need RNs and kitchen workers. Salaries are from $400-900 plus room and board and some travel allowances. Salary based on age, experience and teaching ability. We have a significant return of campers and staff each year, have superior facilities and want to hire people who recognize that camp counseling is a professional responsibility." Apply by May or June to Henry M. Hacker, Dept. SED, 1758 Beacon St., Brookline MA 02146; tel. 617/277-8080.

## Chickawah

Located in Harrison, Maine. Camp for boys, ages 7-16. Member ACA. Openings for college students, teachers and high school seniors, beginning July 1 for 8 weeks. Needs specialist for golf, baseball, basketball, soccer, tennis, riflery, canoeing and sailing (SCI), waterskiing, general swim instructors (WSI); counselors with tripping and pioneering experience, science and nature, dramatics, ham radio, photography, gymnastics; chef, waiters, dishwashers, kitchen helpers, baker, licensed drivers, groundsman, porter, nurse (RN). Salaries are $500 up plus room and board, laundry, travel allowance. Nonsmokers only. Apply to Maurice Steinberg, Box 178, Carle Place NY 11514.

## Cobbossee

Located at Lake Cobbosseecontee, Winthrop. Camp for boys ages 6-16. Openings for college juniors and seniors, college graduates and teachers. Needs counselors for athletics (baseball, basketball, soccer, softball, football), archery, boating, canoeing, crafts, golf, general group, ham radio, photography, riflery, sailing, scuba, swimming, tennis, trampoline, trap and skeet shooting, tripping, waterskiing, wrestling; secretary, nurse (RN). Salaries are $550-800 plus transportation allowance, laundry, basic camp uniform, and increment for each year counseling experience. Sister camp, Camp Somerset; see Somerset listing for address. Apply to Camp Cobbossee, Mianus Dr., Bedford NY 10506.

## Diocesan Camping Center

Located in Poland Spring. Coed agency camp, with Catholic affiliation, for socially integrated children ages 6-13. Openings for college students and teachers from June 26 to August 28. Needs waterfront director (WSI), nurse (RN), and other administrative persons. Salaries are $400-800/season. Apply to Diocesan Camping Center, 87 High St., Portland ME 04101.

## Fernwood

Located in Oxford. Camp for girls ages 9-16. Openings for college students and teachers, minimum age 19, from June 21 to August 24. Needs male and female counselors for tennis, swimming (WSI), jewelry-metal crafts, woodworking, ceramics, canoeing, riflery, archery, sailing, English riding, gymnastics, field sports, piano accompanist (pop, by ear), waterskiing, dramatics (experienced); food service manager; head of pantry; 2 nurses (RN). Salaries are $400-800/season, based on experience. Room, board and laundry provided. Apply to Maxine B. King, 40 Elm St., Topsham ME 04086.

## Jollee for the Physically Handicapped

Goshen, MaineCoed, residential, ages 7-35. Needs director, teacher preferred; assistant director; 4-6 senior female counselors; 4-6 senior male counselors, college student or teacher preferred; 2-3 junior female counselors, 2-3 junior male counselors, college students or high school seniors preferred; nurse and cook. Work 8 weeks beginning end of June through August. "We prefer people who have had either camping experience or experience working with the handicapped." Apply to Camp Director, Camp Jollee, 246 Park, West Springfield MA 01089; tel. 413/788-9695.

## Kamp Kohut
Located in Oxford, Maine, on Lake Thompson. Camp for boys ages 6-16. Openings for 60, minimum age 21, from June 21 to August 25. Needs specialty counselors for archery, athletics, baseball, basketball, canoeing, crafts, dramatics, golf, radio, music, nature, photography, riflery, sailing, scuba, soccer, pioneering, waterskiing, softball, swimming (WSI), tennis, tripping, adventure; nurse (RN); group counselors. Salaries are $450 and up plus room, board, transportation allowance and laundry. Increment is added to base salary for each year of previous acceptable experience. Apply to Malcolm J. Itkin, Kamp Kohut, 451 Buckminster Dr., Norwood MA 02062; tel. 617/769-4685.

## Kennebec Camps
Located at Salmon Lake in North Belgrade, Oakland, Maine. Private camp for boys ages 9-15. Employs college students, administrators and teachers from June 16 to August 20. Accommodations for married applicants. Needs nurses (RN); specialty counselors in archery, baseball, basketball, campcraft, canoeing, ceramics, crafts (wood/metal), cycling, dramatics/entertainment, nature, outward bound, photography, piano, sailing, soccer, swimming, riflery, tennis, track, trip leaders, waterskiing, white water rafting and wrestling. Salaries are $400-1,200/season, depending on specialty and experience. Room, board and laundry services provided. British applicants must apply through BUNACAMP. Others should apply by April 30 to Mr. Bernard Lemonick, Dept. SED, 405 Westview Rd., Elkins Park PA 19117.

## Kippewa For Girls
Located at Lake Cobbosseecontee, Winthrop, Maine. Openings for college students from sophomore year on and teachers from June 22 to August 24. Needs specialty counselors for drama, arts and crafts, nature, canoeing, waterskiing, sailing, field sports, tennis, campcraft, tripping, archery, gymnastics; food service coordinator; 2 nurses (RN). Salaries are $400-750, plus travel allotment, room, board and laundry. Apply to Mr. and Mrs. Martin Silverman, 60 Mill St., Box 307, Westwood MA 02090.

## Laurel
Located 17 miles from Augusta, Maine, in the Central Lakes Region. Coed camp for children ages 8-15. Openings for male and female college students and teachers from June 22 to August 22. Needs specialty counselors for tennis, swimming, sailing, waterskiing, soccer, field sports, dramatics, riding, arts and crafts, ceramics, woodworking, sewing, cooking, archery, gymnastics, piano, photography, AM radio, nature, canoe and mountain trips, early childhood. Salaries are $550 and up, plus room. board and laundry. Apply by April 1 to Ron Scott, Camp Laurel, Box 848, New Paltz NY 12561.

## Matoaka For Girls
Located in Oakland, Maine. Openings for college students and teachers from June 27 to August 22. Needs specialty counselors: 6 WSI, 5 tennis, 5 arts and crafts, 4 waterskiing, 2 drama-music, 2 sewing, 2 gymnastics, 3 photography, 3 land sports, 4 riding, 2 tripping, 4 small-craft, $450 up plus travel allotment; computer operator; secretary, 2 nurses (RN), kitchen supervisor. Apply to Camp Matoaka for Girls, 6 Taylor Rd., Sudbury MA 01776.

## Moose Cove Lodge For Boys
Located at Douglas Hill, Maine. Openings for college students and teachers from June 17 to August 22. Needs head counselor-program director, $800 up for season; specialty counselors: arts and crafts, nature, riflery, archery, kayak, waterskiing, 2 canoeing/whitewater, 2 sailing. Salaries open. Room and board provided. Apply by April 1 to McHenry Gillet, Director, Moose Cove Lodge for Boys, 1739 Circle Rd., Ruxton MD 21204.

## Naomi
Located at Crescent Lake, Raymond, Maine. Coed camp for children ages 8-16. Openings for college students, teachers and foreign students from June 24 to August 24. Needs 30 counselors, $300-600; 4 unit heads, $650-1,200; 10 aquatics (WSI); director, assistant director, sailing, waterfront assistants, boating, waterskiing, canoeing, $350-1,000; 10 program specialists for tennis, arts and crafts, photography, nature, riflery, archery, campcraft, tripping, music, drama, land sports, $400-850; nurses (RN); kitchen and laundry workers. Apply by March to Leonard M. Katowitz, Executive Director, Dept. SED, Jewish Center Camps, 50 Hunt St., Watertown MA 02172; tel. 617/924-2030.

## New England Camping Association, Inc. (ACA)
Located throughout Maine. Camp counselor referral service; for children ages 8-16. Openings for college students and teachers, minimum age 19, for 8 weeks. Needs specialty counselors for advanced lifesaving, archery, arts and crafts, bicycling, boating, campcraft, canoeing, drama, golf, guitar, gymnastics, horseback riding, land sports, music, nature-ecology, photography, piano, radio-electronics, riflery, sailing (SCI), scuba, tennis, waterskiing, WSI; trip leader, unit leader, administrative, chef, baker, kitchen workers, clerical, maintenance, doctors, nurses (RN). Salaries start at $400 and are commensurate with age, education, camp experience and type of position. Room and board provided. $2 application fee. Apply to New England Camping Association, Inc., Room 410, 29 Commonwealth Ave., Boston MA 02116.

## Oceanward
Located in Friendship, Maine. Coed camp for children with wide range of developmental handicaps. Openings from June 21 to August 25. Needs energetic, flexible leaders in elementary education for woodshop, physical education, vocal and instrumental music, folk dance, drama, distance running, 2 WSI, trip leaders. Send resume or write for application to Camp Director, Dept. SED, Box 67, Lancaster MA 01523.

## Pinecliffe
Located in Harrison, Maine. Camp for girls ages 8-16. Openings for college students, teachers and foreign students from June 20 to August 23. Needs program director; 2 unit leaders; specialty counselors: 5 waterfront, 3 tennis, 2 performing arts, 3 crafts, $500-800; nurse (RN, first aid), $700. Apply by spring to Camp Pinecliffe, 200 E. 71st St., New York NY 10021.

## Rapputak
Located on Lovewell Lake in the foothills of the White Mountains (in Fryeburg, Maine). Private camp for 170 girls ages 8-15. Openings for college women,

graduates, and teachers, from June 15 to August 22. Needs camp doctor; nurse (RN); secretary; instructors in archery, arts and crafts, canoeing, choral singing, dramatics, field sports, gymnastics, piano accompaniment, riding, sailing, swimming (WSI), tennis, trampoline, tripping and waterskiing. Salaries are $500-1,200, with allowance for transportation, room and board, and camp clothes. Free laundry, linen, and medical service. Apply by April 1 to Mr. and Mrs. Howard J. Rymland, Stevenson MD 21153.

### Samoset II
Located in Casco, Maine. Camp for boys ages 7-16. Openings for college students, teachers and high school seniors from June 23 to August 21. Needs 4 general counselors familiar with all sports; instructors for soccer, volleyball, baseball, basketball, tennis, archery, lacrosse, riflery, photography, wrestling, nature, universal weight training, drama, canoeing, karate, WSI, scuba, sailing, waterskiing, bicycling; directors for hiking and assistant, crafts and assistant. Salaries are $500-1,000 plus room, board, laundry and insurance. Apply by April 15 to Stephen Feinstein, Director, 140 Waterman St., Providence RI 02906; tel. 401/421-5675.

### Skylemar
Located in Naples, Maine. Camp for boys ages 8-16. Openings for college students, college graduates and teachers from June 27 to August 21. Needs counselors for lacrosse, tennis, golf, arts and crafts, waterfront (WSI), waterskiing, basketball, baseball, riflery, dramatics, photography; general counselors; nurse. Salaries are $600-800 plus transportation allowance and laundry. Apply by April 1 to Lee Horowitz, 7900 Stevenson Rd., Baltimore MD 21208; tel. 301/653-2480.

### Somerset For Girls
Located in Oakland, Maine. Openings for college students and teachers. Needs counselors for archery, athletics, canoeing, crafts, dramatics, fencing, golf, riding, riflery, skeet shooting, sailing, scuba, swimming, synchronized swimming, tennis, tripping, waterskiing, general group; nurse (RN); secretaries; dining room supervisor. Salaries are $500-850 plus transportation, clothing allowance, laundry, room and board. Brother camp, Camp Cobbossee. Apply by May 1 to Camp Somerset, 444 E. 86th St, New York NY 10028.

### Takajo
Located in Naples, Maine. Boys camp. Staff openings for teachers, upper college level students and graduate students (age 20 and up). Vacancies are in athletics, tripping, swimming (WSI), canoeing, sailing, dramatics, music, photography, radio and electronics, nature study, crafts, riflery, archery and general counseling for younger boys. Would prefer high school coaching level applicants for head baseball, basketball, soccer, and tennis. Salary are $450-750 plus maintenance and transportation. Apply to Morton J. Goldman, 3 Puritan Court, Princeton NJ 08540.

### Tapawingo
Located in Sweden, Maine, in the foothills of the New Hampshire White Mountains. ACA accredited camp established 1919. (The "Tap" family consists of 175 girls, ages 8-16; 68 counselors). Over 1,000 acres on private lake. "Reputation as one of New England's most dedicated camps with excellent facilities and equipment." Openings for college juniors, seniors, graduate students, teachers with

genuine interest in teaching and living with children from June 20 to August 23.
Needs counselor staff in arts and crafts, backpacking, canoeing, dramatics,
gymnastics, land sports (including hockey and soccer), riding, sailing, swimming
(including diving, competition and synchronized, WSI only), pianist (accompanist
and transposer), tennis, waterskiing; nurses (RN). Limited accommodations for older
women, men and married couple counselors. Excellent salary, commensurate with
age, experience and skill. Transportation allowance plus board, room and laundry.
Send for application, brochure and detailed information. Apply to Mr. and Mrs. M.
H. Rogers, Directors, 1890 S. Ocean Dr., Box 911, Hallandale FL 33009.

**Vega**
Located on Echo Lake at Kents Hill. Private camp for girls, ages 8-15. Openings
for college students and teachers. Needs counselors for swimming (WSI), sailing,
waterskiing, canoeing, pioneering, tripping, English riding, tennis, drama,
landsports, arts and crafts. Salaries are $400-800/season plus room, board and
laundry. Apply by April to Richard Courtiss, Camp Vega, Dept. SED, Kents Hill ME
04349.

**Wild Goose**
Located at Great Moose Lake in Harmony, Maine. Camp for 70 boys ages 8-14;
includes all land and water sports. Openings from June 20 to August 20. Needs
nurse (RN or LPN), $800-900/season; secretary/typist with car, $800-900/season;
assistant to chef, some experience in kitchen work, salary open depending on age
and experience; counselors with sports background, $400-600/season depending
on age and experience. Apply by April 30 to William E. Trauth, Dept. SED, 328
Summit Ave., Leonia NJ 07605; tel. 201/944-6271.

**Wildwood**
Located at Wood Pond, Bridgton, Maine. General 8-week camp for boys ages
7-15. Openings from June 18 to August 24. Needs 1 arts and crafts head, college
students and teachers preferred, $700-850/season; 4 water safety instructors, 1
sailing instructor, 4 general counselors, college students preferred,
$450-700/season; 2 each baseball and basketball instructors, 2 soccer counselors,
college students and teachers preferred, $450-750; 2 nurses (RN), college students
and teachers preferred, $700-800/season; 4 tennis staff and head, college students
and teachers preferred, staff $450-750/season-head $1,000/season; 2 water ski
counselors, college students and teachers preferred, $500-750/season. "Must like
working with children." Apply by April 15 to Wally Case, Director, Camp Wildwood,
2 Joni Place, West Sayville NY 11796; tel. 516/589-7277.

**Wyonegonic Camps**
Located in Denmark, Maine, near the White Mountains of New Hampshire. 3 small
private girls camps adjacent to one another with separate facilities, program and
staff. Openings for college students, teachers, graduate students and married
couples, from late June to mid-August. Needs specialty counselors (minimum age
21) for waterfront, canoeing and mountain trips, sailing, tennis, riflery, gymnastics,
piano, archery, waterskiing, riding, arts and crafts. Salaries are $400-700 depending
on age, experience and responsibility. Apply by May to Mr. and Mrs. George N.
Sudduth, 30 Hancock Rd., Hingham MA 02043; tel. 617/749-5515.

# Maryland

## Business and Industry

**Kelly Services, Inc.**
More than 450 branches coast to coast, Puerto Rico, Canada, England and France. Temporary work assignments. Offers over 100 job classifications (office, marketing and light industrial assignments) to college students, teachers and other qualified people during summer breaks and year 'round. Kelly Services also has a special referral system that allows you to register at a Kelly office near your school then work near your home during summer recess—or register near your home then work on temporary assignments during the school year. Assignments available include clerks, typists, secretaries, keypunch operators, word processors, bookkeepers and a variety of marketing and light industrial. Offers flexible schedule with "attractive hourly pay rates equal to or higher than the accepted industry standards in most cities." No paycheck deductions except Social Security and income tax. No employment fee for temporary work. See the White Pages for the branch of Kelly Services nearest you. Apply in person or write to: Summer Employment, National Headquarters, Kelly Services, GPO 1179, Detroit MI 48266.

**Mature Temps Inc.**
Located in Baltimore. National temporary employment service. Openings for college students, teachers, high school seniors, local applicants and foreign students from May to September or year-round. Needs secretaries, clerks, typists, bookkeepers, stenographers, accountants, demonstrators and marketing research persons. High hourly rates based on skills. Apply to Mature Temps Inc., 10 E. Baltimore St., Suite 700, Baltimore MD 21202; tel. 301/837-2444.

**Temp Force**
Tempororary office personnel contractor. Openings for college students, teachers, high school seniors during vacations and holidays. Needs secretaries, typists, stenographers, clericals and accountants. Salaries based upon experience. Apply to Temp Force, 1 Investment Place, Towson MD 21204; tel. 301/828-0778.

## Resorts, Ranches, Restaurants, Lodging

**Jonah & The Whale**
Located on the Boardwalk in Ocean City. Ocean resort restaurant. Openings for college students, teachers, high school seniors and foreign students from May 1 to Labor Day; must stay through season. Needs 20 waitresses, 6 general dining room and kitchen workers, 2 food preparation persons, 3 hostesses ($2.90), 4 cooks and receiving clerk. Salaries are hourly plus bonus. Apply to Manager, Jonah & The Whale, Dept. SED, Box 160, Ocean City MD 21842.

**Longhorn Family Steakhouse**
Located in Ocean City. Resort restaurant. Openings from May 24 to Labor Day; must stay through season. Needs 15 waitresses, 3 hostesses, 5 dining room help, 10 kitchen help and receiving clerk. Apply to Alberta Lee Smith, Longhorn Family

Steakhouse, Box 160, Ocean City MD 21842.

## Paul Revere Smorgasbord

Located in Ocean City. Resort restaurant. Openings from March 24 to October 30; must stay through Labor Day. Needs 50 waitresses, 10 hostesses, 30 kitchen help, 10 dining room help, 3 cooks, 2 accounting and receiving clerk. Salaries are $2.90/hour. Apply to Alberta Lee Smith, Manager, Paul Revere Smorgasbord, Box 160, Ocean City MD 21842.

# Summer Camps

### Airy, Louise

Hebrew camp for boys and girls. Openings for college students, teachers and foreign students from June 22 to August 22. Needs 70 counselors with skills in WSI, riflery, crafts, music and outdoor living. Salaries are $300-500 with annual increments, travel and laundry allowance plus room and board; program specialists and unit leaders are paid differentials for additional skill and responsibility. Apply by May 10 to Sidney N. Chernak, 5750 Park Heights Ave., Baltimore MD 21215.

### Children's Fresh Air Society, Inc.

Located thirty miles north of Baltimore. Resident coed camp for children from lower-income families. Openings for 60 teachers and college students. Needs general counselors and waterfront, canoeing, nature crafts, dramatics and photography specialists. Salary plus maintenance. Apply by May 31 to Paul C. Mitzel, Executive Director, 615 Cherry Hill Rd., Street MD 21154.

### Elk's Camp Barrett

Located in Annapolis. Summer camp for boys ages 9-14. Openings for college students and teachers (local applicants also for cooks) from early June to late August. Needs business manager, 2 lifeguards/counselors (WSI), 5 counselors (camping experience and skills in sports, archery, campcraft or nature), rifle range instructor/counselor (NRA), $1,000/season; cook, $2,000/season. Room and board provided. Applicants should "not be afraid of hard work and the rewards of hard work." Send resume by March 1 to Robert Broody, Executive Director, Elk's Camp Barrett, 1001 Chesterfield Rd., Annapolis MD 21401; tel. 301/224-2945.

### Greentop

Located at Lanz. Camp for physically disabled children (ages 6-18) and adults (18 and up). Needs 14 senior counselors and 26 junior counselors. "Counselors work with cabin groups and in activity areas; water safety instructor required for swimming; crafts and sports require experience with children. Salary plus room, board and transportation from Baltimore to camp. Experience working with children and adults desired." Also needs clerical, business and kitchen personnel and nurses/LPNs. Needs counselors for adult camp session from mid to late August, usually 2 weeks; salary plus room and meals. For children's camp, work from late June to mid-August. Apply to Chad M. Casserly, Director, Camping Recreation, The League for the Handicapped, Inc., 1111 E. Cold Spring Lane, Baltimore MD 21239; tel. 301/323-0500.

## King's Landing

Located 6 miles north of Prince Frederick on the Patuxent River. YMCA resident coed camp for children ages 7-15; day, ages 6 to 12. Openings for college students, teachers, high school seniors and foreign students, minimum age 18, from approximately June 20 through August 25. Needs 25 counselors, $400-700/season; 8 junior counselors (minimum age 17 with counseling experience), $100-150/season. Salary depends on experience. Room and board provided. Apply by April to YMCA King's Landing Camp, Box 88, RR1, Dept. SED, Huntingtown MD 20639.

## Letts

Located in Edgewater. Coed YMCA camp. Openings for college students, teachers and high school seniors from mid-June to mid-August. Needs 30 counselors, $350 up; 3 assistant waterfront-pool directors, $350-600; 7 unit leaders, $500 up; 2 waterfront-pool directors, $650 up; land activities director, $550 up; program director, $750 up. Room and board provided. Application deadline: March, but may accept applications until June. Apply early to YMCA Camp Letts, Box 208, Dept. SED, Edgewater MD 21037.

## Tockwogh

Worton, Maryland. Coed YMCA camp for children ages 8-5. Openings for 84 college students from June 15 to August 23. Needs specialty counselors for boating, canoeing, sailing, skiing, swimming, WSI, archery, riflery, tennis, arts and crafts, photography, riding, nature, dramatics, dancing, campcraft, tripping, athletics, soccer; counselors and village chiefs, nurse (RN), graduate nurse's aide. Apply by March 1 to YMCA Camp Tockwogh, 11th and Washington Sts., Wilmington DE 19801.

# Summer Theaters

## Jewish Community Center of Greater Washington

Located in Rockville. Openings from June 14 to August 1. Needs 2 directors, 1 movement choreographer (oriented), college student or teacher preferred, $1,000/season; assistant director, costumer, technical director, musical director, college student or teacher preferred, $750/season; 5 apprentices, local applicants, college students, high school seniors preferred. Send full resumé, or if interested persons are in Washington area (even in winter months) would like to meet them personally. Apply to Bruce Silver, Theater Director, Jewish Community Center of Greater Washington, Dept. SED, 6125 Montrose Rd., Rockville MD 20852; tel. 301/881-0100, ext. 74.

# Massachusetts

# Business and Industry

## Mature Temps Inc.

Located in Boston. National temporary employment service. Openings for college students, teachers, high school seniors, local applicants and foreign students from May to September or year-round. Needs secretaries, clerks, typists, bookkeepers, stenographers, accountants, demonstrators and marketing research persons. High hourly rates based on skills. Apply to Mature Temps Inc., 47 Winter St., Boston MA 02108; tel. 617/482-7628.

### Kelly Services, Inc.
More than 450 branches coast to coast, Puerto Rico, Canada, England and France. Temporary work assignments. Offers over 100 job classifications (office, marketing and light industrial assignments) to college students, teachers and other qualified people during summer breaks and year 'round. Kelly Services also has a special referral system that allows you to register at a Kelly office near your school then work near your home during summer recess—or register near your home then work on temporary assignments during the school year. Assignments available include clerks, typists, secretaries, keypunch operators, word processors, bookkeepers and a variety of marketing and light industrial. Offers flexible schedule with "attractive hourly pay rates equal to or higher than the accepted industry standards in most cities." No paycheck deductions except Social Security and income tax. No employment fee for temporary work. See the White Pages for the branch of Kelly Services nearest you. Apply in person or write to: Summer Employment, National Headquarters, Kelly Services, GPO 1179, Detroit MI 48266.

### Olsten Temporary Services
Located in Boston. Office and industrial employment service. Positions available for loaders-unloaders, packers, warehouse, kitchen help, typists, secretaries, clerks, key punchers, SBO. Positions are daily, long- and short-term assignments. Paid weekly on Fridays, $2.90/hour and up. Apply in person to Olsten Temporary Services, 8 Winter, Boston MA 02108; tel. 617/423-7426.

### Temp Force
Temporary office personnel contractor. Openings for college students, teachers, high school seniors during vacations and holidays. Needs secretaries, typists, stenographers, clericals, accountants. Salaries based upon experience. Apply to Temp Force: 1 Village Square, Chelmsford MA 01824, tel. 617/256-4126; 623 Pleasant St., Brockton MA 02401, tel. 617/588-0500; 140 Union St., Lynn MA 01902, tel. 617/593-6000; 339 Hancock St., N. Quincy MA 02171, tel. 617/328-6400; 446 Main St., Worcester MA 01608, tel. 617/798-2010.

---

**Temporary employment services offer a wide range of job openings for summer job seekers. SED lists temporary employment services in each state that are very anxious to hear from qualified persons.**

# Commercial Attractions

### Midway Park
Located at Salisbury Beach. Amusement park. Openings for local college students, teachers, and high school seniors. Needs 40 ride operators and 3 maintenance persons. "The park's good name depends on your relationship with the public so impeccable personal appearance and courtesy is a necessity." Apply to Michael Mulcahy, Park Manager, Midway Park, 422 North Blvd., Salisbury MA 01950; tel. 617/465-0946.

# Resorts, Ranches, Restaurants, Lodging

### Oak 'N' Spruce Resort
Located in heart of the Berkshires in South Lee. Year-round resort, 440 acres with swimming pools, golf, tennis, skiing and hiking. Openings from early June through Labor Day. Must work through Labor Day. Needs 2 cooks, 12 waiters/waitresses, dining room manager, 3 dishwashers, 3 bartenders, 3 groundskeepers, pool attendant, 3 office/front desk personnel, 6 chambermaids, $120-250/week depending on job skills and position. "Room and board are not included though for some positions a meal would be part of the shift worked. Housing locally costs upwards of $100/month and is readily available in May and June. Applicants should have some experience and interest in the hotel/restaurant/hospitality industry, and have their own transportation." Send resume by May 1. Apply to Roy A. Prinz, Manager, Dept. SED, Oak 'N' Spruce Resort, South Lee MA 01260; tel. 413/243-3500.

# Summer Camps

### Association of Independent Camps
Openings at 100 children's (ages 6-16) summer camps located in New England and Middle Atlantic States. Needs head counselors, group leaders, general and all specialty counselors. Apply by July to Association of Independent Camps, Dept. SED, 55 W. 42nd St., New York NY 10036; tel. 212/695-2656.

### Avalon
Located at Cape Cod. Girls camp. Openings for college students for 9 weeks during the summer. Needs instructors for sailing, tennis, swimming (WSI), gymnastics, trampoline, crafts, archery; program aide, nurse (RN). Salaries are $500 and up, plus room and board. Apply to Mr. and Mrs. George N. Laffey, Jr., Camp Avalon, Chatham MA 02633.

### Clara Barton
Located in North Oxford. Camp for diabetic girls ages 7-17. Openings for college students and teachers from approximately June 22 to August 22. Needs 20 specialty counselors for arts and crafts, canoeing, boating, sailing, swimming (WSI), campcraft, nature, gymnastics, bicycling, team and individual sports, dance, apparatus, Indian lore, $450-600; waterfront director, $750-800; assistant waterfront director, $650-700; 5 unit directors, $650-1,000; program director and

assistant camp director, $1,200-1,500; 3 nurses (RN or graduate nurse), $800-1,000; head dietitian, $1,000; assistant dietitian, $700-900; 3 nurse's aides, 3 lab technicians, $500-800; head cook, $1,200-1,500; assistant cook, $700-900; 3 kitchen aides, 2 maintenance aides, $350-550. College credit can be arranged through respective colleges if program is available. Apply by February 15 to Elizabeth Kruczek, Camps Complex Administrator, UUWF, Dept. SED, 6 Betty St., Auburn MA 01501.

### Becket

Located in Becket. State YMCA resident camp for upper middle class boys; concerned with Christian character development. Openings for college students and teachers from June 14 to August 16 (except waterfront directors, June 12 to August 16 or 24). Needs 25 cabin counselors (serve 7-8 boys, help instruct in skilled activity), $500-700/season. 2 waterfront directors (WSI, YMCA certification), $100 and up/week; music director (choral and instrumental music program), $700-1,000/season; tripping director (minimum age 21, experienced in backpacking and canoe trips), $800 up/season. Salaries include room and board. "Working here is hard work, requiring patience and a real interest in and concern for young people. Earn an advanced lifesaving certification; it means a better salary." Send for application, returning it by May 1 to Don Shellenberger, Director, State YMCA, 6 St. James Ave. Suite 1003, Boston MA 02116; tel. 617/426-8802.

### Belvoir Terrace

Located in Lenox. Fine arts summer school for "talented, motivated teenage women." Openings for college graduates from June 24 through August 24. Needs specialty counselors for art, music, theater, gymnastics, waterfront (WSI) and tennis. Salaries are commensurate with experience; provides room, board and "chances to take classes with the girls." Apply to Nancy Goldberg, 31 Sheffield Rd., Newtonville MA 02160.

### Dorothy Carlton
### Favorite

Dorothy Carlton located in Plymouth; Favorite located in Brewster. Girl Scout camp for girls ages 7-17. Openings for 60 college students, teachers, high school seniors and foreign students from the end of June to the end of August. Needs staff for waterfront, swimming (WSI), boating (small-craft); CIT director, unit leaders, assistant unit leaders, specialty counselors for bicycling, crafts, primitive camping, mentally retarded; assistant cook, kitchen aides. Salaries are $200 and up, depending on position and experience. Apply to Blue Hill Girl Scout Council, Inc., 57 Revere Rd., Quincy MA 02169.

### Chimney Corners Camp

Located in Becket. Christian-oriented YMCA resident camp for girls, ages 8-15. Openings from mid-June to August 20. Needs 30 cabin counselors (college students, graduate students, teachers with skills in program areas), minimum $475/season; program specialists, minimum 1 each, in the areas of photography, nature, waterfront (WSI), sailing, tennis, dramatics, music, arts & crafts, riding, $475-1,200/season depending upon age, skills and experience; service staffers, minimum 1 each, as nurses (RN), office workers, kitchen assistants, maintenance people, cooks, drivers, minimum $475 depending upon position; administrative staffers, minimum age 22, as unit directors, program directors, leader-in-training director (camping and supervising experience), minimum $900 depending upon experience. Room and board included. "We seek the highly skilled and motivated only. Apply early. Most positions are filled by March." Send for application to Jeanne Shellenberger, Camp Director, State YMCA, Dept. SED, 6 St. James Ave., Suite 1003, Boston MA 02116; tel. 617/426-8802.

### Crane Lake

Located in West Stockbridge, Massachusetts, 3 miles from Tanglewood Music Festival in the Berkshire Mountains. Private coed camp. Openings for college students and teachers from late June to late August. Needs physical education majors and teachers to coach basketball, baseball, football, soccer, tennis; specialty counselors: 6 waterfront (WSI), small craft, hiking, gymnastics, drama, music, fine arts, painting, sculpturing, nature, riflery, arts and crafts, guitar. Salaries are $350 up plus room and board, depending on age and experience. Apply by May to Ed Ulanoff, Crane Lake Camp, 4465 Douglas Ave., Riverdale NY 10471.

### Danbee

Located at Peru, Massachusetts. Girls camp. Openings from June 22 to August 22. Needs specialty instructors for swimming (WSI), sailing, boating, canoeing, diving, competitive swimming, synchronized swimming, gymnastics, volleyball, basketball, archery, ceramics, sculpturing, painting, jewelry, weaving, dramatics, cooking, sewing, guitar, piano (accompanist), typing, tennis, campcraft, waterskiing, soccer, bicycling, yearbook, recreational games, golf, dance, and field hockey. Salaries are $500 and up depending on age, background and experience. Apply to Ann B. Miller, Camp Danbee, 2031 Rittenhouse Square, Philadelphia PA 19103.

### Frank A. Day

Located at East Brookfield. YMCA camp for children ages 7-14, CITs ages 15 and 16. Openings for college students, teachers, high school seniors and foreign students from mid-June to the end of August. Needs 2 waterfront specialists, $600-800/season; 12 senior counselors, $400-600/season; 2 unit leaders, $600-900/season; nurse (RN), $700-1,000. Apply to Richard McKnight, Director, Newton YMCA, Dept. SED, 276 Church St., Newton MA 02158.

### Good News

Located at Forestdale, Massachusetts, on Cape Cod. Christian, coed. Openings for college students and teachers from June 23 to August 18. Needs 40 counselors, kitchen staff, laundry workers, store help, office worker, maintenance, nurse. Salaries are $450-600. Apply to Dr. Hope Brooks, 533 Darlington Rd., Media PA 19063.

### Greylock For Boys
### Romaca For Girls

Located in Becket, Massachusetts. Brother-sister camps. Openings from June 19 to August 19 for university and college students and teachers, minimum age 20. Needs 4 group leaders/department heads, $700-1,000; 24 waterfront (ARC, WSI, SCI), $500-800; 60 specialists for all land and water sports, popular/jazz/rock/folk music, art, drama, handcrafts, carpentry, hiking, radio, electronics, nature, kitchen and maintenance, top salaries; 2 doctors, 4 nurses (RN). All salaries include full room and board. Apply by June 10 to Bert Margolis, Camps Greylock for Boys,

Romaca for Girls, Dept. SED, 25 E. 83rd St., New York NY 10028; tel. 212/861-2450.

## Half Moon

Located in Monterey. Nonsectarian boys camp. Openings from June 24 to August 26 for persons age 18 or older. Needs general athletic counselors for all land and water sports; specialty counselors for riflery, sailing, skiing, canoeing, woodworking, wrestling, ceramics, photography; nurses (RN). Salaries are $500-900 plus room, board and laundry. Some accommodations for married couples. Apply to Edward Mann, Box 188, Great Barrington MA 01230.

## Elliott P. Joslin

Located in Charlton. Private, nonprofit, specialty camp for boys with diabetes, ages 7-15½. Needs 1 assistant (WSI) waterfront director, $600-825; 2 waterfront, e.g. canoeing, boating, sailing, kayaking, $600-775; 2 senior counselors, $550-775; 1 accountant/bookkeeper, $800-950. College students preferred. Also needs 2 junior counselors, $450-575, college students or high school seniors preferred. Work from June 16 to August 20. "Salaries depend on previous experience and training. Waterfront personnel must be certified by the American Red Cross in areas they are applying for. Applicants should be looking for a challenging and busy position." Apply by May to Paul B. Madden, Camp Administrator/Director, Elliott P. Joslin Camp, 1 Joslin Place, Boston MA 02215.

## Lenore-Owaissa

Located in Hinsdale, Massachusetts, in the Berkshires. Camp for girls ages 7-17. Openings for upper-class college students, graduate students and teachers from June 26 to August 22. Needs specialty counselors for tennis, arts and crafts, WSI, sailing, soccer, waterskiing, pioneering, archery, fencing, drama, dancing, gymnastics and music. Salary open. Apply to Director, Camp Lenore-Owaissa, 851 E. 23rd St., Brooklyn NY 11210.

## Mah-Kee-Nac

Located in Lenox, Massachusetts. Private boys camps; 52nd summer. Three camps, separated by ages. Openings for 90 upper classmen, graduate students, faculty teachers, and upper classmen from June 22 to August 24. Needs specialty counselors: 26 waterfront (WSI, swimming, canoeing, sailing, waterskiing), 6 overnight camping, 15 tennis, nature, music, ceramics, woodworking, sculling, kayaks, ham radio, electronics, riflery, baseball, soccer, basketball. Attractive salaries match skill and experience. Room, board and laundry provided. Apply to Joseph Kruger, 20 Allen Ct., South Orange NJ 07079.

## Meadow Lark Camp, Inc.

Located at Monterey in the Berkshire Hills. Coed private camp. 41st year. Openings for 60 persons from June 20 to August 25. Needs specialists in arts and crafts, woodwork, nature, sports (non-competitive); nurse. Applicants must be over 21, graduates and teachers preferred. Also needs assistant counselors (minimum age 18½). Salary commensurate with training and experience. All counselors have cabin duties. A personal interview, if at all possible, is preferred. Applicants must love children and be interested in the children's development and in furthering their potential in all areas. Apply to Eric H. Craven, Meadow Lark Camp, Inc., Box 248, Monterey MA 01245.

## Mohawk in the Berkshires

Located at Lanesboro, Massachusetts. Private coed camp for children ages 8-15. Openings for college students and teachers from June 28 to August 24. Needs counselors (ages 19 and older) for music (play piano and sight-reading), sailing, nature, canoeing, drama, dance, tennis, soccer, basketball, softball, ceramics, woodworking and skiing, 2 teen-age trip leaders (skills in canoeing, campcraft, bike riding, minimum age 21), $475-850. Include self addressed stamped envelope with correspondence. Apply to Ralph Schulman, Mohawk in the Berkshires, Dept. SED, 107 Davis Ave., White Plains NY 10605.

## Namequoit

Located in Orleans. Boys sailing camp with general program; ages 9-15. Openings for college students from June 19 to August 18. Needs counselors: 3-4 sailing (salt water, racing—college or club experience preferred); 2-3 swimming (WSI, camp, club or college experience preferred); 1-2 tennis (college or club experience preferred); 1-2 sports (basketball, baseball, soccer—college experience preferred); 1-2 riflery (minimum age 21, NRA/ROTC experience); 1-2 archery (CAA or college certification); 1-2 woodworking (shop or manual of arts); gymnastics (all apparatus—college varsity experience). Pays $500-900/season. "All counselors are cabin counselors, male only. Personal interviews desired if possible. Camp application and brochure sent upon receipt of inquiry." Apply by March 1 to A. E. Farnham, Jr., Director, Camp Namequoit, Box 306, Dept. SED, Orleans MA 02653; tel. 617/255-0377.

## New England Camping Association, Inc. (ACA)

Camp counselor referral service. Openings for college students and teachers, minimum age 19, for 8 weeks. Needs specialty counselors for advanced lifesaving, archery, arts and crafts, bicycling, boating, campcraft, canoeing, golf, drama, guitar, gymnastics, horseback riding, land sports, music, nature-ecology, photography, piano, radio-electronics, riflery, sailing (SCI), scuba, tennis, waterskiing, WSI; trip leader, unit leader, administrative, chef, baker, kitchen workers, clerical, maintenance, doctors, nurses (RN). Salaries start at $400 and are commensurate with age, education, camp experience and type of position. $2 application fee. Apply to New England Camping Association, Inc., Room 410, 29 Commonwealth Ave., Boston MA 02116.

## New England Tennis Camp

Located in Groton, Massachusetts, and Pawling, New York. Specialty camp. Openings for college students and teachers from June 23 to August 25, two 4-week sessions, with a 1-week break between sessions. Needs 29 counselors who have strong tennis background (college team or tournament experience), $700-800. Apply to Jay Norek, New England Tennis Camp, South Rd., Harrison NY 10528.

## Romaca

Located in Hinsdale, Massachusetts. Camp for girls in grades 1-9. Openings for college students and teachers, minimum age 20, from approximately June 25 to August 26. Needs specialty counselors for tennis; waterfront: swimming (WSI), sailing, small craft (SCI), canoeing, waterskiing; performing arts: music (camp piano-other), show directors, modern dance; creative arts; land sports; individual sports: fencing, golf, archery, gymnastics, horseback riding (English), photography, radio; electronics; outdoor living skills: woodslore, hiking, overnights, nature; general counselors experienced in working with young children (grades 1-3); secretary-bookkeeper. Salaries are $350 and up plus room, board and laundry. "Medical insurance coverage available at small cost to counselor." Apply to Romaca for Girls, 55 Hampton Pl., Freeport NY 11520.

### Sandy Brook
Located at Norwich Lake, Huntington. Girl Scouts; resident tent camp for girls ages 7-17. Openings from June 22 to August 24. Needs 4 unit leaders, minimum age 21 (college students, teachers, foreign students and local applicants, experience in working with and leading groups, knowledge of girl scouting and camp counseling preferred), $71-93/week; 7 unit assistants, must be high school graduate (college students, foreign students, local applicants, experienced with group leadership, camp program skills), $50-68/week; waterfront director, minimum age 21 (WSI, college student, teacher, local applicant, experience teaching swimming and small crafts on organized waterfront), $79-114/week; 3 waterfront assistants, must be high school graduates (college students, foreign students, local applicants, WSI, Life Saving), $54-71/week; head cook, minimum age 21 (college student, teacher, local applicant, training and experience in menu planning, food ordering and cooking for large numbers), $114-164/week; assistant cook, must be high school graduate (college student, teacher, local applicant, interested in quantity cooking, ability to take direction), $50-86/week; nurse (local applicant, RN in Massachusetts, first aid training, able to work with children), $96-129/week; riding instructor (college student, teacher, local applicant, Massachusetts license, ability to instruct Western riding and supervise riding program), $100-125/week; craft specialist, must be high school graduate (college student, teacher, foreign student, local applicant, ability to teach hand arts, especially nature crafts), $50-96/week. Salaries include room and board; tax deductions based on including value for room and board. "Applicant must like children and living outdoors in all kinds of weather." Send for application. Apply by April 1 to Priscilla Wahlen, Camp Director, Dept. SED, 46 Millers Falls Rd., Turners Falls MA 01376; tel. 413/863-2115.

### Viking
Located at South Orleans, Cape Cod. Summer sailing camp for boys. Needs 4 sailing counselors, 3 swimming counselors (WSI required), 2 shop counselors, 2 athletic counselors, 2 archery counselors, 2 tennis counselors, college students and teachers preferred, $450-650/8 weeks; 3 kitchen help, college students and high school seniors preferred, $65/week. Dates of employment, June 26 through August 21. "Although Viking has a number of sound activities, we specialize in teaching small boat sailing, and have for fifty years. A great deal revolves around the water, including overnight sailing expeditions, which almost everyone is involved in at one time or another. Applicants should be interested in camping and working with young boys." Write for application to Tom Lincoln, Director, Camp Viking, Box 405, South Orleans MA 02662; telephone (617)255-2739.

### Watitoh
Located in Center Lake, Becket, Massachusetts. Private coed camp. Openings for college students and teachers from June 28 to August 24. Needs instructors: 6 WSI, 2 small craft, 3 tennis, waterskiing, all team and individual sports. Salaries are $500-1,000. Apply to Sheldon Hoch, 28 Sammis Lane, White Plains NY 10605.

## Winadu
Located in Pittsfield, Massachusetts. Sports camp for children ages 6-16. Openings from June 25 to August 22. Needs 14 head tennis counselors and 20 head waterfront counselors, $600-2,000/season; many basketball, baseball, and soccer counselors, $600 plus/season; 1 karate and 1 ham radio counselor, $600 plus/season; and 4 arts and crafts counselors, $600 plus/season. "Please send letter for an application or call." Apply to Mr. Shelley Weiner, Director, 5 Glen Lane, Mamaroneck NY 10543; tel. 914/381-5983.

## Wind-in-the-Pines
Located in Plymouth. Girl Scout resident camp for ages 6-17. Openings for high school graduates, college students and teachers from mid-June to mid-August. Needs waterfront director, water safety instructors, smallcraft director, canoeing and sailing instructors, unit leaders, unit assistants, business manager, cooks and nurse. Salaries are $300-1,700 plus room and board. An equal opportunity employer. Apply to Plymouth Bay Girl Scout Council, Inc., Box 711, Taunton MA 02780.

## Wonderland
Located in Sharon. Salvation Army, church, welfare camp; ages 7-12. Openings from late June to Labor Day. Needs 30 counselors, 5 waterfront, $500 and up; 7 program specialists for nature, crafts, athletics, pioneering, etc., $600; nurses, $1,000 and up. Room and board provided. Apply by March 31 to Salvation Army Camp Wonderland, 147 Berkeley St., Boston MA 02116.

# Summer Theaters

## College Light Opera Company, The
Located in Highfield Theatre, Falmouth, Massachusetts. Music theater, light opera, Gilbert and Sullivan. Openings for college students and high school seniors from June 15 to September 1. Needs 10 staff members, all positions, salary available; 35 singers, 6 technical backstage workers, 6 costume shop, 2 piano accompanists, orchestra (all instruments), room and board, no salary. Deadline for applications: March 1, "but openings in some areas until May 1." Apply to Robert A. Haslun, The College Light Opera Company, 162 S. Cedar St., Oberlin OH 44074.

## South Shore Music Circus
Located in Cohasset. Summer theater serving families, teenagers, senior citizens. Needs office, box office, press, management personnel, April 15 to September 15, salary open; technical personnel, May 15 to September 15, salary open; apprentices, June 1 to September 15, $50/week. Local housing listings made available by theater. Send for application. Apply by April 1 to Ronald Rawson, Producer, South Shore Music Circus, Box 325, Cohasset MA 02021; tel. 617/383-9850.

## Tufts Summer Theater
Located in Medford. Summer stock. Openings for college students and recent graduates from May 26 to August 5. Needs technical, costume and publicity assistants; stage and house managers; actors. Salaries: $300-1,000/season plus

room. Apply by March 1 to Patricia Fina, Tufts Arena Theater, Dept. SED, Talbot Ave., Medford MA 02155.

### Williamstown Theatre Festival
Located in Williamstown. Summer theater. Openings for college students, teachers, high school seniors and foreign students from approximately June 11 to September 1. Needs 10 staff members, salary open; 45-50 apprentices, tuition charged by contract; Equity and non-Equity actors. Apply by May 1 to Gail Bryson, Williamstown Theatre Festival, Box 517, Williamstown MA 01267.

# ——————— Michigan ———————

## Business and Industry

### Joann's Fudge Shop
Located on Mackinac Island. Openings for students from May to October. Peak season, July 1 to Labor Day. Needs clerks and fudge maker's helpers. Enclose stamped return envelope with resume. Apply to Frank Nephew, 261 Altorf Strasse Rte. 4, Gaylord MI 49735.

### Kelly Services, Inc.
More than 450 branches coast to coast, Puerto Rico, Canada, England and France. Temporary work assignments. Offers over 100 job classifications (office, marketing and light industrial assignments) to college students, teachers and other qualified people during summer breaks and year 'round. Kelly Services also has a special referral system that allows you to register at a Kelly office near your school then work near your home during summer recess—or register near your home then work on temporary assignments during the school year. Assignments available include clerks, typists, secretaries, keypunch operators, word processors, bookkeepers and a variety of marketing and light industrial. Offers flexible schedule with "attractive hourly pay rates equal to or higher than the accepted industry standards in most cities." No paycheck deductions except Social Security and income tax. No employment fee for temporary work. See the White Pages for the branch of Kelly Services nearest you. Apply in person or write to: Summer Employment, National Headquarters, Kelly Services, GPO 1179, Detroit MI 48266.

### Temp Force
Temporary office personnel contractor. Openings for college students, teachers and high school seniors during vacations and holidays. Needs secretaries, typists, stenographers, clericals and accountants. Salaries based upon experience. Apply to Temp Force, 3126 Davenport, Saginaw MI 48602; tel. 517/792-9197.

## Resorts, Ranches, Restaurants, Lodging

### Brocato's Knife and Fork
Located on Mackinac Island, Michigan. Resort restaurant, established 1945. Openings for college students and high school seniors from June to Labor Day.

Season ends Labor Day. Needs waitresses, bus boys, dishwashers and cooks who are reliable. Salaries plus sizeable tips; housing provided, employee pays rent. "We are interested in students to apply who need money to further their education—not a vacation." Apply by April 1 to Samuel C. Brocato, Box 776, Scottsdale AZ 85251.

## Chippewa Hotel

Located on Mackinac Island, Michigan. Openings for college students, teachers and high school seniors. Needs maids, cooks, salad makers, bellboys, dock porters, bartenders, bar help, housekeepers, bus boys, hostesses, waitresses, lifeguards, dishwashers, porters, etc. Give earliest arrival date in spring and latest departure date in fall. Enclose a stamped return envelope. Apply by August 1 to Nathan Shayne, Box 325, Scottsdale AZ 85252.

## El Rancho Stevens, Inc.

Located in Gaylord. Western-style resort-ranch. Openings from May through Labor Day for 40 college students, teachers, high school seniors and local applicants. Waiters, waitresses, cooks, bus boys, kitchen helpers, maids, waterski instructor, riding instructors, trail guides, lifeguard, children's counselor, recreational directors, guitar and banjo players, musicians, bartender, typist, office help, gift shop clerk. Excellent salaries based upon applicant's maturity, experience and training; room and board provided. "The ranch is not a swinging night-life sort of place but offers a wholesome out-of-doors kind of summer. Staff all work together in their leisure time to produce little informal entertainments, skits, etc. Sound morality and character are essential." Send self-addressed stamped envelope for application. Apply to C. Stevens, Co-owner, El Rancho Stevens, Inc., Dept. SED, Box 366, Gaylord MI 49735; tel. 517/732-5090.

## Fidelman's Resort

Located at South Haven. American Plan for families. Openings from May to October 15 for college students, teachers and foreign students. Needs 12 waitresses/waiters, 3 broiler cooks, 2 salad makers, 6 bus boys, 4 dishwashers, 4 office personnel, 2 child counselors, 2 lifeguards, bartender, 2 maintenance, gardener, sports director and entertainment director. Prefer those with entertainment talent. Approximate seasonal earnings are $700-2,000 after room and board charges. "Plan on seeking room and board at resort—last year's rate was $28/week, including room and meals. Or seek room in town." Enclose stamped return envelope for application. Apply to Barry Fidelman, Dept. SED, Fidelman's Resort, RFD 4, South Haven MI 49090.

## Flora-dale Resort

Located in Mears. American plan for families. Openings for 14 college students from June 11 through Labor Day. Needs 5 waitresses, 2 cottage cleaners, 2 office workers, recreation director, 2 handyman-dishwashers, cook's helper and all around girl. Salaries are $1,400-2,100/season. Prefers employees with some musical talent. All live in at moderate room and board charge. Send stamped return envelope for application and details to D. Bauer, Flora-dale Resort, Dept. SED, Mears MI 49436.

## Michillinda Beach Lodge

Located on the shore of Lake Michigan in Whitehall. Summer resort. Openings from June 15 to Labor Day. Needs 8 waitresses and dining room hostesses, college student preferred, $400/month; 4 kitchen staff, college students preferred, $350-400/month; and 6 maids, college students or high school seniors preferred, $350-400/month. A service charge is distributed as a bonus at the season's end. "Board and room at nominal charge. (1979 rate was $15/month for room and $45/month for board). Applicants should write for employment application after January 1. Applications must be received prior to March 1 with notifications sent out April 10." Apply to Don Eilers, Manager, Dept. SED, Michillinda Beach Lodge, 5207 Scenic Dr., Whitehall MI 49461.

## Pennellwood Resort

Located at Berrien Springs. Openings for college students and teachers, minimum age 18, from Memorial Day to Labor Day. Needs 15 waitresses. Salary plus excellent tips. Dormitory lodging mandatory. Applications taken after January 1. Apply early to Jack Davis, Dept. SED, Pennellwood Resort, Route 2, Box 51, Berrien Springs MI 49103.

## Sunny Brook Farm Resort

Located at South Haven. Openings from early June through Labor Day for 31 college students, teachers and high school seniors, minimum age 17 (refreshment stand only, minimum age 16). Needs waitresses, waiters, cooks, desk clerk, lifeguard-recreation director, kitchen helpers, chambermaids, children's counselors, maintenance helpers, yardman, musicians (part-time only—piano), night watchman, refreshment stand workers, assistant cook, assistant maintenance foreman. Seasonal earnings after room and board charges are met, $500-1,200. Send stamped return envelope for application form and salary scale to Mary C. Ott, Sunny Brook Farm Resort, South Haven MI 49090.

## Ye Olde Pickle Barrel Restaurant (Cafeteria)

Located on Mackinac Island. Openings for students from May to September. Peak season July 1 to Labor Day. Needs cooks, fry cooks, kitchen help and counter girls. Enclose stamped return envelope with resume. Apply to Frank Nephew, 261 Altorf Strasse, Rt. 4, Gaylord MI 49735 (winter address).

# Summer Camps

## American Camping Association/Illinois Section

Located in Illinois and surrounding states including Wisconsin, Indiana, Michigan and Minnesota. The American Camping Association/Illinois Section is an association of persons involved with camps operated by social agencies, and private camp owners. More than 100 camps in Association. Openings for college students, teachers, foreign students and local applicants from late June to late August. Needs persons over 18 years of age who possess a variety of camp leadership skills for positions such as counselors, cooks, waterfront staff, camping and athletic skills teachers, nurses and program directors. Salaries are $500-1,000 for eight weeks or more. Room and board provided. Apply by writing or calling the American Camping Association/Illinois Section, 19 S. LaSalle St., Room 1024, Chicago IL 60603; tel. 312/332-0833.

## Camp O' The Hills

Located at Brooklyn. Girl Scout camp for girls ages 6-17. Openings for college students, teachers, high school seniors and foreign students from July to August. Needs program director, nurse, $600; CIT director, $500; waterfront director, $550; 3 unit leaders, $460; 5 unit assistants, $400; 3 waterfront assistants, $435; cook, $660; assistant cook, $450; business manager, $410. Apply to Sandra Moyer, Irish Hills Girl Scout Council, Box 1362, Jackson MI 49204.

## Chief Makisabee

Located in Eau Claire. Coed camp for inner city, interracial children ages 7-14; also special unit for mentally retarded. Openings for 52 college students and teachers from June 16 to August 22. Needs 34 unit counselors, 2 nature directors, $500-850; 8 unit leaders, $650-800; waterfront director (minimum age 21, WSI), $800-1,000; 6 lifeguards and boating instructors, $500-700; 3 craft instructors (emphasis on use of local materials, campcraft), $500-700; 2 campcraft/archery instructors (minimum age 21), $500-850; nurse, $1,000-1,500; 2 pottery instructors; also director of small games activities. Apply by May 1 to Juanita L. Ryzner, Director, Camp Chief Makisabee, Chicago Youth Centers, Dept. SED, 8800 Black Lake Rd., Eau Claire MI 49111.

## Crystalaire

Located in Frankfort. Private/independent camp for children ages 8-15. Openings from late June to mid-August. Needs 14 counselors (male and female), college students and teachers preferred, $50-90/week; waterfront director/sailing master, college student or teacher preferred, $100-plus/week; art instructor, teacher preferred, $75/week; barn and garden coordinator, college students preferred, $60-75/week; 2 cooks, college students and teachers preferred, $100-150/week; 2 ecology/trips program people, college students and teachers preferred, $60-90/week. "We are a loosely structured camp which demands staff members be highly flexible and have skills or interests in a number of program areas—music, art, waterfront, etc." Apply as early as possible (including up to opening time) to David S. Reid, Director, Crystalaire, Frankfort MI 49635; tel. 616/352-7589.

## Happy Hollow

Located in Mayville. Private camp for mentally and emotionally impaired persons ages 7-50. Openings from mid-June to the last week in August. Needs waterfront director, 3 program specialists, $750/season; 4 senior counselors, 12 counselors, $550-650/season. All salaries are for live-in positions and room and board is provided. "The earlier applicants apply the better, since positions are filled by early spring." Apply by March 1 to Marsha A. Reid, Executive Director, Camp Happy Hollow, Inc., Route 1, Box 105A, Harmon Lake Rd., Mayville MI 48744; tel. 517/673-3666.

## Lake of the Woods
## Greenwoods

Located in Decatur, Michigan. Private camp for boys and girls ages 8-15; separate but adjacent camps. Openings for college students and teachers, minimum age 19, from approximately mid-June to mid-August. Needs counselors for swimming (WSI or Life Saving), sailing, canoeing, rowing, English and Western riding, waterskiing and boat driver, tripping, guitar, arts and crafts, archery, campcraft, riflery, gymnastics, tennis, golf, land sports, nature, dramatics, fencing, storekeeper, secretary, kitchen help, dishwashers, groundskeepers, maintenance, bus driver. Also, nurses (RN), program staff, waterfront director. Salaries are $500-900 depending on age, position and experience. Salaries include room and board. Apply to Laurence Seeger, 1765 Maple St., Northfield IL 60093; tel. 312/256-2444. Summer phone 616/423-3091.

## Maplehurst

Located in Kewadin. Coed camp, ages 7-17. Openings for college students, teachers and foreign students from mid-June to mid-August. Needs 30 general and specialty counselors for waterfront (WSI), riding (English and western), sailing, boating, canoeing, arts and crafts, photography, dramatics, tennis, waterskiing, scuba (NAUI). Salaries are $400-1,000. Apply by June 1 to Camp Maplehurst, 7366 Balsam Court, West Bloomfield MI 48033; tel. 313/661-0271.

## Miniwanca

Located in Shelby, Michigan, on Lake Michigan and Stony Lake. Christian-oriented camp for boys. Also operates Camp Merrowvista, Ossipee, New Hampshire. Openings for college students, graduates, teachers and high school seniors for varying periods from mid-June through August. Needs workstaff (high school seniors and above); counselors (minimum age 18) with skills in archery, bicycling, canoeing, crafts, photography, riflery, sailing, sports, swimming, tennis; directors (upper college and above) for waterfront, tripping, program, unit, workstaff. Salaries are based on age and experience. Room, board, travel allowance, laundry and insurance provided. Apply by April 15 to Wayne Parton, American Youth Foundation, 3460 Hampton Ave., St. Louis MO 63139.

## Newaygo

Located in Newaygo. YWCA camp for children ages 7-17. Openings for college students and teachers during July and August. Needs 12 general counselors, $400-550/season; waterfront director, $500-700/season; arts and crafts director, CIT, tripping director, nature director, $450-600/season; specialty counselors in backpacking/ecology, waterfront including sailing (WSI, SLS, SCI), and drama, $400-600/season. Room and board provided. Apply by April or May to Beverly Cassidy, YWCA Camp Newaygo, Dept. SED, 25 Sheldon Ave. SE, Grand Rapids MI 49337.

## O'Fair Winds

Located at Columbiaville. Girl Scout camp. Openings for college students and teachers from June 15 to August 17. Needs unit assistants, $540-675; waterfront assistants, $585-675; unit leaders, $720-990; craft director, small craft director, business manager, nature specialist, pool director, $675-1,000; cooks, nurse, $900-1,245. Room and board provided. Apply to Camp Director, Dept. SED, Fair Winds Girl Scout Council, 202 E. Boulevard Dr., Room 110, Flint MI 48503.

## Shawadasee

Located at Lawton, Michigan. Girl Scout camp with emphasis on trips and waterfront. Openings for college students, teachers and foreign students from June to August. Needs camp director, unit leaders, unit counselors, waterfront director, waterfront assistants, small-craft instructors, trip director, business managers, kitchen staff, nurse (RN). Apply to Theresa Arneson, Dept. SED, Girl Scouts of

Singing Sands, Inc., 1635 N. Ironwood Dr., South Bend IN 46635.

### Douglas Smith
Located in Ludington, Michigan. Four-week session of girl's camp and 4-week session of boy's camp. Openings from June 13 to August 19 or September 2. Needs specialty counselors for archery, riflery, tennis, canoeing and tripping, waterskiing, waterfront (WSI), sailing, arts and crafts, and photography. Also needs female counselors from June 13 to July 15, and male counselors from July 19 to August 19. Salaries are $650 and up. Cooks, nurse (RN) and maintenance salaries arranged. Apply by April to Dick Martin, Camp Douglas Smith, 620 Lincoln Ave., Winnetka IL 60093.

### Soni Springs
Located at Three Oaks, Michigan. Girl Scout camp with emphasis on horseback riding. Openings for college students, teachers and foreign students from June to August. Needs camp director, unit leaders (minimum age 21), unit counselors (minimum age 18), waterfront director, business manager, program director, nurse (RN or LPN). Submit resume and request for application to Theresa Arneson, Dept. SED, Girl Scouts of Singing Sands, Inc., 1635 N. Ironwood Dr., South Bend IN 46635.

### The Timbers
Located at Traverse City. Girl Scout camp for junior and senior high school girls. Openings for college students and teachers from June 15 to August 17. Needs unit assistants, waterfront assistants, $540-675; craft director, nature specialist, $540-810; unit leaders, $675-945; small-craft director, $750-945; waterfront director, $900-1,200; assistant waterfront director, $750-945; nurse, $750-1,125; business manager, $675-855; cooks, $700-1,500. Room and board provided. Apply by May 15 to Camp Director, Fair Winds Girl Scout Council, 202 East Boulevard Dr., Flint MI 48503.

### Tocanja
Located at Twin Lake. Girl Scout camp for girls ages 9-17. Openings for college students, teachers and high school graduates from mid-June to mid-August. Needs unit leaders, unit and waterfront assistants, waterfront director, business manager, program directors. Salaries are $450 and up. Apply by May 15 to Director, Camp Tocanja, Girl Scouts of the Calumet Council, 8417 Kennedy Ave., Highland IN 46322.

### Walden
Located in Cheboygan. Private coed camp. Openings for college students, teachers and foreign students from June 20 to August 21. Needs cabin counselors; specialty counselors for English riding, arts and crafts, tennis, golf, modern dance, ballet, folk dancing, drama, radio, fencing, photography, waterfront, sailing, rowing crew, canoeing, kayaking, campcraft, tripping, land sports, gymnastics, music, puppetry; 2 nurses (RN), drivers, secretaries. Salaries are $550-1,350. Cabins, tents and dorms provided for housing. Apply to Larry Stevens, 31070 Applewood Lane, Farmington Hills MI 48018.

# Summer Theaters

### BoarsHead Theater
Located in Lansing. Non-Equity professional year-round theater. Openings from early to mid-June through early September; but prefers qualified candidates available for full year. Needs scenic designer, lighting designer and costumer, $130/week; properties master and seamstress, $100/week; technical director, $120/week; 2 stage managers, $110/week; and 2 carpenters, $100/week. "Salaries negotiable based on experience. Send resume and two letters of reference from different sources if possible." Apply by May 1 to Carol Cleveland, Production Manager, Dept. SED, 425 S. Grand Ave., Lansing MI 48933; tel. 517/484-7800.

### The Cherry County Playhouse
Located in Traverse City. Summer Equity Star stock theater presenting six plays and musicals in a 9-week season. Openings from June 1 or 5 to September 1, 3 or 7. Needs box office treasurer (prior box office experience required, college student or teacher preferred), $150/week; 2 box office assistants (prior box office experience required, college students preferred), $110-120/week; administrative secretary (good typing, bookkeeping and shorthand helpful, college student preferred), $125/week; 2 property/wardrobe assistants (college students and teachers preferred), $120-130/week; assistant technical director (college student or teacher preferred), $120-130/week; director of apprentices (teacher preferred), $150-160/week; promotion/publicity assistant (college student preferred), $110/week; promotion assistant/house manager, $125/week; 16 apprentices (to learn and present 4 children's plays, no fees, college and high school students preferred), $30/week. "Rooming houses and some apartments for share; room about $30/week. Have a serious interest in theater and be willing to work long hours under considerable pressure. Must be punctual and responsible at all times." Send resume by April 15 to William J. Hooton, General Manager, Dept. SED, Box 661, Traverse City MI 49684; tel. 616/947-9560.

# ——————— Minnesota ———————

# Business and Industry

### Anytime Temporaries, Inc.
Located in Edina, a Minneapolis suburb. Employment service. Openings for 2,000 people/year. Has an unlimited number of openings for college students, teachers, and high school seniors during the summer, holidays, vacations and year-round. Needs clerks, secretaries, accounting personnel, receptionist, typists, data processing personnel, warehouse and light industrial employees. Salaries are $2.90-6/hour. No fee, no service charge. Apply to Kim Howard, Manager, Anytime Temporaries, Inc., 5305 Vernon Ave., Edina MN 55436; tel. 612/925-3317.

### Associated Staffing, Inc.
Located at St. Louis Park. Clerical temporary service. Openings for college students, teachers, high school seniors and foreign students from June through September. Needs 80 general typists, $3.40-3.75/hour; 40 file clerks,

$3-3.25/hour; receptionists, $3.40-3.60/hour; 60 dictaphone typists, $3.75-4.25/hour; 100 general office (light typing), $3.40-3.60/hour; 50 junior bookkeepers (10 key, accounts receivable, accounts payable), $3.40-3.60/hour; 70 secretaries, $3.75-4.25/hour. Apply to Associated Staffing, Inc., 5050 Excelsior Blvd., St. Louis Park MN 55416.

## Kelly Services, Inc.
More than 450 branches coast to coast, Puerto Rico, Canada, England and France. Temporary work assignments. Offers over 100 job classifications (office, marketing and light industrial assignments) to college students, teachers and other qualified people during summer breaks and year 'round. Kelly Services also has a special referral system that allows you to register at a Kelly office near your school then work near your home during summer recess—or register near your home then work on temporary assignments during the school year. Assignments available include clerks, typists, secretaries, keypunch operators, word processors, bookkeepers and a variety of marketing and light industrial. Offers flexible schedule with "attractive hourly pay rates equal to or higher than the accepted industry standards in most cities." No paycheck deductions except Social Security and income tax. No employment fee for temporary work. See the White Pages for the branch of Kelly Services nearest you. Apply in person or write to: Summer Employment, National Headquarters, Kelly Services, GPO 1179, Detroit MI 48266.

## Temp Force
Temporary office personnel contractor. Openings for college students, teachers and high school seniors during vacations and holidays. Needs secretaries, typists, stenographers, clericals and accountants. Salaries based upon experience. Apply to Temp Force, 7362 University Ave. NE, Fridley MN 55432; tel. 612/571-4235.

# Resorts, Ranches, Restaurants, Lodging

## Grand View Lodge and Tennis Club
Located in Brainerd. Resort. Openings from May through late September for college students, teachers and foreign students with work permits. Needs 20 waitresses, 3 desk clerks, 10 maids, 5 clerks, 3 beach boys, 4 bus boys, 4 dishwashers, 3 cooks and 5 kitchen help. Salaries are open, depending upon job and experience. Room and board available for $150/month. Apply by March 15 to Joel Connor, Grand View Lodge and Tennis Club, RFD 6, Brainerd MN 56401.

## Gunflint Lodge, Inc.
Located in Grand Marais. Resort with family and fishermen clientele. Openings from May 15 to October 15 for college students, teachers, high school seniors and foreign students. Needs 2 maids; 3 waitresses; 4 kitchen helpers; first, second and third cooks; 3 dock attendants; 4 guides; 3 naturalists; and handyman. Salaries are $275-600/month plus room and board. Enclose stamped return envelope. Apply by March 1 to Bruce Kerfoot, Gunflint Lodge, Inc., Box 100ND, Grand Marais MN 55604.

## Izatys Lodge
Located in Onamia. Family resort. Openings for college students from May 1 to

October 15. Needs 8 waitresses, 2 bus boys, 2 bartenders, 6 maids, 2 playground supervisors, 2 yard workers, 2 dishwashers, 4 kitchen helpers and office help. Salaries are $2.90/hour plus season bonus. Room and board provided for $4.95/day. Apply to J. L. Dubbs, Manager, Dept. SED, Izatys Lodge, Onamia MN 46359.

## Lutsen Resorts, Inc.
Located in Lutsen. Alpine slide and ski area. Openings for college students, teachers and foreign students from June 21 to October 10, December 15 to April 1 and some year-round. Needs 18 waiters/waitresses and 1 bellhop, minimum wage plus tips; 2 bartenders and 2 hostesses, $3/hour plus tips; 10 housekeeper-laundry workers, 2 stream guides (fly fishing), minimum wage; 12 ski lift operators, 3 ski patrols, 2 ski rental-repair persons, $3/hour; 2 secretaries, salad maker, baker's helper, first cook, 4 second cooks, salary open. Housing on premises or can be arranged nearby. Send resume to Lutsen Resort and Ski Area, Dept. SED, Lutsen MN 55612.

## Madden Resorts
Located in Brainerd. Openings for college students, teachers and high school seniors from June 1 to September 15; some positions open late April to late October. No foreign applicants. Needs assistant managers, front desk clerks, waitresses, waiters, shop manager, bartenders, bus boys, service boys, store clerks, craft instructor, cabin maids, children's hostess, assistant caddy masters, cooks, cook's helpers, kitchen helpers, dishwashers, boat attendants and yard help. Salaries and applications available on request. Enclose stamped return envelope. Only those considered will be contacted further. Apply to Madden Resorts, Box 387, Brainerd MN 56401.

## Nelson's Resort
Located at Crane Lake. Family resort with conventions in fall. Openings for college students, teachers, high school seniors and foreign students from May 1 to October 15. Needs 6 waitresses, 2 bus boys, 2 dock attendants, 2 dishwashers, kitchen helper, store clerk, yard help and cook's helper. Salary is Federal minimum wage plus tips, less room and board; 40-hour week. "Minnesota law states charges at $1.50/night board, $1.15/meal, deductible from wages." Apply between February 1 and May 1 to Ms. G.N. Pohlman, Nelson's Resort, Dept. SED, Crane Lake MN 55725.

# Summer Camps

### American Camping Association/Illinois Section
Located in Illinois and surrounding states including Wisconsin, Indiana, Michigan and Minnesota. The American Camping Association/Illinois Section is an association of persons involved with camps operated by social agencies, and private camp owners. More than 100 camps in Association. Openings for college students, teachers, foreign students and local applicants from late June to late August. Needs persons over 18 years of age who possess a variety of camp leadership skills for positions such as counselors, cooks, waterfront staff, camping and athletic skills teachers, nurses and program directors. Salaries are $500-1,000 for eight weeks or more. Room and board provided. Apply by writing or calling the

American Camping Association/Illinois Section, 19 S. LaSalle St., Room 1024, Chicago IL 60603; tel. 312/332-0833.

## Birchwood
Located at Steamboat Lake, LaPorte. Resident girls camp; wilderness boys camp. Openings for college students and graduates, teachers and married couples from June 10 to August 18 and 30. Needs canoe wilderness guides, counselors for riding, tennis, archery, canoeing, riflery, swimming (WSI), crafts, ceramics, $450-700; activity directors (married couples), $500-800 each. Send resume to James C. Bredemus, Camp Birchwood, Dept. SED, Steamboat Lake, LaPorte MN 56461.

## Buckskin Inc.
Located at Lakes MacDougal, 29 miles southeast of Ely. Coed camp for children ages 8-13. Openings for college students and teachers from June 10 to August 21. Needs program director; counselors for archery, camping and canoeing, swimming (WSI), reading, riflery, arts and crafts, ecology and campcraft, $500-750; head cook, assistant cook, camp secretary, salary open. Room and board provided. Send for room and board as early as possible to R.S. "Duffy" Bauer, Camp Buckskin, Dept. SED, Box 389, Ely MN 55731; in winter, 5400 45th Ave. N., Minneapolis MN 55422; tel. 612/533-9674 (evenings).

## Courage
Located at Maple Lake. Camp for physically handicapped, speech and hearing handicapped children and adults. Openings for college students, teachers and high school seniors from June 8 to August 28. Needs 42 counselors, $650; 25 program specialists, $675-1,200; 12 speech therapists, $1,600; 2 nurses (RN), $850; 8 kitchen staff, $525. Some counselor scholarships also available. Apply by May 1 to Robert Polland, Courage Center, 3915 Golden Valley Rd., Minneapolis MN 55422.

## Greenwood
## Ruby Lake
## Lockeslea Arts Camp
Three Girl Scout camps for girls ages 8-18. Openings from June 15 to August 15. Needs 3 directors, teachers preferred, $1,200-2,000; 3 assistant directors, teachers preferred, $800-1,300/season; 3 cooks, local applicants preferred, $600-900/season; 2 waterfront directors, college students or teachers preferred, $500-900/season; 2 nurses, degree required, $500-900/season; 6 general counselors, high school seniors, foreign students, local applicants and college students acceptable, $500-800/season; 9 program specialists, college students and teachers preferred, $500-1,000/season; 3 unit leaders, college students and teachers preferred, $600-900/season; 2 assistant cooks, college students, teachers, high school seniors or local applicants preferred, $500-800/season; CIT director, college students and teachers preferred, $850-1,000/season. Salaries include room and board. Send letter of application to receive more information. Apply by June 1 to Colleen J. Edwards, Outdoor Program Director, Attention Dept. O.P.D., Greater Minneapolis Girl Scout Council, 200 Gorham Building, 127 N. 7th St., Minneapolis MN 55403; tel. 612/338-0721.

**Kici Yapi**
Located at Prior Lake. YMCA day camp for children ages 4-11. Openings for college students, teachers, foreign students and high school volunteers from June 11 to August 17. Needs counselors, $625-700; unit directors, $850; riding director and instructors, $525-975; bus drivers, plus camp salary, $352. No overnight facilities; counselors provide own housing; free bus service from metropolitan area of Minneapolis. Personal interviews required. Apply by May 15 to Southdale YMCA, Attn: Bob Ecklund, 7355 York Ave. S., Edina MN 55435.

**Lakamaga**
Located 30 miles north of the Twin Cities near Forest Lake. Camp serving girls ages 6-14 from rural and urban areas; basic Girl Scout camping program of camp-craft, swimming, boating, nature, plus special programs in environmental education, dramatics, biking and sailing. Openings for college students, teachers and high school seniors from mid-June to Mid-August. Needs camp director (minimum age 25, must have car, camp experience, knowledge of Girl Scout program and valid driver's license), $1,400-2,200/season; assistant camp director (must have car, camp experience, knowledge of Girl Scout program and valid driver's license), $880-1,200/season; 5 unit leaders (experienced in working with groups of children, and preferably in camp counseling or Girl Scouting, and Red Cross Lifesaving and/or First Aid), $720-960/season; 10 assistant unit leaders (experienced in working with groups of children, and preferably in camp counseling or Girl Scouting, and Red Cross Lifesaving and/or First Aid), $640-880/season; waterfront director (WSI, experienced in canoeing, and preferably camping), $760-1,040; 2 waterfront assistants (ALS, prefers camp experience), $680-840/season; health supervisor (RN, LPN, EMT, prefers First Aid training), $800-1,200/season; food superviser (experienced in quantity cooking, prefers training in food management), $880-1,200/season; cook's assistant (prefers experience in cooking), $800-1,000/season; packout person (physical stamina and basic math skills required), $640-760/season. Room and board provided. Equal Opportunity/affirmative action employer. Request application to Kay Kramer, Camping Services Director, Girl Scout Council of St. Croix Valley, 400 S. Robert, St. Paul MN 55107; tel. 612/227-8835.

**Manakiki**
Located at Lake Waconia. Camp for children ages 8-14. Openings for college students, college graduates and teachers from mid-June to mid-August. Needs cabin counselors; specialty counselors for arts and crafts, nature study, WSI waterfront (swimming and smallcraft); nurse (RN); business manager; supervisors; and cooks. Salaries are $550-800/season, depending on qualifications and position. Room, board and health insurance provided. Apply by May 1 to Camp Personnel Coordinator, Pillsbury-Waite Neighborhood Services, Inc., 720-22 E. 26th St., Minneapolis MN 55404.

**Mishawaka**
Located at Grand Rapids, Minnesota. Private, ACA accredited, separate camps for children ages 8-16. Openings for college students and teachers, minimum age 20, from June 21 to August 20. Needs boys' camp: 8 general counselors with skills in arts and crafts, nature study, campcraft, Indian lore, riflery, sailing, dramatics, swimming, camp newspaper, track, canoeing, backpacking or athletics, $500-700 according to skill and experience. Needs girls' camp: 10 counselors with skills in

swimming, canoeing, tennis, music, drama, dance, riding, archery, $500-700. Also needs driver (minimum age 21), $600-750; cooks, $1,300-1,500 for 10 weeks from June 14; nurse (RN), $750-900. Room and board provided. Apply by April 15 to Ernest S. Cockrell, Box 252 Marion MA 02738.

## Northland For Girls
Located in Ely, Minnesota. Camp for girls ages 7-17. Openings for 30 male and female college students and teachers, minimum age 19, from June 19 to August 19. Needs instructors skilled in one or more: sailing, canoeing, tennis, English riding, gymnastics, trampoline, drama, arts and crafts, waterskiing, archery, riflery, synchronized swimming, nature study, waterfront (WSI). Also canoe trip guides, and inquiries for program director (minimum age 25), nurse (RN), kitchen staff and maintenance. Salaries are $500 and up plus room and board, laundry and travel expenses. Apply January through June to A.O. Berglund, Jr., Director, Camp Northland, Dept. SED, 2583 Hickory Lane, Deerfield IL 60015.

## Sherwood Forest Camp
Located at Deer Lake, Deer River. Private camp for girls ages 7-17. Openings for college students and teachers from June 13 to August 13. Needs specialty counselors for English riding, swimming, lifesaving, diving, water ballet, waterskiing, sailing, canoeing, campcraft, archery, dramatics, dancing, tennis, arts and crafts, gymnastics, riflery; program director, CIT director, secretary-driver, cooks, nurse (RN). Salaries include room and board and are based on skills and experience. Apply early to Maxine Gunsolly, 805 2nd Ave. NW, Grand Rapids MN 55744.

## T.T.T. Camps for Girls
Located at Rice Lake, Eden Valley, Minnesota with second camp at Dallas Lake, Wolcottville, Indiana. Camps for disadvantaged children, ages 9½ and 10½. Openings for college sophomores (minimum age 19) in two resident camps; Rice Lake, June 16-August 20 and Dallas Lake, for 4 weeks. Needs 8 counselors for waterfront (WSI), craft, nature, music leader, recreation; general counselors, nurse, cook/manager and assistant cook. Salaries open. Prefers to hire staff with background in volunteer services and with empathy for the children. Apply to Mrs. Charles Fitzgibbons, Dept. SED, 205 E. Henry, Mt. Pleasant IA 52641.

## Tanadoona
Located in Excelsior. Camp Fire camp for children ages 7-17. Openings for college students, teachers, high school seniors and foreign students from mid-June to mid-August. Needs directors: riding, waterfront, tripping, 4 unit (minimum age 21), $600 and up/season; cabin counselors, assistant waterfront, assistant riding, (minimum age 18), $400 and up/season. Room and board provided. Apply by July to Karen Williams, Dept. SED, Camp Tanadoona, 4100 Vernon, St. Louis Park MN 55416.

## Thunderbird for Boys, Thunderbird for Girls
Located in Bemidji, Minnesota. Independently owned brother-sister camps for children ages 8-15. Openings for 140 college students, teachers and foreign students from mid-June to mid-August. Needs supervisory staff; swim director; riflery instructor (NRA); riding directors; counselors for backpacking, bicycling, riding, nature lore, Indian lore, sailing, arts and crafts, waterskiing, canoe tripping,

cabin; laundry helpers, food service workers; kitchen helpers; and cooks. Salaries are commensurate with skills. Apply to Allen L. Sigoloff, 10976 Chambray Court, St. Louis MO 63141.

**Villa Maria**
Located in Frontenac. Private camp for girls ages 9-16. Openings for college students from June 15 to August 8. Needs instructors for water safety, canoeing, tennis, dancing/gymnastics, riding; also assistants for kitchen and maintenance. Salaries are commensurate with skills and experience. Room and board provided for $3.85/day. Apply by February 28 to Directress, Camp Villa Maria, Dept. SED, Frontenac MN 55026; tel. 612/345-3455.

# Mississippi

## Business and Industry

**Kelly Services, Inc.**
More than 450 branches coast to coast, Puerto Rico, Canada, England and France. Temporary work assignments. Offers over 100 job classifications (office, marketing and light industrial assignments) to college students, teachers and other qualified people during summer breaks and year 'round. Kelly Services also has a special referral system that allows you to register at a Kelly office near your school then work near your home during summer recess—or register near your home then work on temporary assignments during the school year. Assignments available include clerks, typists, secretaries, keypunch operators, word processors, bookkeepers and a variety of marketing and light industrial. Offers flexible schedule with "attractive hourly pay rates equal to or higher than the accepted industry standards in most cities." No paycheck deductions except Social Security and income tax. No employment fee for temporary work. See the White Pages for the branch of Kelly Services nearest you. Apply in person or write to: Summer Employment, National Headquarters, Kelly Services, GPO 1179, Detroit MI 48266.

**Temp Force**
Temporary office personnel contractor. Openings for college students, teachers, high school seniors during vacations and holidays. Needs secretaries, typists, stenographers, clericals and accountants. Salaries based upon experience. Apply to Temp Force, 201 Lameuse St., Biloxi MS 39533; tel. 601/432-0418.

**Notice of many job openings come to us after our deadline for including them in this book. For an update to your 1980 *SED*, see page 15 for details.**

## Commercial Attractions

### Farrow Amusement Co.
Headquartered in Jackson. Carnival touring Arkansas, Louisiana, Mississippi, Tennessee, Illinois, Wisconsin. Openings for college students, local applicants and foreign students from May 25 to October 13. Needs 15 laborers (semiskilled), and 15 truck drivers, $125/week plus bonus at end of season. "Hard work, long hours, plenty of travel; plenty of blue jeans or other work clothes needed." Apply by March to E.E. Farrow Jr., Assistant Manager, Farrow Amusement Co., Box 6747, Jackson MS 39212.

# Missouri

## Business and Industry

### CDI Temporary Service
Located in the Kansas City and St. Louis area. Office, marketing, light industrial personnel. Offers college students, teachers, high school students and other qualified people interesting temporary work at a variety of companies in diversified industries during summer vacation, semester breaks and year 'round. Work 1 to 5 days, 2 weeks at a time, a month, or for entire summer. Top hourly pay according to skills on a weekly basis. Never a fee. Needs all office, marketing and light industrial skills, e.g., receptionists, typists, secretaries, transcribers, word processors, keypunch operators, figure clerks, bookkeepers, switchboard operators, sorters, stuffers, inventory workers, product demonstrators, market researchers, machine operators, factory workers, assemblers and many others. Suggest contacting office prior to availability. Apply to CDI Temporary Service, 4635 Wyandotte Ave., Kansas City MO 64112, tel. 816/753-3575; or Progress West Plaza, 100 Progress Pkwy., Maryland Heights (St. Louis area) MO 63043, tel. 314/878-6225.

### Kelly Services, Inc.
More than 450 branches coast to coast, Puerto Rico, Canada, England and France. Temporary work assignments. Offers over 100 job classifications (office, marketing and light industrial assignments) to college students, teachers and other qualified people during summer breaks and year 'round. Kelly Services also has a special referral system that allows you to register at a Kelly office near your school then work near your home during summer recess—or register near your home then work on temporary assignments during the school year. Assignments available include clerks, typists, secretaries, keypunch operators, word processors, bookkeepers and a variety of marketing and light industrial. Offers flexible schedule with "attractive hourly pay rates equal to or higher than the accepted industry standards in most cities." No paycheck deductions except Social Security and income tax. No employment fee for temporary work. See the White Pages for the branch of Kelly Services nearest you. Apply in person or write to: Summer Employment, National Headquarters, Kelly Services, GPO 1179, Detroit MI 48266.

# Commercial Attractions

### Mark Twain Cave
Located in Hannibal. Natural and historical cave. Openings in May for college students, teachers, high school students, local applicants and retired people (minimum age 16). Needs 5 tour guides or groundskeeper, minimum wage. "Must have neat appearance and good personality. We have trailer parking facilities nearby." Send resume by April 1 to R.C. Bogart, General Manager, Box 913, Hannibal MO 63401; tel. 314/221-1656

### Silver Dollar City
Located at Marvel Cave Park. Theme park based on 1880s offering authentic crafts demonstrations, attractions and entertaining shows. Openings for 300/season from April 19 to October or June to August. Needs front gate ticket sellers/tour guides, parking attendants, cave guides (must wear state park image uniforms provided by employer); actors, ride attendants (musical or acting abilities, will wear 1880 costumes provided by employer); sales personnel, food service workers, craft demonstrators, waiters/waitresses; housekeeepers, groundskeepers. "Pay varies from $2.65/hour plus end-of-season bonus if you stay through your agreed upon ending date to minimum wage depending on your qualifications. We provide a list of available housing but it is up to each employee to secure housing." Apply as soon as possible by contacting Personnel Office, Dept. SED, Silver Dollar City, Inc., Marvel Cave Park MO 65616; tel. 417/338-2611.

# Resorts, Ranches, Restaurants, Lodging

### Jellystone Campgrounds
Located in Branson. Campground. Openings available for couple or family (1 man and 1 woman) from June to August to clean bathrooms. "Couple must work 7 days a week, but not necessarily 8 hours a day. Must have a recreational vehicle and live on the campgrounds. A waterslide, pool and playground are available for use." Free camping. Send for application or phone by May 15 to Sam Groves, Manager, Jellystone Campgrounds, Branson MO 65616; tel. 417/334-4131.

### Marriott's Tan-Tar-A
Located in Osage Beach. Resort. Openings approximately from Memorial Day to Labor Day. Positions available for waiter/waitress, $1.60/hour; busperson, $1.80/hour; front desk clerk, $3.15/hour; groundskeeper, $2.90/hour; housekeeper, $2.90/hour; bellperson, $1.60/hour. Local applicants, college students, teachers, high school seniors, foreign students all acceptable. Also needs cocktail waiter/waitress, $1.60/hour; bartender, $3/hour. Local applicants, college students, teachers, foreign students all acceptable. Provides 1 meal/day. Write for personal interview. Apply to Bob Gordon, Personnel Director, Dept. SED, Marriott's Tan-Tar-A, State Road KK, Osage Beach MO 65065; telephone (314)348-3131, ext. 6556.

# Summer Camps

### Blue Sky

Located in St. Louis County. Resident and day camps for mentally retarded persons ages 3 and older. Openings for college students, teachers, high school seniors, and local applicants from June 18 to August 15. Needs 75 counselors, WSIs, campcraft and outdoor education specialists. Salaries are $300-400/season. "Special education majors are given preference; experience in working with trainable and educable retarded citizens ideal. Call or write for camp brochure, application and personal interview date." Apply by March 15 to Mrs. Elizabeth Gilbert, Director of Camping, Camp Blue Sky, 1240 Dantel Lane, St. Louis MO 63141; tel. 314/569-2211.

### Cedarledge

Located in Pevely. Resident Girl Scout camp for girls ages 7-17. Openings from June 8 to August 10. Needs 3 administrative persons, college students and teachers preferred, $1,000-2,500/season; 3 nurses, $1,100-1,400/season; 11 troop leaders, college students and teachers preferred, $600-900/season; 20 assistant troop leaders, college students, teachers and foreign students considered, $350-500/season; 3 specialists: nature, crafts, canoeing, college students and teachers preferred, $600-900/season; 12 swimming, wranglers, college students, teachers and foreign students considered, $350-500; 2 maintenance workers, supply clerk, college students and high school seniors preferred, $300-500. Room and board provided. Apply to Doris Winnemann, Camping Services Director, Camp Cedarledge, Girl Scout Council of Greater St. Louis, 915 Olive St., St. Louis MO 63101; tel. 314/241-1270.

### Forty Legends/The Aud Homestead

Located in Osage County. Private resident camps serving children ages 8-15. General camping activities include canoeing, backpacking, campcraft, archery, horsemanship, ecology, swimming (lake and pool), music, crafts, climbing, Indian lore and a special emphasis on homestead skills such as blacksmithing, broommaking, log construction, draft horses, spinning/weaving, animal husbandry, furniture making and gardening. Salary commmensurate with skills and experience with children. Openings for college students, teachers and independent adults from June 8 to August 16 (includes 1 full week of training). Spring "school camp" program (April and May) offers additional employment opportunities. Needs cabin counselors, skilled specialists, kitchen personnel, nurse, maintenance staff and junior staff (minimum age 17). Salaries are $300-1,500/season, commensurate with skills and experience with children. Room and board provided. "We do not hire persons who smoke or have a dependency on drugs or alcohol. We are inter-faith, inter-racial and coed." Apply to Joseph C. Soete Sr, Owner/Director, Forty Legends, Rt. 2, Box 836, Washington MO 63090; tel. 314/239-6087.

### Latonka

Located in Wappapello. Girl Scout camp for girls ages 8-17. Openings for college students, teachers and foreign students from mid-June to early August. Needs 7 unit counselors and 3 waterfront assistants, $250-400; 3 consultants (sports, canoeing, crafts) and waterskiing instructor, $250-400; 5 unit leaders and waterfront director, $300-500; wrangler, $350-500. Room and board provided.

Apply by March to Evelyn Workun, Cotton Boll Girl Scout Council, Box 684, Sikeston MO 63801.

### Shawnee

Located in Waldron, just north of Greater Kansas City. Camp Fire resident camp for girls ages 7-17. Openings available early June to early August. Needs program director (prefers college student or teacher), $600-800/season; CIT director, minimum age 25 (prefers college student or teacher), $500-600/season; waterfront director (WSI), minimum age 21 (prefers college student or teacher), $550-625/season; 1-2 waterfront assistants (WSI, prefers college students or teachers), $475-550/season; 4 unit directors, minimum age 21 (prefers college student or teacher), $475-525/season; 12 cabin counselors, minimum age 18, $450-500/season; nurse (RN or awaiting board), $600-700/season. Room and board provided. "Laundry facilities are available at no cost to the counselors. Program includes arts & crafts, games, songs, simple folk and square dancing, nature lore, orienteering, outdoor cooking and campcraft skills, dramatics and swimming. We have opportunity for both the generalist and the specialist. If you are strong in one specific area, we plan to utilize that skill." Send resume or send for application by March 21; interview required. Apply to Dorothy Stanley Moore, Camp Director, Kansas City Council of Camp Fire, Dept. SED, 8733 Sni-A-Bar Rd., Kansas City MO 64129; tel. 816/737-3256.

### Woodland

Located in Albany. Girl Scout camp for girls ages 7-17. Openings for college students, teachers, high school seniors and foreign students from mid-June to early August. Needs camp director, assistant camp director, 5 unit leaders, 13 assistant unit leaders, 3 riding counselors, dining hall hostess and 2 cooks. Send for application to Barbara Braxdale, Camp Woodland, Midland Empire Girl Scouts, 402 City Hall, St. Joseph MO 64501.

# ——————— Montana ———————

## Business and Industry

### Kelly Services, Inc.

More than 450 branches coast to coast, Puerto Rico, Canada, England and France. Temporary work assignments. Offers over 100 job classifications (office, marketing and light industrial assignments) to college students, teachers and other qualified people during summer breaks and year 'round. Kelly Services also has a special referral system that allows you to register at a Kelly office near your school then work near your home during summer recess—or register near your home then work on temporary assignments during the school year. Assignments available include clerks, typists, secretaries, keypunch operators, word processors, bookkeepers and a variety of marketing and light industrial. Offers flexible schedule with "attractive hourly pay rates equal to or higher than the accepted industry standards in most cities." No paycheck deductions except Social Security and income tax. No employment fee for temporary work. See the White Pages for the branch of Kelly Services nearest you. Apply in person or write to: Summer

Employment, National Headquarters, Kelly Services, GPO 1179, Detroit MI 48266.

# National Parks

### Glacier Park, Inc.
Located in Glacier National Park, Montana. Resort hotels, motor inns. Openings for 900 college students and teachers from June 1 (some May 1) to September 10-16 (some October 1). Also, midseason replacements. Needs stenographers, chief room clerks, room clerks, night clerks, auditors, front office cashiers (including some N.C.R. posting machines No. 42), information clerks, switchboard operators, reservation office clerks, bellmen, porters, cabin porters/bellmen, housekeepers, assistant housekeepers, linen room attendants, housemen, maids, cleaners, dormitory matrons, chefs, first cooks, second cooks, cook's helpers, head bakers, baker's helpers, salad-pantry helpers, vegetable preparers, kitchen workers, assistant dish machine operators, cafeteria servers, grill cooks, fountain clerks, kitchen storekeepers, dining room managers, dining room cashiers, waiters, waitresses, bus boys, grill waiter/waitresses, head bartenders, bartender-waiters, gift shop senior and junior clerks, warehouse receiving clerks, accounting clerks, truck drivers, bus drivers (minimum age 21), service station attendants, night watchmen, deckhands, full time combos (3-piece), full time string trios, organists, laundry workers, washer extractors, seamstress, golf pro, assistant golf pro, undergardeners and lifeguards. "Talented students given additional consideration as are hotel and restaurant majors. Our guest entertainment programming is an important part of our schedule." Recruitment begins January 1. Salaries are all described and listed in Employment Circular, sent when applying. Apply by April or May to Ian B. Tippet, Vice President, Personnel, Glacier Park, Inc., 1735 E. Ft. Lowell, Suite 7, Tucson AZ 85719.

### Granite Park & Sperry Chalets
Located in Glacier National Park. "Hotel and dining rooms reached only by trails; serving backcountry hikers, horseriders, and active professional families." Openings 19 for college students and local applicants from June 21 through the day after Labor Day. Needs cooks, bakers, dishwashers, waitresses, laundry personnel, $2,000/season. "Must room and board on premises, $50/week. This is a work situation, 7 days a week, for 11 weeks in semi-primitive living conditions." Send for application by May 1 to L.R. Luding, Chalet Coordinator, Belton Chalets, Inc., Box 188, Dept SED, West Glacier MT 79936; tel. 406/888-5511.

### Hamilton Stores, Inc.
Located in Yellowstone National Park, Montana. General merchandising. Openings for 500-600 college students, teachers and high school seniors (minimum age 18) from late May to mid-September. Needs salesclerks, fountain clerks, dishwashers, grocery stock clerks, maintenance workers, kitchen helpers, housekeepers, cashiers, security guards, federal minimum wage. Also needs cooks (for employees' dining rooms), office workers, construction workers, salaries based on experience. Room and board provided at a minimal daily charge. Write for applications and descriptive brochure after January 1 to Personnel Department, Hamilton Stores, Inc., Dept. SED, Box 2700, Santa Barbara CA 93120.

**Yellowstone Park Service Stations**
Located in Yellowstone National Park. Concessionaire. Openings from May 1 to October 31 for college students and teachers, US citizens only (minimum age 18); minimum work period is June 10 to Labor Day. Needs 85 male or female gasoline service station attendants, 10 service station cashiers, 6 warehouse/office/clerical help, 8 journeyman automobile mechanics and 8 mechanic helpers. Wages for all positions are based on hourly rates, with none being less than the federal minimum wage. Apply by May 1 to Employment Department, Box 11, Dept. WDB, Gardiner MT 59030.

# Resorts, Ranches, Restaurants, Lodging

**Flathead Lake Lodge**
Located in Big Fork. Dude ranch. Openings for college students from May 1 to September 10. Needs 2 cooks, $300-600/month; 3 wranglers, $150-300/month; 10 cabin maids, 6 waitresses, hostess, 2 waterfront attendants, $150-200/month. Room and board provided. Enclose long, stamped return envelope. Apply to Doug Averill, Flathead Lake Lodge, Box 248, Big Fork MT 59911.

**Lazy K Bar Ranch**
Located in Big Timber; isolated in a mountain canyon. Working Dude ranch, 100-years-old, serving families (primarily Eastern). Openings for college students, teachers, and high school students from June 15 to Labor Day. Must stay through the season. Needs head cook, $300/month; second cook, $250/month; 4 male wranglers (with Western horse and riding experience, bonus for horse shoeing), $200/month; female wranger (children's wranger), $200/month; laundress, $175/month plus one-half guests' laundry bills; chore man (able to milk, or learn to milk cows by hand), $175/month; 4 dining room and/or kitchen workers, $130-150/month; 3 cabin workers, $130-150/month. Room, board and tips are provided. "No drinking. Ability to work happily without complaining is necessary. We place great value on our employees' loyalty to us as an employer." Send for application; enclose long, stamped return envelope. Apply by March 1 to Barbara K. Van Cleve, Dept. SED, Lazy K Bar Ranch, Big Timber MT 59011; tel. 406/537-4404.

**Nine Quarter Circle Ranch**
Located in Gallatin Gateway. Family dude and livestock ranch. Openings for college students from June 5 to September 15. Needs 2 cabin maids, dishwasher, kitchen helper, laundry worker, $200-225; second cook, $225-275. Room and board provided. Apply by May 1 to Mr. H.T. Kelsey, Nine Quarter Circle Ranch, Dept. SED, Gallatin Gateway MT 59730.

**St. Mary Lodge Motels**
Located at the east entrance to Glacier National Park, St. Mary, Montana. Summer resort. Openings for 150 college students (minimum age 19) from May 1 to October 15. Needs waiter/waitress/pantry/fry cooks, gas station attendants, maids, gift shop/supermarket/sporting goods store clerks, bartenders/cocktail waitresses, dishwashing/kitchen helpers, lodge desk/office personnel. Waiters/waitresses, $320/month including room and board, plus $45/month bonus; others $500/month including room and board, plus $20/month bonus. Apply by May 15

to Roscoe Black, General Manager, St. Mary Enterprises, Box 1808, Sun Valley ID 83353.

## Summer Camps

### Big Sky Girl Scout Council, Camp Scoutana
Located in Augusta in the Bob Marshall Wilderness area. Openings from June 25 to August 8. Needs unit leaders, $60-65; counselors, $50-55; handyman, $65; cook, $90-100; assistant cook, $60-75; nurse, $65. Room and board provided. Send for application. Apply early to Pat Phelps, Dept. SED, Suite 11, Holiday Village, Great Falls MT 59405.

### Shining Mountain Ranch
Frontier living on a high mountain ranch in southwestern Montana. Private coed camp for children ages 10-18. Openings for college students and teachers from early June through August. Needs 6 cowboys, 16 general counselors, specialty counselors (arts and crafts), $500/season; 2 waterfront directors, $550 up/season. Room and board provided. Cowboy and counselor staff must all be good to excellent riders with strong educational and talent qualifications. Apply by May 25 to Shining Mountain Ranch Camp, Box 251N, Sula MT 59871.

## Summer Theaters

### Bigfork Summer Playhouse
Located in Bigfork. Openings for 25 people from early June to Labor Day. Needs directors, actors, instrumentalists, technicians, designers, choreographers, costumers and box office personnel. Salaries are $50-100/week plus housing. Apply by March 1 to Bigfork Summer Playhouse, Bigfork MT 59911.

# Nebraska

## Business and Industry

### Kelly Services, Inc.
More than 450 branches coast to coast, Puerto Rico, Canada, England and France. Temporary work assignments. Offers over 100 job classifications (office, marketing and light industrial assignments) to college students, teachers and other qualified people during summer breaks and year 'round. Kelly Services also has a special referral system that allows you to register at a Kelly office near your school then work near your home during summer recess—or register near your home then work on temporary assignments during the school year. Assignments available include clerks, typists, secretaries, keypunch operators, word processors, bookkeepers and a variety of marketing and light industrial. Offers flexible schedule with "attractive hourly pay rates equal to or higher than the accepted industry standards in most cities." No paycheck deductions except Social Security and income tax. No employment fee for temporary work. See the White Pages for

the branch of Kelly Services nearest you. Apply in person or write to: Summer Employment, National Headquarters, Kelly Services, GPO 1179, Detroit MI 48266.

# Nevada

## Business and Industry

### Kelly Services, Inc.
More than 450 branches coast to coast, Puerto Rico, Canada, England and France. Temporary work assignments. Offers over 100 job classifications (office, marketing and light industrial assignments) to college students, teachers and other qualified people during summer breaks and year 'round. Kelly Services also has a special referral system that allows you to register at a Kelly office near your school then work near your home during summer recess—or register near your home then work on temporary assignments during the school year. Assignments available include clerks, typists, secretaries, keypunch operators, word processors, bookkeepers and a variety of marketing and light industrial. Offers flexible schedule with "attractive hourly pay rates equal to or higher than the accepted industry standards in most cities." No paycheck deductions except Social Security and income tax. No employment fee for temporary work. See the White Pages for the branch of Kelly Services nearest you. Apply in person or write to: Summer Employment, National Headquarters, Kelly Services, GPO 1179, Detroit MI 48266.

## Resorts, Ranches, Restaurants, Lodging

### Cottonwood Cove Resort & Marina, Inc.
### Callville Bay Resort & Marina, Inc.
Cottonwood Cove Resort & Marina is located on Lake Mohave, an hour from Las Vegas, in the Lake Mead National Recreation Area; Callville Bay Resort & Marina is located on Lake Mead, near Las Vegas. Resort with boat rentals, boat tours, campgrounds, fishing charters, lodging, restaurants, service stations and boat and car repair shops. "Our primary season runs from Easter through mid-October although open year-round, presenting a continuous need for qualified employees." Needs marina mechanics, boat pilots, dockhands, housekeepers, cashiers, food servers, cooks, accounting clerks, office clerks, maintenance people, service station attendents and houseboat maids and instructors. "Employees are housed primarily in mobile homes. Housing for married couples is limited and available only when both partners are willing to accept shift work and work Sundays and holidays. We encourage semi-retired people to work for short periods in spring, summer and/or fall. Living in this beautiful, but remote, desert area provides the opportunity to take advantage of all the water and outdoor activities. Please specify beginning and ending dates of availability." Equal opportunity employer. Send resume to Personnel Office, Del Webb Recreational Properties, Inc., Box 29040, Phoenix AZ 85038.

### Echo Bay Resort
Located 20 miles south of Overton. Hotel, restaurant, national park

concessionaire. Openings for college students, teachers, high school students, foreign students and local applicants for all jobs from May or June to October (except no high school students as waiters, waitresses, bartender, cocktail waitress, cashiers, front desk personnel and auditors). Needs 5-8 waiters/waitresses; bartender, cocktail waitress (latter two should be experienced in basic and exotic drinks); 5-8 cooks and kitchen helpers; 5-8 motel and houseboat maids and laundry persons; 10-15 cashiers, front desk personnel, and auditors (cash handling experience necessary); 15-18 dockhands to pump gas and help boats in/out of marina (boat handling experience helpful); 4-6 maintenance persons for grounds, electricity, refrigeration, plumbing and carpentry (experience helpful); 4-6 mechanics for maintenance of outboards and inboard-outboards (mechanical experience necessary). "Most wages are hourly, none pay less than federal minimum wage. There are some salaried supervisory positions with additional benefits open. Housing is provided for a minimal rent charge or if one wants to bring their own camper, mobile home or travel trailer, space and utilities will be provided. Some housing units will have kitchenettes; otherwise meals are served in employees side hall at cost (approximately $2/meal)." Resort includes houseboat, ski boat, fishing boat and patio boat rentals. Customers consist of fishermen (older folks), skiers (young people), and houseboaters (families and young people); substantial group of young ski boaters and visitors from Las Vegas on weekends. "Be able to acclimate to hot, dry climate. Should enjoy lake and beach recreation. Resort is located in remote area but only 60 miles from Las Vegas." Send for application by April 1; include brief description of past experience. Apply to Don Willard, Assistant General Manager, c/o Echo Bay Resort, Dept. SED, Overton NV 89040; tel. 702/394-4000.

## Summer Camps

**Galilee**
Located at Lake Tahoe. Episcopal Church camp for children and adults ages 8 and older. Openings for college students from June 12 to September 1. Needs 3 program counselors (arts and crafts, music, recreation), 1 program counselor/lifeguard. Pays $500/season plus room and board. Also needs many weekly cabin counselors on volunteer basis. "Inquire early, as soon after January 1 as possible. Apply to The Right Reverend Wesley Frensdorff, Camp Galilee, Box 6357, Reno NV 89513; tel. 702/747-4949.

# ——— New Hampshire ———

## Business and Industry

**Kelly Services, Inc.**
More than 450 branches coast to coast, Puerto Rico, Canada, England and France. Temporary work assignments. Offers over 100 job classifications (office, marketing and light industrial assignments) to college students, teachers and other qualified people during summer breaks and year 'round. Kelly Services also has a special referral system that allows you to register at a Kelly office near your school then work near your home during summer recess—or register near your home

then work on temporary assignments during the school year. Assignments available include clerks, typists, secretaries, keypunch operators, word processors, bookkeepers and a variety of marketing and light industrial. Offers flexible schedule with "attractive hourly pay rates equal to or higher than the accepted industry standards in most cities." No paycheck deductions except Social Security and income tax. No employment fee for temporary work. See the White Pages for the branch of Kelly Services nearest you. Apply in person or write to: Summer Employment, National Headquarters, Kelly Services, GPO 1179, Detroit MI 48266.

## Resorts, Ranches, Restaurants, Lodging

### Lake Shore Resort
Located in Northwood. Openings for college students and high school seniors from mid-June to mid-September. Needs 2 waitresses, 3 chambermaids, laundress, general worker, 2 dishwashers, kitchen helper, groundskeeper and tennis pro. Salaries to be arranged. Apply to E.A. Ring, Lake Shore Resort, Dept. SED, Jenness Pond Rd., Northwood NH 03261.

### Wayside Inn and Motel
Located at Bethlehem. Hotel and restaurant. Openings for college students, teachers and foreign students from June 6 to October 16. Needs 6 waiters/waitresses, 3 dishwasher-kitchen helpers and 3 laundress-chambermaids. Send resume and application request. Apply to Wayside Inn and Motel, Box 452, Bethlehem NH 03574.

### Wild Goose Lodges  Motel
Located on Lake Sunapee. Resort. Openings for college students, high school seniors and foreign students, minimum age 18, from mid-June to Labor Day. Needs 4 chambermaids, also to do some housework. Salary plus room and board. Send resume. Apply to Nellie R. Pieczaika, Dept. SED, Box 69, Newbury NH 03255.

## Summer Camps

### The Aloha Foundation, Inc.
Located 20 miles from Hanover (Dartmouth College). Aloha Camp (for girls ages 12-17) and Lanakila (for boys ages 8-14) located at Lake Morey in Fairlee area; Aloha Hive (for girls ages 8-12) located at Lake Fairlee in West Fairlee. Openings for males and females from June 21 to August 18. Needs 75 counselors in the area of arts & crafts, campcraft, canoeing, sailing, swimming, music, archery, photography, ecology. Includes room and board, and free laundry service. "Applicants must posess a high degree of skill in their field." Send for application by May 1. Apply to John R. Emery, Jr., Executive Director, Box 929, Hanover NH 03755; tel. 603/643-5101.

### Alton
Located at Wolfeboro, New Hampshire. Camp for boys. Openings for college students, nurses and teachers from approximately June 25 to August 25. Needs specialty counselors: sports and tennis, 2 arts and crafts, 5 waterfront (WSI), 2

boating (SCI), 3 campcraft and hiking, 2 nature, 2 music, 2 drama; kitchen workers (high school). Salaries are $450-750 and up. Room and board provided. Personal interview necessary. Apply to Peter Guralnick, Middle St., West Newbury MA 01985.

## Calumet Lutheran

Located at West Ossipee. Coed religious camp for ages 8-16. Openings for college students, teachers and high school seniors from June 20 to September 1. Needs 25 counselors, $300-500/season; 8 program department heads, $500-700/season; and 4 maintenance helpers, 10 kitchen helpers, $200-400/season; 2 nurses, $300-600/season. Room and board provided. Send for applications. Apply by March 1 to Donald Johnson, Director, Camp Calumet Lutheran, Dept. SED, West Ossipee NH 03890.

## Camp Union/Otter Lake Conservation School

Located in Greenfield. Nonprofit summer camp and outdoor education school with year-round programs. Staff training is June 20-30; work through August 26 (four 12-day sessions with 2 vacant days between sessions). Season lasts 7 weeks. Needs 2 waterfront directors, college students or teachers preferred, $900/season; 2 trip directors, college students or teachers preferred, $600-800/season; 2 unit directors, college students or teachers preferred, $700-900/season; 12 cabin counselors, college students or high school seniors preferred, $400-700/season; 4 waterfront skill instructors, college students, teachers or high school seniors preferred, $600-800/season; 2 camping/survival skill instructors, college students, teachers or high school seniors preferred, $500-800/season; and 2 forestry/gardening/conservation instructors, college students, teachers and high school seniors preferred, $500-800/season. Room, board and insurance provided. "As with most summer camp experiences, the various positions involve a quite intensive time and energy commitment and a continual projection of an enthusiastic and pleasant disposition. It is necessary for any applicants to become acquainted with the program and personalities at Camp Union well in advance of the summer." Apply to Cy Johnson, Director, Camp Union, Greenfield NH 03047; tel. 603/547-3412.

## Cardigan Mountain School

Located in Canaan. Summer session for children ages 10-15. Needs 20-25 teachers of English, math, and reading (undergraduate degree, minimum) $800 and up. Employment from June 22 to August 9, including orientation days. "Teachers must be able to assist with activities program (many are offered, ranging from waterfront to land sports to crafts) and dormitory supervision. Beautiful and complete school facilities on Canaan Street Lake. Established program with long record of success with youngsters needing remedial English, math or reading help." Apply to Jeffrey D. Hicks, Director, Summer Session, Cardigan Mountain School, Canaan NH 03741; tel. 603/523-7156.

## Chase Tennis & Golf Camps

Located in Bethlehem, New Hampshire. Ranch. Openings from mid-June to August 25. Needs 4 tennis counselors, 3 golf counselors, teachers, college students, foreign students all acceptable, $400-1,000/season; 2 nurses (RN), $800/season; 3 kitchen trainees, local applicants, college students or high school seniors preferred, $500/season. "Apply early and expect to work hard in order to be a part of the spirit and fun." Apply to Neil Chase, Chase Tennis & Golf Camps, Dept. SED, Box 1446, Manchester MA 01944; tel. 617/526-7514.

## Cody for Boys
Located in West Ossipee, New Hampshire. Camp for boys ages 7-16, established 1926. Fifty openings for mature counselors, coaches, and instructors in all athletics (team and individual sports), archery, canoeing, arts and crafts, drama/music, nature, photography, ham radio, riflery, tripping/woodcraft, swimming, sailing, waterskiing, scuba, etc. Salaries $400-800 and up, based on experience. "Room, board and laundry provided. Staff autos OK. State is tax free for salaries and purchases." Also needs physician, nurse (RN), waiters, groundsmen, kitchen assistants and secretary. National/international clientelle and staff. Contact Director Alan J. Stolz, winter office: Dept. SED, 5 Lockwood Circle, Westport CT 06880; tel. 203/226-4389.

## Coniston
Located in Croydon on Lake Coniston. YMCA coed camp. Openings for college students and teachers from June 17 to August 16. Needs counselor/programs instructors for arts and crafts, archery, gymnastics, riding, swimming, drama, riflery, sailing, canoeing, campcraft, soccer, waterskiing, tennis, ecology, $600-1,000; nurse, cook, salary open. Fringe benefits. Apply by March 1 to Robert V. Sanders Jr., Director, Camp Coniston, Dept. SED, Box 1, Claremont NH 03743.

## Foss
Located in Barnstead. YMCA camp for girls ages 7-15. Openings for college students, teachers and high school seniors from June 15 to August 20. Needs 12 cabin leaders, directors for aquatics and programs, riding and tennis instructors, nature counselor, kitchen assistants, nurse (RN). Salaries are $400-1,100. Room and board provided. "An opportunity to apply yourself in a challenging yet comfortable environment. Applicants from northeast US preferred." Apply by June 1 to K.R. Goebel, YMCA Camp Foss, 14 Farrington St., Rochester NH 03867; tel. 603/332-4340.

## Huckins YMCA Camp
Located at C. Ossipee. Resident camp for girls ages 9-15. Openings for college students for 9 weeks, from June 16 to August 19. Needs senior counselors in areas such as waterfront, arts and crafts, $500-600/season. Apply in January and February to Zaven K. Vorperian, Director, YMCA Camp Huckins, Dept. SED, Box 521, N. Conway NH 03860; tel. 603/356-2019.

## Lincoln
Located in Kingston. YMCA resident camp for boys. Openings from approximately June 25 to August 25 (9 weeks). Needs waterfront director, college student or teacher preferred, $600-800/season; campcraft/trip director ($400-600/season), craft instructor ($300-600/season), riflery instructor ($300-600/season), archery instructor ($300-600/season), 9 cabin counselor/activity instructors ($300-600), college students preferred; program director ($800-1,000/season), CIT director ($600-800/season), teacher preferred. Send for applicaton to Fran Marchand, Director, YMCA Camp Lincoln, Dept. SED, 4-F Pine Isle, Derry NH 03038.

## Merrimac

Located in Contoocook, New Hampshire. Private coed camp for children. Openings for college students and teachers from June 27 to approximately August 24. Needs mature group leaders; specialty counselors for pioneering, water safety (ARC), nature, golf, science; instructors for waterskiing, sailing, diving, athletics, riflery, tennis, archery, electronics, ham radio, chemistry, crafts (all phases), riding, judo, wrestling, canoeing, soccer, softball, basketball, fencing, dancing, cheerleading, fine arts, dramatics; ice hockey coaches; figure skating instructors; nurse (RN); kitchen help; bus driver; and maintenance person. Salaries are $250-650/8-week season plus orientation. Apply to Robert Bomze, Camp Merrimac, 6 Orchard Place, Harrison NY 10528.

## Merriwood

Located in Orford, New Hampshire. Private camp for girls. Openings for college students and teachers from June 28 to August 18. Needs counselors for arts and crafts, canoeing, archery, riflery, drama, gymnastics, land sports, riding (English), sailing, tennis, waterskiing; boat drivers; water safety instructors; and nurse (RN). Salaries are $500 and up plus travel allowance. Apply by May to Gary D. Miller, 7 Field Rd., Riverside CT 06878; tel. 203/637-4674.

## Moosilauke

Located in Orford, New Hampshire. Private camp for boys ages 8-16. Openings for college students and teachers from June 28 to August 18. Needs general and specialty counselors for tennis, baseball, basketball, canoeing, soccer, outdoor life, sailing, crafts, gymnastics, archery and swimming, $500-1,000. Room, board, laundry and travel allowance provided. Apply by April to Dr. Gordon Porter Miller, 570 Colonial Ave., Pelham Manor NY 10803.

## New England Camping Association, Inc. (ACA)

Camps located in New Hampshire. Camp counselor referral service. Openings for college students and teachers (minimum age 19) for 8 weeks. Needs specialty counselors for advanced lifesaving, archery, arts and crafts, bicycling, boating, campcraft, canoeing, golf, drama, guitar, gymnastics, horseback riding, land sports, music, nature-ecology, photography, piano, radio-electronics, riflery, sailing (SCI), scuba, tennis, waterskiing, WSI; trip leader; unit leader; administrative staff; chef; baker; kitchen workers; clerical; maintenance; doctors; and nurses (RN). Salaries start at $400 and are commensurate with age, education, camp experience and type of position. $2 application fee. Apply to New England Camping Association, Inc., Room 410, 29 Commonwealth Ave., Boston MA 02116.

## New Hampshire 4-H Camps, Spruce Pond and Bear Hill

Located in Bear Brook State Park, Allenstown. Agency sponsored coed residential camps for children ages 8-15. Openings from approximately June 24 to August 25. Needs 2-4 program directors, camp administrative experienced necessary, $700-1,200/season; 8-10 waterfront staff, college students or teachers preferred, $400-800/season; 15-18 program staff, $400-700/season; 2 trip leaders, college students or teachers preferred, $800/season; 8 unit heads, college students, teachers, and foreign students preferred, $500/season; 20 counselors, college students, high school seniors, and foreign students preferred, $200-300/season; 10 kitchen/maintenance, college students, teachers, and foreign students preferred, $200-800/season. "Qualifications: love of kids and outdoors, willingness to work hard and share with others, understanding of the vital role of camps and staff in the development of youth." Apply to Bruce Matthews, Director, New Hampshire 4-H Camps, State 4-H Office, Moiles House, U.N.H., Durham NH 03824; tel 603/862-2180.

## Pierce Camp Birchmont

Located at Wolfeboro, New Hampshire. Coed camp for ages 7-16. Openings for high school seniors or college students from June 26 to August 25. Needs sports counselors—tennis, rifle, archery, trampoline and water. Apply to F.W. Pierce, Director, Dept. SED, Mineola Ave., Roslyn NY 11576; tel 516/621-2211.

## Pleasant Valley Camp

Located on Lake Wentworth, S. Wolfeboro, New Hampshire. Resident girl's camp. Openings from June 2 to August 2. Needs program director, teacher preferred, $900-1,000/season; CIT director, college student preferred, $800-900/season; 3 waterfront counselors (WSI), high school seniors or college students preferred, $500 minimum/season; sailing instructor, college students preferred, $600 minimum/season; arts and crafts director, college student preferred, $600 minimum/season; and tennis instructor, college student preferred, $600 minimum/season. "Write for application. Selections made February to April. All activity staff have cabin responsibilities." Apply to Barbara E. Damon, Resident Director, 25 Central Ave., Danvers MA 01923.

## Robin Hood

Located at Center Ossipee, New Hampshire. Private camp for boys, ages 7-16. Openings for college students, teachers and coaches from June 22 to August 22. Needs counselors: 15 general bunk, 5 WSI, trips, pioneering, canoeing, tennis, baseball, basketball, soccer, trampoline, ham radio, arts and crafts, sailing, piano, drama scuba, waterskiing and archery. $400 up depending upon age, experience and position. Room and board provided. Apply to John C. Klein, 2250 Par Lane No. PH10, Willoughby Hills OH 44094.

## Runels

Located in Pelham, New Hampshire. Girl Scout camp for girls ages 7-17. Openings for college students, teachers and high school seniors from June 23 to August 18. Needs 30 counseling staff: unit leaders, counselors, $350-600/season; arts and crafts, $350-600/season; environmental studies $400-600/season; waterfront (WSI), $400-800/season; small craft (sailing, boating, canoeing), $400-800/season; nurse (RN), $700-1,000/season; CIT director, $500-700/season; biking and backpacking, $400-700/season. Apply by June 15 to Camping Services Director, Summer Employment, Merrimack River Girl Scout Council, Inc., 89 N. Main St., Andover MA 01810.

## Sunapee

Located in New London. Private camp for boys. Openings for college undergraduates, graduate students and teachers of all faiths, races and nationalities (minimum age 18) from mid-June through the end of August. Needs chef, chef's helper, head counselor, unit leaders, trip leader and trip counselors; directors: program, CIT, waterfront, creative arts, land sports; specialty counselors for riflery, archery, track and field, tennis, soccer, baseball, basketball, street hockey, golf, swimming (WSI preferred), waterskiing, sailing, scuba diving, boating, canoeing, music, rocketry, photography, dramatics, arts and crafts, woodworking, nature, campcraft, fishing; dining hall steward; kitchen workers; and maintenance workers. Salaries are commensurate with age, position and experience. Room, board and insurance provided. Apply by June 1 to Mr. and Mrs. Jan Kater, Camp Sunapee, New London NH 03257.

## Trinity House
Located in Atkinson. Camp for underprivileged children: resident camp for girls (ages 6-15) and boys (ages 6-10); day camp for boys and girls (ages 4-11). Openings for college students and teachers from middle of June to end of August. Needs specialty counselors for swimming (WSI), arts and crafts, nature, sports and campcraft; and unit heads. Salaries are $300-800. Room, board and insurance provided. Staff openings for commuters, Monday through Friday. Pays $300-450. Apply to Susan Noble, Director, Trinity House Camp, Atkinson NH 03811.

## Wa-Klo
Located in Jaffrey Center, New Hampshire. Camp for girls, ages 5-18; established in 1938. Openings from June 28 to August 28. Needs specialists in swimming, small-craft, gymnastics, waterskiing, arts and crafts, tennis, golf, music, nature, riflery, dance, dramatics, riding, $400-600; and nurse, salary open. Needs college students and teachers as counselors. Write to Director, Dept. SED, 506 Devonshire Rd., Baldwin NY 11510.

## Walt Whitman
Located in Pike, New Hampshire. General coed camp for children ages 7-15. Openings for college students and teachers from June 23 to August 24. Needs 2 WSI counselors, $600-800/season; counselors: 4 tennis, 2 woodworking, 2 art, 2 music, 2 campcraft, $500-700/season. Please state experience with children. Apply to Mr. L.C. Soloway, 80-83 Kent St., Jamaica NY 11432; tel. 212/380-5330.

## Winamac Riding Camp
Located in Bennington, New Hampshire. Private riding and waterfront camp for children ages 6-16. Openings from June 20 to August 20. Needs 6 English riding instructors, 3 Western riding instructors, college students preferred, $400-700/season; 10 waterfront counselors, college students and high school seniors preferred, $400-600/season; 2 riflery instructors, college students preferred, $500/season; 4 athletic instructors, college students and high school seniors preferred, $500/season; 3 ceramics and arts and crafts instructors, college students and high school seniors preferred, $400-500/season; 10 cabin counselors, college students, teachers, and high school senior preferred, $300-600/season. Apply to George Athans, Director, Winamac Riding Camp, R.F.D. 2, Mt. Kisco NY 10549.

# Summer Theaters

## New London Barn Players
Located in New London. Summer Theater. Openings for college students and teachers from early June through Labor Day. Needs stage manager, technical

director, scenic designer, costume designer, box office treasurer, properties coordinator, costume assistant, musical director, percussionist, publicity coordinator, $25-100 plus room and board; 2 journeymen, $15 plus room and board; 14 acting apprentices, 1 technical apprentice, 1 administrative apprentice, room and board only. Apply by March 15 to Norman Leger, Producer, New London Barn Players, Box 285, New London NH 03257.

# New Jersey

## Business and Industry

### Kelly Services, Inc.
More than 450 branches coast to coast, Puerto Rico, Canada, England and France. Temporary work assignments. Offers over 100 job classifications (office, marketing and light industrial assignments) to college students, teachers and other qualified people during summer breaks and year 'round. Kelly Services also has a special referral system that allows you to register at a Kelly office near your school then work near your home during summer recess—or register near your home then work on temporary assignments during the school year. Assignments available include clerks, typists, secretaries, keypunch operators, word processors, bookkeepers and a variety of marketing and light industrial. Offers flexible schedule with "attractive hourly pay rates equal to or higher than the accepted industry standards in most cities." No paycheck deductions except Social Security and income tax. No employment fee for temporary work. See the White Pages for the branch of Kelly Services nearest you. Apply in person or write to: Summer Employment, National Headquarters, Kelly Services, GPO 1179, Detroit MI 48266.

### Olsten Temporary Services
Located in Trenton. Temporary personnel employment services. Openings from May to September for 15 secretaries ($3.75-4.25/hour), 25 typists ($3.50-4/hour), 25 clerk typists ($3.10-3.40/hour), 15 key punchers ($3.75-4/hour), 20 figure clerks ($2.90-3.30/hour), college students, teachers and local applicants preferred. "Apply on spring break if possible. There are no fees. Weekly pay." Apply in person, Olsten Temporary Services, 1510 Pennington Rd., Trenton NJ 08618; tel. 609/771-0400.

### Temp Force
Temporary office personnel contractor. Openings for college students, teachers and high school seniors during vacations and holidays. Needs secretaries, typists, stenographers, clericals and accountants. Salaries based upon experience. Apply to Temp Force: 389 Passaic Ave., Fairfield NJ 07006, tel. 201/227-9350; 210 River St., Hackensack NJ 07601, tel. 201/342-1777; 500 Elizabeth Ave., Somerset NJ 08873, tel. 201/469-6100; 1460 Morris Ave., Union NJ 07083, tel. 201/687-1812.

### Temp Staff
Temporary office personnel contractor. Openings for college students, teachers and high school seniors during vacations and holidays. Needs secretaries, typists, stenographers, clericals and accountants. Salaries based upon experience. Apply to

Temp Staff: 1099 Wall St. W., Lyndhurst NJ 07071, tel. 201/939-3443; 333 Littleton Rd., Parsippany NJ 07054, tel. 201/263-2300; 2401 Morris Ave., Union NJ 07083, tel 201/964-6900.

# Resorts, Ranches, Restaurants, Lodging

### Atlas-Motor Inn and Seashore Food Distributor
Located in Capenay. Motel restaurant and wholesale food distributor. General positions available. Apply to Harry Satt, President, Madison-Beach Dr., Capenay NJ 08204; tel. 609/884-7000.

### Pierre's Holiday Enterprises, Inc.
Located on the Boardwalk at Wildwood. Restaurant. Openings for college students, teachers, high school seniors and foreign students from May 15 to September 20. Needs 30 waitresses, 6 bus boys, 6 short order cooks, 2 cashiers, 3 hostesses. New Jersey minimum wage plus tips for some positions. Apply to Pierre's Holiday Enterprises, Inc., 117 E. 23rd Ave., North Wildwood NJ 08260; tel. 609/522-6354.

# Summer Camps

### The Appel Farm
Located in Elmer. Art and music center for children. Openings for college students, teachers, foreign students, artists and musicians, minimum age 21, from June 18 to August 21. Nonsmokers only. Needs bunk counselors, water safety instructors (ARC), specialty counselors for dance (modern, ballet, jazz, folk), photography, video/audio and film, arts and crafts (painting, weaving, batik, sculpture, ceramics, printing), music (orchestral and band instruments, jazz, rock); nurse (RN), doctor. Salaries are $500 and up plus room and board. Must be motivated and interested in working with children. Apply by April 30 to The Appel Farm, Dept. SED, Elmer NJ 08318.

### Central New Jersey YMCA Camps
Located at Blairstown. Coed camps for ages 8-16 and camping and conference center with golf course, tennis courts, recreation center, etc. Openings from June 16 through August; earlier and later dates possible; college students or teachers preferred. Needs 2 aquatics directors, 2 horseback directors, 2 minibike/motorcycle directors, $1,000-2,000/season; 2 AM radio directors, $800-1,000/season; 15-20 general counselors, $500-1,000/season; 2 arts and crafts directors, $1,000/season. "Apply immediately for summer position; do not wait till first of year." Apply to J.H. Wilkes, Executive Director, YMCA Camp Mason, Rd. 3, Box 41, Blairstown NJ 07825; tel. 201/362-8217.

### Dark Waters
Located in Medford. Camp for boys and girls ages 7-13. Openings from June 22 to August 23. Needs cook (college student, teacher, local applicant) to prepare menus, order supplies, cook meals, supervise campers and counselors in kitchen, $1,000-1,500/season; assistant cook (college student, local applicant), $700-800/season; camp nurse, $800-1,000/season; 18 counselors (college students, teachers, high school students, local applicants), $250-600/season.

Room and board provided. Applicants "must like children and people in general; must be bright, creative and flexible." Send for application by April 1. Apply to Stephen A. Edgerton, 231 West Winona St., Philadelphia PA 19144; tel. 215/438-9035.

### Eagle's Nest
Located in Delaware. Christian-residence coed camp for children, ages 8-16. Openings from late June through late August. Needs 16 general counselors, $500/season; 3 WSI's, $600 and up/season; 1 driver (must have school bus license), $600/season; 1 pool director-WSI, $1,000/season; 1 nurse, $800/season. Apply to Joan Lodge, Eagle's Nest Camp, 11 Central Ave., Caldwell NJ 07006; tel. 201/226-1853.

### Fairview Lake YMCA Camps
Newton, New Jersey. YMCA coed camps: 2 residential camps, boys and girls (ages 8-16) on opposite sides of a 100-acre lake; residential unit for 3rd and 4th graders, both boys and girls; a day camp, coed for ages 6-12. Openings for college students and teachers from June 22 to August 17. Needs 2 program directors (teachers preferred), salary open; 40 general counselors (responsible for cabin of 7-9 campers, teaching 1 program area, assisting in other programs), $400-650/season; 10 specialty counselors for waterfront, riding, riflery, sailing, arts and crafts, minimum $550/season. Room and board provided. "We are looking for enthusiastic, mature, intelligent, outgoing people with high energy levels, a love of the out-of-doors, and a love for kids. Previous experience in a camp setting is a plus. Moody and/or defensive personalities need not apply." Send resume or send for application. Apply to W. Daniel McCain, Camp Executive, Fairview Lake YMCA Camps, Dept. SED, RD 5, Box 210, Newton NJ 07860; tel. 201/383-9282.

### Gramercy
Located in Blairstown, New Jersey. Coed camp for underpriviledged children. Openings for college students, teachers, high school seniors and foreign students from late June to early September. Needs 10 CITs, 10 junior counselors, 20 general counselors, 3 waterfront staff, 6 program specialists, 6 kitchen aides, nurse (RN or LPN), salaries open. Apply to Murray Struver, C.C.D. Camp Gramercy, 2169 Grand Concourse, Bronx NY 10453.

### Hartley Farm
Located at Lincoln Park, New Jersey. Social service agency camp for children ages 6-12. Openings for college students, teachers and high school seniors from June 28 to August 29. Needs 3 specialty counselors for crafts, sports, nature, $500-600; 20 counselors, $350-400; 2 unit heads, $550-650. Salaries are for season. Apply to Hartley Farm Camp, Dept. SED, 413 W. 46th St., New York NY 10036.

### Hudson Guild Farm
Located in Andover. Nonsectarian Neighborhood House Camp serving families, single adults and senior citizens. 550 acres. Convenient to New York City. Families of many ethnic and economic backgrounds. Program for children (5-15 years of age), parents and senior citizens. Openings from end of June to end of August. No cabin duties. Needs program director, single persons and couples with camp, group or teaching experience with specialties in folk music (guitar), dramatics,

outdoor education, recreation and waterfront. Also office clerk, dining room and kitchen workers, cooks and auto driver. Most salaries range from $500-800 for season, plus room and board. Write to Curtis R. Ream, Hudson Guild Farm, Andover NJ 07821.

## Lenape Scout Reservation
Located at Medford in the pinelands of New Jersey. Boy Scout Camp for ages 11-18. Openings from July 1 through August 20. Needs camp director (minimum age 21, scouting background), teacher preferred, $1,500-2,000/season; ecology director, camp commissioners, rifle range instructor, waterfront personnel, maintenance director, $100-1,000/season. Send resume or request application. Apply by April 15 to Gerard M. Connell, Scout Executive, Burlington County Council Boy Scouts of America, Dept. SED, Box 295, Medford NJ 08055; tel. 609/871-1050.

## Merry Heart
Located in Hackettstown. Coed camp for the physically handicapped. Openings for college students and teachers from approximately June 16 to September 1. Needs 4 specialists, $600-900; 20 counselors, $500-800. Apply by May 1 to Mary Ellen Ross, Director of Camping, Camp Merry Heart, Dept. SED, RFD 2, Hackettstown NJ 07840.

## Nejeda
Located in Stillwater. Residential camp for diabetic children, ages 5-15. Openings for college students, teachers, high school seniors from June 22 to August 23. Artistic, musical, arts and crafts and sports skills. Needs 16 counselors, $450-800; salary negotiable. Also needs 2 WSIs. Deadline for applications: April 1. Apply early to Camp Nejeda, 153 Roseville Ave., Newark NJ 07107.

## Star Lake Camp
Located in Ramapo Hills, Bloomingdale, New Jersey. Camp for boys and girls. Operated by The Salvation Army since 1923 for Metropolitan New York children ages 7-12. Member: ACA, FPWA, participant in the Community Council. Staff of 160. Openings for teachers, college students and high school seniors from mid-June to August 19 or September 1. Program directors, social workers, $650 and up; 2 head counselors, $600 and up; 70 general counselors, $400 and up; 16 specialists, $400 and up; WSIs, $550 and up. 5 nurses (RN), $650 and up; nurse's aide, $350 and up; and CITs. Room and board provided. Wonderful opportunity for intercultural service and learning. Write by May 1 to Director, The Salvation Army Star Lake Camp, 50 W. 23rd St., New York NY 10010.

## Tecumseh
Located in Pittstown. Coed camp for children, ages 6-14, on 300 beautiful acres. Openings for 60 persons for 10 weeks during summer. Needs counselors: general, program, nature, pioneer, crafts, athletic, waterfront, $350-1,000; camp secretary, cooks, nurse, dining hall, kitchen and maintenance personnel, $250-1,400. Room and board provided. Serves New Jersey youth with a special ministry to the underprivileged. Member of ACA. Apply to Divisional Youth Secretary, The Salvation Army, Box 679, Newark NJ 07101.

## Trail Blazer

Located in New Jersey with 1,000 acres of forest and a large lake. Interracial, interfaith camp for low-income children. Openings for college students and teachers (minimum age 20) from June 20 to August 27. Needs counselors, $500-600/season; lakefront (WSI and senior lifesaver), $650-750/season, 2 dieticians (no cooking), $700-800/season; typist-mimeographer, $550-650/season; pot scrubber-kitchen aide, $500-600/season; nurses, $800-950/season. Mature professional attitude and dedication required. Apply to Lois Goodrich, Trail Blazer Camps, 56 W. 45th St., New York NY 10036.

## Vacamas Association

Located on 600 acres in the Ramapo Mountains in New Jersey; only an hour from New York City. Nonsectarian social agency camp for boys and girls from low-income families. Needs counselors, specialists and service staff. No experience required. Men and women in their junior year of college or high school preferred and given salary increments. Education, social work, psychology and related majors preferred. Salaries $300-500, based on qualifications. Write to Camp Vacamas Association, Irving Topal, Executive Director, 215 Park Ave. S., New York NY 10003.

## Willow Lake Camp

Located on 35 acres of mountainous property in West Milford. Day camp for children ages 5-14 and family center; designed "to develop Christian values through a variety of recreational activities, such as team sports, swimming and group games." Openings from June 30 to August 22. Needs health director (EMT or RN, minimum age 21, previous experience in nursing or emergency squad), aquatics director and assistant aquatics director (WSI, ALS, Standard or Advanced First Aid, CPR), 3 village directors (minimum age 21, 3 years camping experience), $800-1,100/season; archery/tennis instructor, $600-800/season; outdoor education instructor, 4 lifeguard/swimming instructors (ALS and Standard First Aid, minimum age 18), $500-700/season; 10 counselors (minimum age 18), $400-700/season. Send resume and call for interview. Apply by May 1 to Camp Director Montclair YMCA, 25 Park St., Montclair NJ 07042; tel. 201/744-3400.

## YMCA Camp Bernie

Located at Port Murray. Resident coed camp for girls, 3rd to 9th grade, and boys, 3rd to 10th grade. Openings for college students from June 25 to August 17; staff training is the week of June 17-23. Needs 15-20 cabin counselors, $450-700/season plus room & board; 1 riflery instructor and about 4 tripping leaders, $600-800/season plus room & board; 1 riflery instructor and about 4 tripping leaders, $600-800/season plus room & board; 1 swimming instructor, $450-650/season plus room & board; 1 nature & ecology instructor,

---

**A personal interview is required for many of the jobs listed in *SED*. Read the article "Applying for a Job" for tips on how to conduct yourself during an interview.**

$700-850/season plus room & board; and 1 truck driver, $600-800/season. Apply by June 20 to Neil VanBodegon-Smith, Camp Director, Dept. C, Rd. #1, Port Murray NJ 07865, tel. 201/689-1318 or 832-5315.

### YMCA Silver Lake

Located in Stockholm. Coed YMCA resident camp for ages 7-15; operates Western riding program. Openings from June 23 to August 17 or 24. Needs 14 general and 6 ranch camp counselors (minimum age 18, college students preferred, previous camping experience), $500-600/season; 8 junior counselors (ages 16-18, previous camping experience preferred), $250-300/season; waterfront director (minimum age 21, Red Cross WSI, ability to teach swimming), $115-130/week. Room and board provided. Apply early (April 1 deadline) to David J. Montanye, Camp Director, Silver Lake Rd., Stockholm NJ 07460; tel. 201/827-7212.

# ——————— New Mexico ———————

## Business and Industry

### Kelly Services, Inc.

More than 450 branches coast to coast, Puerto Rico, Canada, England and France. Temporary work assignments. Offers over 100 job classifications (office, marketing and light industrial assignments) to college students, teachers and other qualified people during summer breaks and year 'round. Kelly Services also has a special referral system that allows you to register at a Kelly office near your school then work near your home during summer recess—or register near your home then work on temporary assignments during the school year. Assignments available include clerks, typists, secretaries, keypunch operators, word processors, bookkeepers and a variety of marketing and light industrial. Offers flexible schedule with "attractive hourly pay rates equal to or higher than the accepted industry standards in most cities." No paycheck deductions except Social Security and income tax. No employment fee for temporary work. See the White Pages for the branch of Kelly Services nearest you. Apply in person or write to: Summer Employment, National Headquarters, Kelly Services, GPO 1179, Detroit MI 48266.

## Resorts, Ranches, Restaurants, Lodging

### Bishop's Lodge

Located in Santa Fe. Openings for college students May to Labor Day, some through mid-October. Needs 1-2 lifeguards, $3.50/hour; 3-4 counselors, $4/hour; 10-12 waitresses, 6-8 waiters, $2.65/hour plus tips; 4 wranglers, $3.50/hour; 4-5 busboys, $2.65/hour plus tips; also bartenders, minimum age 21, and desk clerks. Salaries depend on ability and experience. Apply to James R. Thorpe, The Bishop's Lodge, Box 2367, Santa Fe NM 87501

# Summer Camps

### Brush Ranch
Located in Tererro. Private camp for children ages 8-17 (girls) and 8-14 (boys). Openings for college students from June 11 to August 9. Needs instructors who also serve as boys' and girls' cabin counselors for music, western riding (boys), English riding (girls), tennis, riflery, fencing, fishing, certified WSI and synchronized swimming, art, dance, drama and nature. Apply to James S. Congdon, Brush Ranch Camps for Boys and Girls, Tererro NM 87573; tel. 505/757-8772.

### Philmont Scout Ranch and Emplorer Base
Located in Cimarron. Summer camp for Boy Scouts with approximately 19,000 campers annually. Openings from June 7 to August 22 for 550 staffers who must be registered members of the Boy Scouts of America, minimum age 18. Majority of staffers hired from outside New Mexico. Needs 160 back country staffers, 140 or more ranger staffers and 250 base personnel staffers. Within these three basic areas, persons are needed for the following positions: cooks, photographers, rangers, security, maintainence, activities, wranglers, group leaders, tent manager, conservation services, museum staff. Especially needs staff for food service, trading posts and snack bars on the camp. Base salaries for new employees is as follows: age 18, $260/month; age 19, $270/month; age 20, $280/month. Room and board provided; transportation to and from camp is not. Competition is keen for staff jobs. In 1979 more than 1,200 applications were received. Most staff selections are made by March 15 for each summer. By that time all applicants will have been notified of their status if they have a job, they don't have a job, or they are still being considered. Send a note requesting an application form, mentioning SED in the note. On the back of the form is a brief description of the available jobs and the applicant is asked to note which 3 jobs he is interested in; in order. Apply to Seasonal Personnnel, Philmont Scout Ranch, Cimarron NM 87714.

### Tall Pines
Located in Mayhill, New Mexico. Girl Scout camp for girls, ages 6-17. Openings for college students, teachers and high school seniors from June 14 to August 9. Needs 5 program administrators, $45-60/week; 10 program counselors, $30-35/week; riding director, $45-60/week; assistant riding director, $30-40/week; nurse, $60/week; 3 cooks, $45-70/week; kitchen aide, business manager, $40-60/week; assistant director, $45-60/week. Room and board provided. Applications considered as received beginning January 1. An equal opportunity employer. Apply to Camp Director, Rio Grande Girl Scout Council, 3214 E. Yandell Dr., El Paso TX 79903.

### Mary White
Located in Mayhill, New Mexico. Girl Scout camp for ages 9-17. Openings for college students, teachers, high school seniors and foreign students from June 6 to August 2. Needs 6 unit counselors, $250-350; 9 unit assistants, $200-250; directors: riding, program, $250-350; nurse (RN or graduate); 2 cooks, $250-450; business manager, $250-350. Room and board provided. Apply to Paula Homer, 2708 Sunset Dr., San Angelo TX 76901.

# New York

## Business and Industry

### Allied Temporary Personnel, Inc.
Temporary services. Openings throughout the year for college students and teachers who are US citizens. All phases of office work: secretarial, reception, typists and business machine operators. Hourly pay based on experience and skills. No fee to applicants for placement. Apply to Personnel Director, Summer Positions, Allied Temporary Personnel, Inc., 370 Lexington Ave., New York NY 10017.

### Brook Street Bureau of Mayfair Ltd.
Permanent and temporary personnel agency. Openings for unlimited number. Needs permanent and temporary secretaries, "Fridays," and typists. Salaries are $150-200/week. All fees paid. Room and board available in hotels; residence guide available. Apartment bulletin board provided. Office locations: 958 3rd Ave., New York NY 10022; 1 N. Broadway, White Plains NY 10601; and 8 Winter St., Boston MA 02108. Apply to Administration Office, Brook Street Bureau of Mayfair Ltd., 136 E. 57th St., New York NY 10022.

### Career Blazers Personnel Services
Located in New York City. Has hundreds of employment opportunities for administrative assistants, secretaries, gal/guy fridays, typists, file clerks, word processors, receptionists and many others. Positions available in publishing, advertising, fashion, film, radio, TV, financial, nonprofit organizations, etc. "Highest salaries paid"; full time, part-time or temporary. Write to Career Blazers Personnel Services, 500 Fifth Ave., New York City NY 10036.

### Davidson's Temps
Temporary personnel contractor. Openings for many college students, teachers, high school seniors and foreign students during vacations and holidays. Needs stenographers (minimum 80 wpm), $4.50-6; typists (minimum 50 wpm), $3.50-4.50; secretaries (with/without steno), $3.50-4.50; word processing operators (Mag card, Vydek, etc.), $8-9.50. Apply to W.P. Davidson, Davidson's Temps, 41 E. 42nd St., New York NY 10017.

### Enwood Temporary Services, Inc.
Temporary employment service. Hundreds of jobs available. Openings for college students, teachers, high school seniors, local applicants, and foreign students from May 1 to September 15. Needs secretaries with steno, $4-6/hour; secretaries without steno, $3-5/hour; typists, $3-4.75/hour; statistical typists, $3.25-5/hour; receptionists, $2.75-4/hour; word processors, $6-8/hour; clerks, $2.65-3.50/hour. Apply to Eunice Brill, President, Enwood Temporary Services, Inc., 6 E. 45th St., New York NY 10017, tel. 212/682-4080; or 160 Broadway, New York NY 10038, tel. 212/227-0790.

## Kelly Services, Inc.
More than 450 branches coast to coast, Puerto Rico, Canada, England and France. Temporary work assignments. Offers over 100 job classifications (office, marketing and light industrial assignments) to college students, teachers and other qualified people during summer breaks and year 'round. Kelly Services also has a special referral system that allows you to register at a Kelly office near your school then work near your home during summer recess—or register near your home then work on temporary assignments during the school year. Assignments available include clerks, typists, secretaries, keypunch operators, word processors, bookkeepers and a variety of marketing and light industrial. Offers flexible schedule with "attractive hourly pay rates equal to or higher than the accepted industry standards in most cities." No paycheck deductions except Social Security and income tax. No employment fee for temporary work. See the White Pages for the branch of Kelly Services nearest you. Apply in person or write to: Summer Employment, National Headquarters, Kelly Services, GPO 1179, Detroit MI 48266.

## Mature Temps Inc.
Located in New York City. National temporary employment service. Openings for college students, teachers, high school seniors, local applicants and foreign students from May to September or year-round. Needs secretaries, clerks, typists, bookkeepers, stenographers, accountants, demonstrators and marketing research persons. High hourly rates based on skills. Apply to Mature Temps Inc., 1114 Avenue of the Americas, New York NY 10036, tel. 212/869-0740; 200 Mamaroneck Ave., Suite 200, White Plains NY 10601, tel. 914/428-9050.

## North Shore Studios
Located in Northport. Model services, commercial photography. Needs models (female only), minimum age-18th birthday in 3 months to 36 years old, $5-25/hour; 2 general assistants, college students or teachers preferred, $3.50/hour. Employment not seasonal, but hourly salary when used. "In commercial photography 90 percent of attaining position is beauty of face, then figure. Good manners, proper grooming, good teeth and a healthy disposition are essential. Be yourself, sincere, and study the work you would do in applying for any position." Apply to Alexander D. Jones, Jr., Owner, North Shore Studios, 216 Elwood Rd. E., Northport NY 11731; tel. 516/261-5527.

## Office Help Temporaries
Located in Yonkers. Other locations in Westchester-Rockland, Greenwich-Stamford, and New York City. Temporary openings available throughout the year, 1 week to 3 months and all school holidays, for college students and teachers with office skills including secretarial, typing, mag card, keypunching and others. Salaries are $2.90-5 and up/hour. No fees. Telephone for appointment: Greenwich-Stamford, 203/324-2115; New York City, 212/884-2427; Westchester-Rockland, 914/946-1690; Yonkers, 914/965-1333.

## Temp Force
Temporary office personnel contractor. Openings for college students, teachers and high school seniors during vacations and holidays. Needs secretaries, typists, stenographers, clericals and accountants. Salaries based upon experience. Apply to Temp Force: 1975 Hempstead Turnpike, East Meadow NY 11554, tel. 516/794-9700; 320 Fulton Ave., Hempstead NY 11550, tel. 516/485-5800; 260 N.

Broadway, Hicksville NY 11801, tel. 516/822-4700; 425 Rt. 110, Melville NY 11747, tel. 516/293-7050; 1805D Fifth Ave., Bayshore NY 11706, tel. 516/273-1030; 452 Medford Ave., Rt. 112, Patchogue NY 11772, tel. 516/289-7300; 1621 Hillside Ave., New Hyde Park NY 11040, tel. 516/352-4442; 140 Bay St., Staten Island NY 10301, tel. 212/981-9193; 85 Denison Parkway East, Corning NY 14830, tel. 607/937-5391; 222 Mamaroneck Ave., White Plains NY 10605, tel. 914/761-3838.

**Aubrey Thomas Inc.**
Temporary and permanent personnel agency. Works with over 200 major corporations serving banking, insurance, publishing, advertising and many other fields in the metropolitan area. Positions available for full-time and part-time help from May 1 to September 15. Needs 250 typists ($4-5/hour), 250 secretaries ($4.50-5.25/hour), 200 gal/man Fridays ($4-5/hour), 100 receptionists ($3.50-4/hour), 100 clerk-typists ($3.50-4/hour). No fee charged to applicants. Can apply in person at following locations: Midtown, 400 Madison Ave., New York NY; tel. 212/486-7800; Wall Street, 150 Broadway, New York NY; tel. 212/732-6100; Westchester, 1 N. Broadway, White Plains NY; tel. 914/428-2020.

## Commercial Attractions

**Bronx Zoo—New York Zoological Society**
Located in Bronx. Nonprofit private cultural institution. Openings for college students and teachers (local applicants preferred) from April to October. Needs Wild Asian Monotrail tour guides and Safari tour train guides, $3.50/hour. Also needs Children's Zoo aides, animal demonstration aides, admission attendants, minimum wage. Apply by April to Jeff Franco, Personnel Associate, Zoological Society, Bronx Zoo, 185th St. and Southern Blvd, Bronx NY 10460; tel. 212/220-5126.

**Carousel Mountain Amusement Park**
Located in Owego. Family amusement park. Needs entertainers with skills to produce and perform shows such as magic, puppets, juggler, clowns, dog act, etc. (college students or teachers preferred), June to August, $200-350/week; 30 ride operators and food service personnel (local applicants, college students, high school students preferred), April through October, minimum wage. Room and board negotiable for entertainers only. "I am open to proposals for any type entertainment." Send resume or send for application by April 1. Apply to Mike Kendall, President, Box 37, Owego NY 13827; tel. 607/687-2156.

## Resorts, Ranches, Restaurants, Lodging

**Atlantic Terrace Motel Corp.**
Located in Ocean View Terrace, Montauk, on Long Island. Openings from late June to October. Needs chambermaid, $90/week; lifeguard, maintenance help, groundskeeper, office help, $105/week. Salaries are given out under contract system; part of salary is withheld and given out as a bonus on Labor Day—penalty for premature departure. Salaries include housing and cooking facilities. Apply by

April 1 to Ralph Jakoby, 286 Vanderbilt Pkwy., Dix Hills NY 11746; tel. 516/427-9389.

## Bekarciak's Valley View House, Inc.

Located at Kenoza Lake. Resort. Openings for college students, teachers and high school seniors from May 1 to October 15. Needs 15 waiters/waitresses, lifeguard, groundskeeper, 7 kitchen helpers-dishwashers, New York State minimum wage; 2 bartenders, social director, salary to be arranged. Apply to Bekarciak's Valley View House, Inc., Kenoza Lake NY 12750.

## Blue Water Manor

Located at Diamond Point on Lake George. Resort. Openings for 45 college students and teachers, minimum age 18, from mid-June to Labor Day. Needs waitresses, chambermaids, waiters, cabin boys, secretaries, kitchen help, bartenders, ski-boat drivers, grounds, maintenance personnel and snack bar attendants. Room and board available. Resort experience and talent for staff show and dance band desired. Send stamped return envelope for job information and application form. Apply to Dorothy Long, Blue Water Manor, Diamond Point NY 12824.

## Driftwood on the Ocean

Located in Montauk. Resort. Openings for college students and foreign students from June 15 to September 15. Apply only if available until September 15. Needs telephone operator-office help, chambermaids, 2 lifeguards and maintenance help, $125 plus tips and free lodging (room with kitchen facilities). Apply to Sam Weisbein, Driftwood On The Ocean, Box S, Montauk NY 11954.

## Golden Acres Farm and Ranch

Located in Gilboa. Family farm resort. Openings for 60 college students, teachers and high school seniors (minimum age 16) from late June (some late May) to Labor Day. Needs waitresses, waiters, bus boys, hostess, bartender, snackbar attendants, chef, assistant cooks, kitchen workers, salad maker, baker, baker-trainee, kitchen steward, dishwasher, potwasher. front office clerks, secretary, bellhops/maintenance persons, farm hand, maids, laundry attendant, social director (must know square and folk dancing), nurse, head counselor to supervise teen and children's program, athletic director for adults and teens, general counselors (must swim), arts and crafts counselors, lifeguards, WSI, stable head and assistants (must ride and teach Western riding), craft teacher for adult program, maintenance person, and 3- or 4-piece band or single with electronic equipment. Salary depends on position and experience; most positions have tips plus room and board. A personal interview is required. Send a resume and stamped, legal size return envelope. Apply to Mrs. Jerry Buxbaum, Dept. SED, Golden Acres Farm, Gilboa NY 12076.

## Gurney's Inn

Located in Montauk. International beauty and health spa; complete resort complex and conference center with restaurant. Openings for college students, teachers, high school seniors, foreign students and local applicants from mid-May to mid-September; year-round work available also. Needs 40 waiters and waitresses, $350/week; 25 buspersons, $275/week; 15 maids, $180/week, 10 laundry helpers,

$165/week; 10 cashiers, $165/week; 5 bellhops, $275/week; 20 kitchen help, $165/week; 10 therapists, $200/week; 10 attendants, $165/week; 10 lifeguards, $180/week; 10 masseuses and masseures, $250/week. "Applicants should be nonsmokers and nondrinkers (preferred). Housing available." Apply to Rick O'Neill, Paymaster, Gurney's Inn, Old Montauk Highway, Montauk NY 11954; tel. 516/668-2345.

### Lake House Hotel

Located in Woodridge. Kosher, open April to October. Openings from June through October or minimum July and August working 7 days/week. Needs 2 maids, local applicants, college students, high school seniors, foreign students all acceptable, $50/week plus tips; 3 cooks' helpers, local applicants, college students, high school seniors, foreign students all acceptable, $100-150/week; 3 dishwashers, 2 pantry helpers, college students, foreign students acceptable, $100-150/week; 1 baker's helper, college students, high school seniors, foreign students all acceptable, $100-150/week; 2 lifeguards, college students and high school seniors preferred, $70-100/week; 1 or 2 second cook (experienced only), local applicants, college students, high school seniors, teachers, foreign students all acceptable, $125-250/week. "Write sending as much information as possible. Room and board are provided (Kosher food)." Apply after February 1 to Mr. Kay, Personnel Manager, Lake House Hotel, Box 367, Woodridge NY 12789; telephone only after June 1, 914/434-7800.

### Olympian Village

Located at Lake George, Diamond Point. Resort motel. Openings for 7 college students (minimum age 18) from the last week in June to Labor Day. Needs reservation clerk (general office work) and chambermaids. Apply to Mrs. Henrietta Kopelman, 270 Jay St., Brooklyn NY 11201.

### Peekskill Ranch

Located in Peekskill. Resort. Openings from June through Labor Day. Needs 12 waiter/waitress, 5 outdoor maintenance, 8 housekeeping/chambermaids, 10 wranglers/barnworkers, college students, US and foreign, acceptable; 4 day camp counselors, college students and teachers preferred. Minimum wages less room and board. Apply to Don San Marco, President, Peekskill Ranch, Furnace Wood Rd., Box 112, Peekskill NY 10566.

### Potter's Resort Motor Lodge

Located at Blue Mt. Lake, New York. Family resort. Openings for persons age 18 and older from June 22 through Labor Day. Needs 8 waitresses, 3 dishwashers and 2 chambermaids. Salaries are New York State service help wage plus good tips; live on premises at cost of $34.50/week. Apply by March 15 to Bing Faxon, Manager, Dept. SED, 1612 Treasure Dr., Tarpon Springs FL 33589.

### Sugar Maples Resort, Inc.

Located in Maplecrest. Summer resort. Openings for 100 people, minimum age 18, from May to September 21, some longer. Needs chef, cook's helpers, pot washer, dishwashers, gardener, porter, carpenter, electrician, shuffleboard attendant, lifeguards, bus boys, bellhops, desk clerks, teen-age social director, maintenance, baker, baker's helper, accountant, office clerks, typists, soda fountain help, salad room help, adult social director, reservation clerk, waitresses, children's social director, telephone operators, gift shop sales, chambermaids, housekeeper, employees' dining room servers and dining room hostess. Enclose stamped return envelope with application and a recent photograph. Apply between January and March to M.H. Fuller, Dept. SED, 78 Beacon St., Chestnut Hill MA 02167; in April to Sugar Maples Resort, Inc., Dept. SED, Maplecrest NY 12454.

## Tennanah Lakeshore Lodge

Located in Roscoe. Resort hotel. Openings for 30 college students and high school seniors, minimum age 18, from late June through Labor Day. Needs waitresses, waiters, front office personnel, dining room hostess, kitchen helpers, groundsmen, bartender, office clerks and bellmen. Salaries are minimum wage up plus room and board, tips for some positions. Apply to Michael Pavelka, President, Tennanah Lakeshore Lodge, Roscoe NY 12776.

## Vegetarian Hotel

Located in Woodridge. Openings for college students, teachers, high school seniors and foreign students from May to September. Needs 4 maids, $70.50/week plus tips; porter, gardener, dishwasher, $97.80/week; cook's helper, $112.50/week; 2 office girls, $59/week; lifeguard, $50/week. Salaries include room and board. Enclose stamped return envelope (foreign students, postal coupon) with application. Apply to Vegetarian Hotel, Box 457, Woodridge NY 12789.

## Vineyard Lodge

Located in Ulster Park. Resort hotel for adults. Opening for college student or high school senior from late May to October 1, or any period between. Needs second cook/chef's helper (some grill or short order experience), $150/week plus room and board (sleep-in quarters for men only). Apply to Vineyard Lodge, Ulster Park NY 12487.

# Summer Camps

## Adirondack Swim and Trip

Located at Rainbow Lake, near Lake Placid. Private camp for boys. Openings for college students and teachers from late June to mid-August. Needs waterfront director (WSI), $1,000; instructors: 2 swimming (WSI), 2 sailing, 2 canoeing, 2 campcraft, archery, crafts, riflery, tennis, sports; 5 tripping leaders (canoe/mountain). Salaries for new staff start at $500-600 plus room and board. Apply beginning January 1 to Adirondack Swim and Trip Camp, 39 Mill Valley Rd., Pittsford NY 14534.

## Adirondack Woodcraft

Located at Old Forge. Private camp. Openings for college students, teachers and foreign students from late June to late August. Needs counselors: 4 trip (canoe, mountain), 4 waterfront (ARC, WSI), 3 campcraft and arts, 2 nature study, $500 and up; 5 general, $450 and up. Specialty counselors usually paid more, depending upon age and experience. Room and board provided. Write for application, sending resume. Apply to John J. Leach, Dept. SED, Adirondack Woodcraft Camps Inc., Box 219, Old Forge NY 13420.

## American Camping Association
Private organizational camps for boys, girls, coed and family. Residential camps throughout the northeastern states; day camps in New York metropolitan area. Openings for college students and teachers, minimum age 18, with at least one year of college. Needs general counselors; trained and experienced specialty counselors for land sports, water sports, nature, pioneering, arts and crafts, music, drama, WSI, NRA; nurses (RN), physicians, office secretaries, maintenance, grounds, all kitchen staff. Salaries are commensurate with age, education, camp experience and type of position. "For resident camps, room and board is included." Visit our office or send stamped self-addressed envelope for free staff application. Apply by July 1 to American Camping Association, 225 Park Ave. S., Suite 739, New York NY 10003.

## Association of Independent Camps
Openings at 100 children's summer camps located in New England and the Middle Atlantic states. Needs head counselors, group leaders, general and all specialty counselors. Room and board provided. Apply by July to Association of Independent Camps, Dept. SED, 55 W. 42nd St., New York NY 10036; tel. 212/695-2656.

## Barker
Located at Cropseyville. Camp of the Troy Boys' Club for low-income boys, ages 7-14. Openings for college students (minimum age 18) with one year of college, for 9 weeks during July and August. Needs counselors with backgrounds in athletics, aquatics, arts and crafts, nature study, archery, BB gun shooting, special events, singing and drama, boating. Also needs program director, athletic director, waterfront director (WSI) for lake, driver-maintenance man, nurse (RN or LPN). Students can be accepted on the college work-study program. Contact the school financial aid office for details. Salaries begin at $550 for season plus room and board; some weekends off. Send for application; include resume. Apply by May 18 to Director, Dept SED, Camp Barker Associates Inc., 1700 7th Ave., Troy NY 12180.

## Beaumont
Located in Parksville. Residential camp for children, ages 6-17. Openings from June 26 to August 21. Needs 12 waitresses/office/mother's helpers, high school seniors preferred, $350/season; high school counselors, $400/season; freshman college student counselors, $500/season; sophomore college student counselors, $600/season; junior to graduates up counselors, $750/season; 1 arts and crafts counselor, $850/season, college students preferred; 1 cook, $650/season, college students preferred; and 1 waterfront counselor and 1 assistant waterfront counselor, college students preferred, salary open. Apply to Dr. Gerald Burday, Executive Director, Route 52, Liberty NY 12754.

## Beaver Hollow
Located at Java Center. YWCA camp for children ages 7-16. Openings for college students, teachers and high school seniors from June 30 to August 24. Needs assistant director, $650-850; 4 cooks, kitchen aides, $300-800; nurse (RN), $800; 8 program coordinators: WSI, riding, music, drama, ecology, campcraft-backpacking, sailing, canoeing, crafts, sports, $450-600; 25 unit directors and counselors, $250-600. Send resume by first week in June to Camp Director, YWCA, Dept.

SED, 190 Franklin St., Buffalo NY 14202.

## Beech-Wood
## Pine-Wood

Located in Sodus (Beech-Wood), Arkport (Pine-Wood). Girl Scout resident camps for children ages 7-12 (Beech-Wood) and ages 11-18 (Pine-Wood). Openings from the end of June to the middle of August. Needs 2 camp directors for 9 weeks, administrative ability, group leader experience, teacher preferred, $1,700-2,500; 3 assistant camp directors, 8 weeks, group leader experience, supervisory ability, college students or teachers preferred, $800-1,200; 14 unit leaders, 7 weeks, group leader experience, program skills, college students or teachers preferred, $560-1,050; 8 specialists, 7 weeks, WSI for waterfront, riding, arts, tripping, college students or teachers preferred, $560-1,050; 13 assistant unit leaders, 7 weeks, 1 year college and camp experience, college students, teachers all acceptable, $455-600; 4 assistant specialists, 7 weeks, riding, boating, swimming, skills, college students, teachers acceptable, $455-600; 10 unit assistants, 7 weeks, camping experience, college students, high school seniors acceptable, $350-385; 2 clerks, 7 weeks, liking for details and record keeping, college students, teachers, high school seniors acceptable, $455-600; 2 nurses, 7 weeks, RN, LPN or EMT in New York state, $900-1,200; 2 food supervisors, 7 weeks, experience in quantity cooking, $980-1,500; 2 assistant cooks, 7 weeks, cooking experience, $455-800; 6 aides-kitchen and unit, 7 weeks, graduation from high school, $280-350. Send for application or apply by letter with complete resume including Social Security number, dates available and applicable reference letters. Apply by May 15 to Audrey A. Cooper, Camp Administrator, Girl Scouts of Genesee Valley, Inc., 550 E. Main St., Rochester NY 14604; tel. 716/454-7010.

## Belle Terre Gymnastic Camp for Girls

Located in South Kortright. Openings for college students and teachers from June 25 to August 23. Needs specialty counselors/teachers (also act as bunk counselors): 6 gymnastics; 1 dance (ballet and jazz); 2 waterfront (WSI, pool and lake); 1 tennis; 2 Western horsemanship; 1 arts and crafts. Salaries are $720-1,000, commensurate with skills and experience, plus room and board. Also needs nurse (RN or LPN), cook, 2 kitchen helpers. "Counselors should seek certification in advanced First Aid if at all possible." Apply early (May 1 deadline), enclosing complete resume, to Consuelo G. Haus, Director, Belle Terre Gymnastic Camp for Girls, Dept. SED, South Kortright NY 13842; tel. 607/538-9434.

## Brant Lake Camp

Located in the Adirondack Mountains, Warren County. Founded 1916. Private camp for boys ages 7-16. Openings for college students and teachers from June 24 to August 24. Needs 12 general counselors, $450-600; 12 specialty counselors for tennis, camping, WSI, riflery, athletics, arts and crafts, $400-800; assistant waterfront director, 2 nurses (RN), $600; director of arts and crafts, supervisor of 9 year old division, $1,000 and up (couple accepted). Apply by March to Brant Lake Camp, 84 Leamington St., Lido Beach NY 11561.

## Bergen County Girl Scout Council

Located at Glen Spey. Openings for college students and teachers from late June to late August. Needs program specialists, $500-800; unit leaders, $600-800; waterfront directors, $600-900; nurse, $600-1,200; camp director, $850-2,000 and up. "Beautiful setting on a natural lake." Send resume and application request. Apply to John Hopp, Dept. SED, Girl Scout Council of Bergen County, Bergen Mall, Paramus NJ 07652.

## Che-Na-Wah

Located in Minerva, in the Adirondack Mountains. Private camp for girls ages 6-16; brother camp on same lake. Openings for college students, college graduates and teachers from June 23 to August 23. Needs group leaders; specialty counselors: athletics, archery, arts and crafts, modern and jazz dance, drama, gymnastics, music (piano), guitar and folk singing, pioneering, photography, tennis, waterskiing; ARC instructors in swimming, boating, canoeing, sailing; and nurse (RN). Salaries are open depending on skill, training and experience. Room, board and laundry provided. Apply by June 1 to Mrs. Alice Sternin, Dept. SED, 51 Planting Field Rd., Roslyn Heights NY 11577.

## Comstock
## Egypt Valley
## Yaiewano

Located in the Finger Lakes region. 3 Girl Scout camps serving girls, ages 6-17. Openings for 60 males and females, minimum age 18, from June 24 to August 18. Needs assistant director, unit leaders, assistant unit leaders, nurses, cooks and assistant cooks. Specialists needed for waterfront, horseback riding, sailing, canoeing, tennis, sports, backpacking and arts and crafts. Starting salary is between $475 and $1,700 including room and board; based on position and experience. Apply to Karen D. Fouracre, Seven Lakes Girl Scout Council, Box 268, Geneva NY 14456.

## Eagle Island

Located in Upper Saranac Lake, New York. Girl Scout camp. Openings from approximately June 20 to August 15. Needs program specialists, salaries determined by age and qualifications; assistant director, business manager, directors for waterfront and sailing counselors; arts and crafts consultant, nurse (RN), maintenance staff; security staff. An equal opportunity employer. Send resume and application request to Outdoor Program Manager, Dept. SED, Girl Scout Council of Greater Essex County, 120 Valley Rd., Montclair NJ 07042.

## Echo Lake

Located in Warrensburg, in the heart of the Adirondacks. Private coed camp. Openings for college students, college graduates and teachers from June 21 to August 21. Needs group leaders, $600 and up; instructors: woodcrafts, sculpture, tennis, waterfront (WSI), pioneering and tripping, $500 and up; directors: nature, gymnastics, aquatics, photography, theatre, girls' athletics, folk dance, $600 and up. Apply by March to Staff '80, Camp Echo Lake, Dept. SED, 49 Clubway, Hartsdale NY 10530.

## Educational Alliance Camps

Located in Brewster. Specialized camping services for senior citizens and developmentally disabled children; children ages 8-25, older adults ages 60-90. Openings for college students, teachers and high school seniors from June 21 to August 28; pre- and post-season work available in April and September. Needs 4 unit heads, $1,000-1,600; 10 unit assistants, specialists, $500-900; 40 counselors, $200-600; 40 junior staff, $150; 25 kitchen staff, maintenance staff, $75-700; 3 nurses (RN), $1,000-1,500; office workers. Apply to Educational Alliance Camps, 197 E. Broadway, New York NY 10002.

## Forestburg Scout Reservation
Located in Forestburg, New York, on 1100-acre reservation at the base of the Catskill Mountains. 2 Boy Scout Camps for boys ages 11-18. Openings for 6 weeks during summer for men with prior scouting experience. "Teachers welcome to apply." Also needs area directors, minimum age 21: 2 male waterfront directors, $800/season; 2 male rifle range officers, $700-900/season; 1 male reservation commissary director, $1,000/season; 1 male high adventure direcor, $800-1,000/season; 2 male/female chefs, $1,200-1,500/season; 1 female health officer (RN, LPN, EMT), $800/season. Needs area directors, minimum age 18: 2 male nature/scoutcraft director, 500-700/season; 2 male or female trading post managers, $500-800/season; 6 male camp commissioners, $600-800/season; 1 male commissary director, $500/season. Room and board provided. "An opportunity to give a young person a meaningful experience and a chance for self-improvement and self-growth. Apply by May 30 to Lawrence Feyereisen, Program Director, Monmouth Council of the Boy Scouts of America, Monmouth and Deal Rds., Oakhurst NJ 07755.

## The Fresh Air Fund
Located in Sharpe Reservation, Fishkill. Nonprofit organization sponsoring 4 camps for inner city youngsters. Openings for college students from approximately June 22 to August 25. Needs 175 general counselors, $450-600; 14 village leaders, $700-850; specialists: 5 arts and crafts, nature, $550-650; 14 waterfront staff (WSI and assistants), $650-850. Salaries depend upon experience. Apply to Larry Mickolic, Associate Director, The Fresh Air Fund, 300 W. 43rd St., New York NY 10036.

## Green Twigs
Located in Roosevelt. Cerebral palsy camp for teenagers and adults. Openings for college students and teachers from approximately June 25 to August 23. Needs 10 group counselors, $250-500; 6 activity counselors for games, waterfront, nature, music and dramatics, arts and crafts, $500-800. For residential camp, needs 15 residential counselors, $550; residential director, $1,000-1,500; residential nurse, $1,000-2,000. Apply by April or May to Recreation Department, Camp Green Twigs, 380 Washington Ave., Roosevelt NY 11575; tel. 516/378-2000.

## Greenwich House
Located in Copake Falls. Settlement house for coeds, ages 7-12. Openings for college students from June 28 to August 25. Needs 10 general counselors, $150-350; specialty counselors: 2 pioneering, 2 nature, 2 crafts, $300; swimming head, $650; head counselor, $400-800. Apply by April 15 to Morton S. Horowitz, Greenwich House Camp, 27 Barrow St., New York NY 10014.

## Hatikvah
Located at Livingston Manor. YM and YWHA camp, strictly kosher with traditional Jewish observance. Openings for college students, teachers and foreign students

from June 16 to August 30. Needs 3 division heads, $800 and up; 8 specialty counselors for nature-pioneering, music, drama, arts and crafts, dance, waterfront, archery, photography, $400-1,000; 25 general counselors, $250-600; 6 maintenance, $300-800. Apply by June 15 to David Hirsch, Director, Camp Hatikvah of the YM and YWHA of Williamsburg Inc., 575 Bedford Ave., Brooklyn NY 11211, tel. 212/387-6695; camp, 914/439-4702.

## Hidden Valley
Located in Watkins Glen. 4-H camp for children ages 9-19, whose purpose is outdoor education. Openings for 25 college students and teachers from June 22 to August 16. Needs general counselors, specialty counselors in canoeing, waterfront, nature, horsemanship, crafts, archery, hiking, pioneering. Salaries are $40-75/week plus room and board. Apply to David J. Hillmann, 4-H Office, 208 Broadway, Montour Falls NY 14865.

## Hillcroft
Located in Billings. Nonsectarian coed camp. Openings for college students and teachers, minimum age 20, from June 25 to August 24. Needs 2 group leaders for teenagers, 6 group leaders, $500 and up; instructors: 6 WSI, canoeing-gardening-animal care, 2 archery-tennis, dramatics-folk music and dance, photography, science-hiking, pioneering, $350; 2 nurses (RN), secretary. Apply to Dennis Buttinger, Jan Ridge Rd., Somers NY 10589.

## Huntington Camps
Located in the Catskills Mountains. Camp for learning disabled, brain injured and mentally retarded people ages 6 to adult. Openings for college students and teachers from June 28 to August 22. Needs 25 general counselors, 2 arts and crafts, woodworking, $300-600; 3 academic teachers, 2 speech therapists, 4 water safety instructors, $500-900; 2 home economics counselors, $200-400; head counselor; specialty counselors for perceptual training, controlled reading, music, drama; nurse (RN); unit leaders. Enclose stamped return envelope. Apply to Huntington Camps, 1017 E. 80th St., Brooklyn NY 11236.

## Impala
Located in Woodbourne. Resident coed camp for children ages 6-16. Openings for college students from June 25 to August 25. Needs 12 male and female general workers, $400-500/season; 1 tennis counselor, $500-600/season; 1 WSI counselor, minimum age 22, $800/season; 2 younger WSI counselors, $500/season; 1 pioneering counselor, $450/season; and 2 arts and crafts counselors, $400-450/season. "Applicants should have sincere desire to work with youngsters, enjoy them; be able to participate, show initiative and integrity." Apply to Fredda/Abe Kerner, Directors, 5405 Avenue S., Brooklyn NY 11234.

## Ithaca Speech Clinic, Inc.
Located in Spencer. Residential camp for ages 4-20. Openings from June 28 through August 11 for counselors with a background in speech and hearing primarily and related fields in general. Salary $400-600/6 weeks, plus room and board. "Applicants must enjoy working with all types of children (some are physically and/or mentally handicapped). They should be people planning careers working with children (or seeking experience to decide if this type of work should

be a lifetime career)." For information, contact Dept. SED, Ithaca Speech Clinic, 1408 Lake St., Elmira NY 14901; tel. 607/732-7069.

## Jawonio

Located in New City. Camp for orthopedic physically handicapped people, ages 6-25. Openings for college students and high school seniors from June 25 to August 24. Needs 32 general counselors, $400-500/season; 4 kitchen helpers, $600-800/season; nurse (RN), $1,600-1,800/season. Apply to Camp Jawonio, Rockland County Center for the Physically Handicapped, Inc., 260 Little Tor Rd. N., New City NY 10956.

## Jeanne d'Arc

Located at Merrill on 14-mile Lake Chateaugay in the Adirondacks. Private camp for girls, ages 6-17. Openings for college students and teachers from June 25 to August 20. Needs 20 specialty/cabin counselors with skills in archery, arts and crafts, canoeing (SCI), campcraft, dramatics, golf, guitar, gymnastics, horseback riding, nature and ecology, riflery (NRA), sailing (SCI), tennis, waterskiing, $350-900/season; 5 WSI, trip leader (must have Standard First Aid); 2 nurses (RN), $700-900. Apply to Mrs. A.C. McIntyre, Box 83H, Scarsdale NY 10583.

## Jefferson Park

Located in Woodville, on Lake Ontario. Camp for intercity children, sponsored by the Salvation Army. Openings from June 22 to August 24. Needs waitresses, kitchen help, counselors; specialty counselors for nature, craft, athletics; waterfront safety instructor, lifeguards. Salaries are $300-500/season, specialized positions higher. Room and board provided. Apply by May 1 to Mrs. Major Charles Drummond, The Salvation Army, 749 S. Warren St., Syracuse NY 13202.

## Kennybrook

Located in Monticello. Private coed camp. Openings for college students, teachers and foreign students, minimum age 19, from June 27 to August 27. Needs 40 counselors, $500 and up; specialty counselors for archery, swimming, WSI, pioneering, boating, $500-700; 2 tennis instructors, $500; dramatics instructor, $500. Apply early to Peter Landman, 19 Southway, Hartsdale NY 10530.

## Lenni-Len-A-Pe

Located in Salisbury Mills. Coed camp serving children ages 6-16. Openings for college students and teachers from June 29 to August 24. Needs 40 general counselors, $300-600/season; 10 group leaders, $500-1,000/season; 60 specialty counselors for pool, lake, waterski, tennis, etc., $300-1,500/season. Write or call. Apply by June 15 to Director, Camp Lenni-Len-A-Pe, Dept. SED, 3242 Judith Lane, Oceanside NY 11572; tel. 516/764-2112.

## Lenoloc

Located in Bear Mountain. Small rustic camp for girls, ages 6-13. Openings from June 25 to August 21. Needs 1 program director, $1,000-1,200/season; head cook, $1,000-1,500/season; 2 arts & crafts directors (college students, teachers, high school students), $400-500/season; waterfront director (college student, teacher), $800-1,000/season; 2 waterfront assistants (college students, teachers), $500-700/season; nurse (teacher), $1,000/season; sports director (college student, teacher, high school student), $600-700/season; 2 assistant sports directors (college students, teachers, high school students), $400-600/season; 2 dance/drama directors (college students, teachers, high school students), $400/600/season; nature director (college student, teacher, high school student), $300-500/season; 3 general counselors (college students, teachers, high school students), $300-450/season; chauffer to run errands into town, $300/season. Room and board provided. "Learning, caring, growing, sharing is the camp motto" and should be kept in minds of applicants. Send for application by June 1. Apply to Kareene Bloomgarden, Camp Director, Camp Lenoloc, Dept. SED, YWCA 395 Main St., Orange NJ 07050; tel. 201/672-9500.

## Lincoln Farm
Located in Roscoe. Two adjacent programs: Lincoln Farm Teen Camp for children, ages 12-16, and Lincoln Farm Jr. for children, ages 7-12. Openings for US and foreign college students and teachers. Needs specialists for 34 craft studios, waterfront (pool and lake), athletic supervisors; leaders for construction, farming, forestry, driver-training, typing, science, instrumental and guitar instruction, music, dance and drama; office helpers; food-service workers; mother's helper; bookkeeper; nurse (RN); and groundkeepers and maintenance staff. Salaries are $750-1,500 for administrative staff; $400-800 for specialists; $300-500 for general counselors (salaries include room and board). Apply by May to Lincoln Farm, Box SED, Ardsley NY 10502.

## Long Point
Located in Penn Yan. Salvation Army camp for children ages 7-12. Openings for college students, teachers, high school seniors and foreign students from June 21 to August 29. Needs 12 general counselors, arts and crafts counselor, nature counselor, athletic director, $500; 2 lifeguards, 1 WSI, $500-800; 3 program aides, $400; 5 kitchen help (busing, utility), 3 maintenance, 2 housekeepers, $300; nurse (RN), $1,000. Salaries are seasonal plus room and board. Apply by April to Divisional Youth Secretary, The Salvation Army, 200 Twin Oaks Dr., Dewitt NY 13206.

## Loyaltown, Association for the Help of Retarded Children
Located in Hunter. Organizational coed camp for trainable retarded people ages 8 through adult. Openings for teachers, college students and high school seniors from approximately June 25 to August 28. Needs 70 general counselors, $350-600. Specialty counselors in music, arts and crafts, dance, dramatics, movement, nature, speech, atypical athletics, cooking, sewing, grooming, workshop, $700; swimming (WSI, pool), $500-800; 3 nurses (RN or LPN), $700-1,200. Room and board provided. Apply to A.H.R.C., 189 Wheatley Rd., Brookville NY 11545.

## Lymelight Inc.
Located in Accord. Camp for mentally handicapped children and adults, ages 10 to adult. Openings begin in June. Needs at least 50 general counselors (minimum age 18 with at least one year of college), $300-500/season (sometimes more with BA/BS); 2 specialists in each arts and crafts, minimum $400; 1 specialist each in pioneer, dance, drama, grossmotor (adaptive special physical education), minimum $400; 8 specialists in swimming, minimum $300 with ASL, minimum $400 with WSI. Includes room and board. Must pay $17 medical fee; shirts optional. Send resume or request for application as soon as possible. Apply by March to Stewart

Shein, Dept. SED, 2273 Sultana Dr., Yorktown Hts. NY 10598; tel. 914/962-2559.

## Madison-Felicia

Located in Putnam Valley. Social agency; nonprofit camp for underpriviledged children ages 7-14; CITs ages 16-17; special program for senior citizens ages 65 and up. Openings for college students, teachers, high school seniors and foreign students from June 28 to August 25. Needs 20 general counselors, $300-500; 4 unit leaders; specialists in nature, reading program, arts and crafts, drama, waterfront, WSI, $500-800; 4 trip teaders, $500 and up. Room and board provided. Apply to Jennifer Harris, Camp Madison-Felicia, Dept. SED, RFD 1, Box 153, Putnam Valley NY 10579.

## Metropolitan Baptist Camps, Inc.

Located in Poughquag. Christian outdoor education camp for children ages 9-18 and families. Openings for college students, teachers and a limited number of high school seniors from the end of June to the first week in September. Needs counselors and mature staff; specialists in nature, crafts and music; WSIs; and nurse. Salaries negotiable. Room and board provided. Apply by May 15 to Rev. Preston R. Washington, American Baptist Churches—Metro New York, 225 Park Ave. S., New York NY 10003; tel. 212/254-0880.

## Mogisca

Located in Glen Spey. Girls resident camp. Openings for college students and teachers (except kitchen and stable helpers, high school seniors preferred) from June 28 to August 18. Needs 12 unit leaders (minimum age 21) and 1 assistant waterfront director (minimum age 21), $800-1,000/season; 12 assistant unit leaders (ages 18-21), $350-500/season; 12 counselors, $300-400/season; 1 horseback riding director (minimum age 21), $600-1,000/season; 2 assistant horseback directors, $400-700/season; 1 arts and crafts specialist, $300-800/season; 1 waterfront director (minimum age 21), $850-1,000/season; and 5 waterfront counselors (ages 18-21), $300-500; 7 kitchen as well as stable helpers, $250-350/season. Camp has 1,000 acres including lake, athletic field, stables, pool and farm. Has a diversified program—English riding and older girl trip programs. Apply to Barbara L. Windrow, Camp Administrator, Morris Area Girl Scout Council, 300 Mendham Rd., Mendham NJ 07945; tel. 201/538-4936.

## Normandie

Located in Westport. Waterfront land sports camp—"an international flavor" with emphasis on languages, for children ages 6-16. Openings for college students and teachers, minimum age 19, from June 25 to August 25. Needs general and specialty counselors for waterskiing and boat operation, tennis, baseball, arts and crafts, shop, drama, tripping, waterfront, $350-1,000; waterfront director, $800-1,300; nurse, $700-1,100. Apply early (April 1 deadline) to Camp Normandie, 1199 Park Ave., New York NY 10028.

## North Country Camps (Lincoln and Whippoorwill)

Located in the Adirondack mountains of New York State. Boys' and girls' summer camps. Openings for college students from June 26 to August 23. Needs counselors to live with cabin groups of 4-6 children. Must have trip camping skills, swimming ability, and the skill to instruct such activities as tennis, canoeing, sailing, archery, field sports, crafts or horseback riding. Pays $550 or more, depending upon experience. Apply to Peter L. Gucker, Director, North Country Camps, Dept. SED, 96 Everett Rd., Demarest NJ 07627.

## Northwood

Located in Utica. Camp for children (ages 6-13) with learning disabilities. Openings for college students and teachers from June 28 to August 18. Needs occupational therapist, salary open; 30 general counselors and specialists in crafts, swimming, waterskiing, sports, video equipment, music, $35-200/week. Apply by April 1 to Camp Northwood, Dept. SED, 10 W. 66th St., New York NY 10023; tel. 212/799-4089.

## Oxford-Guilford Camps

Located in Guilford. Private brother-sister camp for teenagers. Openings for 100 college students and teachers for 8 weeks, starting late June. Needs physical education majors and coaches, WSI; specialty counselors for waterskiing, sailing, tennis, land sports, golf, modern dance, gymnastics (apparatus), pianists, nature, pioneering, arts and crafts, ceramics, horseback riding. Salaries are $300 and up, depending on experience and qualifications, plus transportation. Apply by June to: Barry Kingsley, 51 Simpson Dr., Old Bethpage NY 11804; and Arthur Scholder, 1200 Midland Ave., Bronxville NY 10708.

## Point O'Pines

Located at Brant Lake, New York, in the Adirondack Mountains. Camp for girls, 2nd grade to 9th grade. Openings for college students and teachers, minimum age 20 or 2 years of college completed. Needs instructors (ARC) for swimming, boating, canoeing, sailing; many very well-qualified tennis instructors; specialists for waterskiing, diving, golf, athletics, archery, gymnastics, music (pianists), arts and crafts, drama, radio, guitar, photography, pioneering. Salaries include room, board and travel allowance, and depend on age, grade and experience. Apply to Andrew S. Rosen, Dept. SED, 144 Park Ave., Apt. 1A, Swarthmore PA 19081.

## Powell House

Located in Old Chatham. Conference and retreat center. "We hold conferences for groups of the New York Religious Society of Friends (Quakers) and provide recreation periods for them. Outside groups are accommodated as space is available. Families, singles and teenagers come to a variety of programs—some programs with religious and social justice content, some mainly for personal growth, all short term from 2-7 days." Openings for college students, teachers and local applicants. Needs maintenance helper (mow lawns, repairs, janitorial, etc., prefers experience in some areas), May 1 to October 1; 2 cook's helpers/gardeners (prepare vegetables, weed garden, learn to cook for groups of 20-60—life saving cerification helpful), early or mid-June to end of August; program assistant (to be counselor in youth weekends to junior high and senior high students, involves gardening, music and craft skills—lifesaving certification helpful), early or mid-June to August 31. Salaries are minimum $300/month plus room and board. "Availability of jobs depend on configuration of permanent staff. Please do not apply if you are antagonistic to a Christian outlook on life or take drugs. Clientele is asked not to bring liquor onto premises and unmarried couples are not housed together." Send resume by April 1. Apply to Director, Powell House, Dept. SED, RD 1, Box 101, Old Chatham NY 12136; tel. 518/794-8811.

## Raquette Lake Boys' Camp

Located at Raquette Lake. Sister camp across lake. Openings for college students and teachers, minimum age 20, for 8 weeks from late June. Needs head coaches and assistants for football, basketball, hardball, soccer, mountaineering, golf; specialists for aquatics (WSI) competitive swimming, tripping, waterskiing, canoeing, sailing, land sports, tennis, archery, arts and crafts, drama; pianists; drivers; boat pilots; kitchen; maintenance; typists; and nurses. All counselors have bunk assignments. Salaries are $300-1,400, depending on experience and qualifications. Room, board, transportation, clothing allowance, laundry, linens and medical provided. Apply to Jerry Halsband, 300 West End Ave., New York NY 10023.

## Raquette Lake Girls' Camp

Located at Raquette Lake. Brother camp across lake. Openings for college students and teachers, minimum age 19, for 8 weeks from late June. Needs specialists and department heads for performing arts, fine arts, aquatics, synchronized swimming, gymnastics; counselors for land sports, tennis, archery, arts and crafts, drama; pianists; drivers; boat pilots; kitchen maintenance; typists; and nurses. All counselors have bunk assignments. Salaries are $300-1,400, depending on experience and qualifications. Room and board, transportation, clothing allowance, laundry, linens and medical provided. Apply to Jerry Halsband, 300 West End Ave., New York NY 10023.

## Rawhide Ranch

Located in Lake Hill. Coed camp for children ages 8-14. Openings for college students and teachers. Needs 6 cowboy-riding instructors, June 1 to August 24, $750/season; 2 athletic directors, June 24 to August 24, $600/season; 6 cowgirl-riding instructors, June 21 to August 24, $600; 2 lifeguards, June 24 to August 24, $600/season. Room and board provided. "Each child has his/her own horse and takes on new responsibilities. Applicant must enjoy working with children. Contact us as early as possible, give as much information as possible, and don't hesitate to call if you have any questions." Send resume by May 1 to Robert W. Seaman, Owner/Director, Dept. SED, Rawhide Ranch, Lake Hill NY 12448; tel. 914/679-9351.

## Red Wing

Located at Schroon Lake in the Adirondacks. An 8 week camp of 100 girls, ages 7-15. Needs 25 female staff members (total staff-40), for a congenial setting with children eager to learn from qualified specialists in tennis, swimming, gymnastics, sailing, skiing, canoeing, fine and performing arts. Also needs resident MD and 2 RNs. Activities with nearby boys' camps. ACA Accredited. Salaries are $500-1,000. Write full details. Apply by April 1 to Director, Red Wing, Dept. SED, 160 Beach 138 St., Belle Harbor NY 11694.

## Regis
## Apple Jack Teen Camp

Located in Paul Smith's, in the Adirondack Mountains on the shore of Upper St. Regis Lake near Lake Placid. Nonsectarian coed camps with Quaker leadership; for children ages 6-14 (Regis) and ages 14-17 (Apple Jack Teen Camp). Openings July and August for men and women counselors, minimum age 19, single or married couple. Needs specialists and general counselors, nurses, cooks, maintenance. Teachers, graduate students, undergraduates, and others make up international staff. Informal democratic program. Salaries are from $300 and up, plus room, board and transportation allowance. Write to Michael N. Humes, 107 Robinhood Rd., White Plains NY 10605; tel. 914/761-8228.

**Sequoia**
Located in Rock Hill. Private brother-sister camp for children ages 6-15. Member APC, ACA, 49th season. Openings for college students and teachers for 8 weeks from late June to late August. Needs counselors/instructors in tennis, pioneering/camping, nature, self defense, dramatics, music, gymnastics, boating, WSI, basketball, horseback riding, waterskiing, crafts (wood, ceramics, macrame), riflery, archery, land and water sports; general counselors; 2 nurses; kitchen help. Salaries are $400 and up including room, board, laundry and medical coverage. Apply by May 15 to Camp Sequoia, Attn: CS—Sequoia, Rock Hill NY 12775.

**Talako**
Located in Central Valley. Camp for underpriviledged girls ages 8-14. Openings for college students and teachers from June 22 to September 2. Needs 6 general counselors (minimum age 18), $275-350; WSI, $400-600; 3 SLS, $300-450; pioneering, arts and crafts, music, drama, sports, American Indian lore, $300-450. Salaries include room and board. Apply by June 1 to Margarette M. Catalano, Girls Vacation Fund, Inc., 370 Lexington Ave., New York NY 10017.

**Te Ata**
Located in Harriman State Park, Central Valley, New York. Girl Scout camp. Openings for college students, teachers and foreign students from June 23 to August 18. Needs 6 unit leaders (minimum age 21), $600 and up; 15 assistant unit leaders, $400 and up; 5 waterfront (WSI), $700 and up; counselors (minimum age 21) for backpacking, canoeing, $600; nurse, $800 and up; 3 cooks, $800 and up. Apply to Nancy Fisk, Camping Administrator, Lenni Lenape Girl Scout Council, Dept. SED, 555 Preakness Ave., Paterson NJ 07502.

**Ten Mile River Scout Camps**
Located in Narrowsburg, in the Catskill Mountains. "Largest Boy Scout camping operation in the US." Operates 5 camps. Openings for 250 college students or teachers with Boy Scout background, married couples, from mid-June to August. Needs specialists for aquatics, archery, camping and outdoor skills, canoeing, ecology and conservation, field sports, handicrafts, horsemanship, riflery; nurses (RN), doctors, assistant camp directors, program directors, Scoutmasters, bookkeepers, payroll clerk, cooks, bakers, drivers and maintenance personnel. Salaries are $400-1,200/season depending on position and experience. Room and board provided. Apply by May 15 to Director of Camping, Boy Scouts of America, 345 Hudson St., New York NY 10014.

**Timbercrest**
Located in Randolph on 866 acres. Girl Scout resident camp for girls ages 6-16; "primitive type encampment with 33-acre lake for swimming and boating." Openings for college students and teachers (high school students also for handyperson) from June 22 to August 20. Needs 8 counselors (some camping experience desired), $250-400/season; nurse (RN), $600-800/season; 2 handypersons (driver's license required), $80-100/week; waterfront director (WSI,

some canoeing experience required), $400-600/season. "Room and board are provided but are subject to New York state taxation. Housing is in platform tents for all staff. There is an excellent experience for those interested in teaching and recreation or for people who enjoy the out-of-doors. 36-48 hours of time-off allotted to each employee per week." Send for application by June 15 to Donna Dolce, Camp Director, 7 E. Main St., Fredonia NY 14063; tel. 716/679-1559.

### Treetops
Located at Lake Placid. Coed camp for children ages 8-13. Openings for college students, teachers and foreign students from June 24 to August 22. Needs specialty counselors: pottery, music, riding, hiking, drama, carpentry, gardening, weaving, nature, swimming, gymnastics, canoeing, sailing. Salaries are $450 and up/season. Room and board provided. Apply to Colin Tait, Director, Camp Treetops, RFD 4, Winsted CT 06098.

### Troutburg
Located near Hamlin, on Lake Ontario. Camp for children. Openings for college students and teachers from approximately the third week of June to the third week of August (8-week season). Needs 3 lifeguards, lifeguard (WSI), $800; 2 SLG, nature/craft director, 10 counselors (college or graduate students), $550/season; nurse (RN or LPN), $800/season. Salaries include room and board. Apply to Camp Troutburg, The Salvation Army, Box 1010, 60 North St., Rochester NY 14603.

### Wabenaki
Located at Lake Stahahe, Southfields. Camp for boys ages 7-14. Openings for college students, teachers and foreign students from approximately mid-June to September 1; includes 1 week orientation. Needs 15 general counselors, waterfront director (WSI), 2 waterfront counselors (SLS), 2 arts and crafts, music, dramatics, hiking, pioneering, nurse (RN). Salaries include room and board and are based on age and experience. Apply to Ralph Hittman, Executive Director, Boys Brotherhood Republic, 888 E. 6th St., New York NY 10009.

### Williams
Located in Suffern. Coed organizational camp for underprivileged children. Openings for college students and teachers from June 26 to August 30. Needs 12 general counselors, $300; 6 specialty counselors for nature, ceramics, art, dramatics, photography, woodshop, $300-500; WSI, $900. Apply by June to Martin Gordon, 8 Remsen St., Baldwin NY 11510.

---

**Most of the jobs listed in *SED* note time periods for employment. Be sure you can stay the entire employment season before you apply.**

## Wiquanuppek
Located at Bear Mountain. YWCA camp. Openings for college students, teachers and high school seniors from late June to late August. Needs waterfront director, $700-1,000; program director, $700-1,000; advanced first aider, $600-800; specialty-cabin counselors for swimming (WSI), sailing, canoeing, boating, nature, tennis, archery, drama, arts and crafts, music, dance, general athletics, camping and outdoor skills, $250-700 depending on age, position and experience. Apply to Camp Department, YWCA, 795 Main St., Hackensack NJ 07601.

## Woodcliff
Located in Kingston. Private coed children's camp. Openings for 60 people from last week of June to late August, plus precamp orientation. Needs head counselor; assistant head counselor; division heads; waterfront director; specialty counselors for swimming (WSI), canoeing (SCI), waterskiing, gymnastics, tennis, soccer, athletics, arts and crafts, industrial arts, riding, nature, newspaper, photography, electronics and ham radio, overnight camping and backpacking, drama, dance, music (piano, instrumental), guitar and folk singing, fencing, archery, riflery (NRA instructor); nurse (RN); doctor (New York State license); secretary and bookkeeper; drivers. Enclose complete resume of skills and experience with children in letter of application. Apply by August to Mr. and Mrs. S.E. Saphir, 62 Howard Ave., Tuchahoe NY 10707.

## Woodmere
Located at Paradox in the Adirondack Mountains. Girls camp. Opening for college students and teachers, minimum age 19, from June 20 to August 19. Needs instructors for tennis, tripping, archery, canoeing (SCI), 3 swimming (WSI), sailing, waterskiing, athletics, nature, drama, arts and crafts, dancing; pianist; nurse (RN). First aid training required for counselors. Apply to Director, Camp Woodmere, 1464 Rydal Rd., Rydal PA 19046; tel. 215/884-5120.

## YMCA-YWCA Camping Services
Located in Huguenot. Three YMCA-YWCA camps of greater New York (Camps Greenhill, Talcott and McAlister), each self-sufficient with own lake, set on 1,000 acres of forests. Openings from June 22 to September 1 (cooks, May to September). Needs waterfront director, unit leaders, arts and crafts director, outtrip director, teachers preferred, $80-110/week; 70 counselors, college students, high school students, foreign students and local applicants preferred, $40-60/week; 20 junior counselors, high school students preferred, $150/season; 6 cooks, $150-200/week; 4 office helpers, $40-60/week. Room and board provided. "It is a very worthwhile experience. We have jobs for people who like working in gymnastics, volleyball, summer residents camps, outdoor environmental education or in our sports center." Send resume, request application or phone. Apply by June 15 to Peter Moffat, Associate Executive, YMCA-YWCA Camping Services, Huguenot NY 12746; tel. 914/856-4316 or 212/564-1300, ext. 271.

# Summer Theaters

## Melody Fair Corp.
Located in North Tonawanda. 3,000-seat dome theater-in-the-round, playing all major stars. Openings for college students and high school seniors from early June

to September 30. Needs 10 apprenticeships, tuition free; 10 fellowships, $35/week, room and board not included. Apply by April 1 to Jeffrey Fisher, Melody Fair Corp., 674 Main St., Buffalo NY 14202.

# ───── North Carolina ─────

## Business and Industry

### Kelly Services, Inc.
More than 450 branches coast to coast, Puerto Rico, Canada, England and France. Temporary work assignments. Offers over 100 job classifications (office, marketing and light industrial assignments) to college students, teachers and other qualified people during summer breaks and year 'round. Kelly Services also has a special referral system that allows you to register at a Kelly office near your school then work near your home during summer recess—or register near your home then work on temporary assignments during the school year. Assignments available include clerks, typists, secretaries, keypunch operators, word processors, bookkeepers and a variety of marketing and light industrial. Offers flexible schedule with "attractive hourly pay rates equal to or higher than the accepted industry standards in most cities." No paycheck deductions except Social Security and income tax. No employment fee for temporary work. See the White Pages for the branch of Kelly Services nearest you. Apply in person or write to: Summer Employment, National Headquarters, Kelly Services, GPO 1179, Detroit MI 48266.

## Commercial Attractions

### Carowinds
Located in Charlotte. Amusement park. 1,400 seasonal jobs available from March through October in food service, merchandise and games, ride operations, cashier services (front gate and toll plaza), parking lot, special services (maintenance of bathrooms and trash cans, and dispensing cleaning supplies to other departments), night cleanup (must be at least 18 years of age), security (must be at least 20 years of age), first aid (must be registered nurse or certified EMT), warehouse (must be at least 18 years of age), wardrobe, clerical, guest relations, campground, and live shows (musical entertainment in park, operation of petting zoo, bird show, animal characters and guardettes, operation and maintenance of all sound and electronic equipment throughout park—must audition through Live Shows Department). Applicants must be 16 by October 1, 1980 to apply (must be 16 prior to employment), have proof of age, have a Social Security card, and provide own transportation. Apply to Brenda E. Serrell, Director of Personnel, Carowinds, Box 240516, Charlotte NC 28224; tel. 704/588-2606.

## Resorts, Ranches, Restaurants, Lodging

### Cataloochee Ranch
Located in Maggie Valley. Dude ranch. Openings for college students and teachers

from mid-May to late October. Needs 4 waitress-maids, 2 guides for horseback riding, dishwasher/yardman, $75-90; cook, $150. Room and board provided. Apply by April to Judy Coker, Cataloochee Ranch, Route 1, Box 500, Maggie Valley NC 28751.

## Fontana Village Resort

Located at Fontana Dam. Hotel, 300 cottages, recreational complex. Openings for college students and teachers. Federal minimum wage; 40 hour week. Needs 20 cashier/clerk; 5 craft instructors; 30 general laborers (housekeeping, linen, maintenance); 5 registration clerks; 5 lifeguards (WSI and advance LS); 10 kitchen/dining room helpers; 20 waitresses/waiters, ($150/week/wages and tips); 5 cooks (broiler, fry, sautee, general), prefers experienced college students and teachers. Work April 1 to November 1; May 15 to August 15; June 15 to Labor Day. "Lodging available to all applicants for $10/week; must be 18 years of age; meals provided at a discount; recreational privileges granted to all employees; appreciate experience but will train for some positions. Write or call for general employment information and application. Will consider co-op and internship students. Couples considered for full season (April 1-November 1); applicants must be willing to work for a ten-week period minimum. An equal opportunity employer." Apply by April 15 to Andrea Brack, Personnel Manager, Fontana Village Resort, Dept. SED, Fontana Dam NC 28733; tel. 704/498-2211.

## Lee's Inn

Located in Highlands. Mountain inn, "highest inn in eastern United States." Needs 7 waiters, 3 bellmen, youth counselor, and 7 waitresses, $100/month plus tips; and 5 housekeepers, $250/month plus tips. Salaries include room, board and uniforms. Work from May 20 to Labor Day, late August to late October or open to closing. "Working at Lee's Inn can be a very rewarding experience, but you have to work." Apply by April 1 to R.W. Lee, Owner, Lee's Inn, Dept. SED, Highlands NC 28741; tel., winter 305/293-7098, summer 704/526-2171.

## Osceola Lake Inn

Located in the cool and scenic Blue Ridge Mountains, Hendersonville, North Carolina. Resort hotel. Openings for college students and high school seniors from early May to November 1. Needs desk clerks, waiters, waitresses, bus persons, lifeguard, children's counselors, bellhops, kitchen aides, dishwashers, maids, secretary, chauffers, maintenance helper, groundskeeper. Salaries include tips and bonus. Room and board provided. Enclose stamped return envelope with recent photograph, resume, dates available and references with application. State job preference: first, second and third choice. Apply to winter address: Stuart Rubin, 250 Palm Ave., Palm Island, Miami Beach FL 33139.

## YMCA Blue Assembly, Inc.

Located in Black Mountain. Nonprofit conference resort for families, teenagers and adults. Openings for college students, teachers and foreign students from May 27 or 29 to August 26. Needs 80 collegiate staffers working in food service, dining room, swimming pool, craft shop, gift shop, switchboard, etc., pays minimum wage; 30 supervisory staffers, approximately $1,650/season. "Employees are encouraged to live on the campus in staff dormitories. Meals are provided. Cost for these and other services to staff (insurance, transportation, entertainment, etc.) is $7.50/day." Send for application by April 1. Apply to Ken Kelly, Assistant Executive Director,

YMCA Blue Ridge Assembly, Black Mountain NC 28711; tel. 704/669-8422.

# Summer Camps

### American Camping Association, Southeastern Section
Located in Tuxedo. Positions available in North Carolina, South Carolina and Georgia. Openings for college students, college graduates, and teachers, minimum age 19. Needs cabin and unit counselors; guidance specialists; activity leaders; directors for program, boating, waterfront; dietitians; nurses (RN). Apply to Counselor Referral Service, American Camping Association, Southeastern Section, Box 188, Tuxedo NC 28739.

### Blue Star
Located in Hendersonville. Private coed camp. Openings for college students, teachers and foreign students from June 10 to August 25. Needs 100 cabin counselors, $250-600; 20 specialty counselors, $500-1,500. Room, board and laundry provided. Apply by June 1 to The Popkins, Blue Star Camps, Box 1029, Hendersonville NC 28739.

### Carolina for Boys
### Rockbrook for Girls
Located in Brevard. Private camps. Openings for college students and teachers from June 9 to August 16. Needs cabin counselors with skills in tennis, golf, swimming (WSI), riding, canoeing, wrestling, pioneering, crafts, hiking, $350 and up; 3 nurses (RN), $700-1,200; 2 dietitians, $1,200-1,600. Apply to Nath Thompson, Director, Camp Carolina for Boys; Mrs. Teed Lowance, Director, Rockbrook for Girls, Dept. SED, Brevard NC 28712.

### Cheerio
Located in Glade Valley, North Carolina. YMCA camp for children, ages 8-15. Openings for college students, teachers and high school seniors. Girls' camp, June to mid-July; boys' camp, mid-July and August. Needs 30 junior counselors, $40-55/week; 30 senior counselors, $60-85/week; aquatic director (WSI), 10 week job; specialty counselors for riding, photography, riflery, campcraft, golf, tennis, trampoline, canoeing, swimming, dance, baton, cheerleading, athletics, rock climbing and rappelling. Apply by February 1 to Ron Austin, Box 627, High Point NC 27261.

### Chimney Rock
Located in Chimney Rock, North Carolina. Private coed camp. Openings for college students and teachers from June 16 to August 10. Needs 45 counselors, $500-900; 12 specialty counselors, $600-1,000; 5 general workers, $80/week plus board; nurse; dietitian. Apply to Barbara Rankin, Box 717, Stone Mountain GA 30083.

### Easter in the Pines
Located in Carthage. Camp for physically and multiply-handicapped children and adults, ages 6 and older. Openings from May 27 to August 22. Needs 7 activity specialists, (minimum age 21, college students, teachers), $400-800/season; 60

counselors (college students, teachers, high school students, local applicants), $400-850/season; 2 camp nurses (RN), $1,000/season. Room and board provided. Send for application. Apply by March 15 to David Cottengim, Director of Program Services, 832 Wake Forest Rd., Raleigh NC 27604; tel. 919/834-1191.

## Falling Creek Camp for Boys
Located in the Blue Ridge Mountains, Tuxedo, North Carolina. Private mountain boys' camp, Christian centered. Openings for college students and teachers, May 30 to August 25 or June 24 to August 25. Total staff of 80 people; normally 25-30 openings each summer. Average staff age 18-25. Work 9- or 11-week season. First year salary range $500-1,100. Needs general cabin counselors with teaching level skills in one or more program activities—swimming (WSI), sports, tennis, riding, sailing, skiing, canoeing (white water), photography, archery, hiking, rock climbing, crafts, nature. A few openings for women in riding and craft programs or office work. "Apply early so interview can be arranged—a must for serious consideration." Apply to J. Yorke Pharr III, Owner, Falling Creek Camp for Boys, Box 98, Tuxedo NC 28784; tel. 704/692-0262.

## Golden Valley
Located in Bostic, near the South Mountains and Ashville. Girl Scout camp with 15-acre lake; for girls ages 6-17. Openings for college students and teachers from late-June to mid-August. Needs waterfront director (WSI, minimum age 21), $65-90/week; small craft instructor (minimum age 21), $60-85/week; 3 waterfront assistants (must have advanced lifesaving, minimum age 18), $50-70/week; 12 unit assistants (minimum age 18), $55-85/week; nurse (minimum age 21), $55-100/week. Includes room, board and accident insurance. Applicants must "enjoy working with girls in a camp setting with other counselors who are high school graduates, college graduates, and professionals. Program opportunities include swimming, sailing, canoeing, tennis, archery, softball, gymnastics, volleyball, basketball, general camping." Send resume, letter of interest, call or send for application. Apply by May 1 to Ginny Simmons, Camp Director, Pioneer Girl Scout Council, Dept. SED, 324 N. Highland St., Gastonia NC 28052; tel. 704/864-3245.

## Gwynn Valley Camp
Located in Brevard. Independent coed camp for children, ages 5-12. Openings for college students, teachers and foreign students (will accept couples), from June 12 through August 20. Needs cabin counselors with program skills and special interest in the younger child, $500-1,000. Salaries include room and board. Apply by May to Dr. and Mrs. Howard M. Boyd, Gwynn Valley Camp, Route 4, Box 292, Brevard NC 28712.

## Hinton Rural Life Center
Located in Hayesville. Methodist church center "dedicated to working with small churches and groups of rural churches to enable them to be more active in their ministry." Openings for 12 college students and foreign students from May 30 to August 6. Work includes "1 week of training at Hinton Center and 7 weeks service in a rural church or parish, primarily helping with Vacation Church Schools, recreational programs, work and day camps, outreach, and some social work." Workers given $500 honorarium. Room, board and transportation provided. "Employee is responsible for transportation to Hinton Center at the beginning of the project and from Hinton Center at the close. Personal expenses are provided

by employee during project." Send for application and return by March 1 to Ann Janzen, Associate for Church and Community, Box 27, Hayesville NC 28904; tel. 704/389-8336.

## Kanuga

Located in Hendersonville, 6 miles southwest in the Blue Ridge Mountains. Coed camp for children ages 8-15; conference center, all ages. Openings for teachers, college students and high school seniors from May 15 to September 1. Needs children's program director; male and female youth coordinators (minimum age 25); canteen manager; organist and chaplain's assistant; nurse; 12 counselors, preferably with special skills (crafts, etc.); 4 waterfront. Salaries include room and board. Apply by April 1 to Edgar Hartley, Jr., Kanuga, Drawer 250, Dept. SED, Hendersonville NC 28739.

## Keystone Camp, Inc.

Located in Brevard. Private camp for girls ages 7-17. Openings for college students and teachers beginning in June. Needs CIT leader; waterfront head; 15 activity/cabin counselors for gymnastics, nature, canoeing, swimming (WSI), crafts, tennis/badminton, riflery (NRA), archery, dance (ballet, tap), volleyball/basketball, hiking/camping, golf drama; 4 forward seat riding counselors; assistant to dietitian. Salaries are $500 and up/season. Apply by March 31 to William E. Ives, Box 829, Brevard NC 28712.

## Occoneechee

Located on Lake Lure, North Carolina. Girl Scout camp for girls, ages 9-17. Openings for college students and teachers from June 9 to August 11. Needs 2 specialists (arts and crafts, small craft) and 7 troop leaders, $80/week; 12 assistant troop leaders, 3 waterfront assistants, $60/week; 1 cook, $80/week; kitchen manager/head cook and nurse (RN), $100/week. Experience raises base salary. Apply early to Director of Outdoor Program, Hornet's Nest Girl Scout Council, Inc., 7007 Idlewild Rd., Charlotte NC 28212.

## Our Lady Of The Hills

Located in Hendersonville. Religious coed camp for ages 7-16. Openings for college students and high school seniors from June 9 to August 20. Needs 2 waterfront directors, $500-700/season; 20 cabin counselors, $225-375/season; 15 specialty counselors for sailing, canoeing, archery, 2 nature lore, $225-375/season; 2 nurses (RN); 2 riding instructors, $350-700/season. Salaries include room and board. Apply by May 1 to The Rev. J.J. McSweeney, PO Drawer 420, Dept. SED, Waynesville NC 28786.

## Pinewood

Located in Hendersonville, North Carolina. Private coed camp for children, grades 2-9. Openings for college students from June 17 to August 19. Needs 70 cabin counselors, $400-450; 15 specialty counselors for archery, riflery, tennis, golf, waterskiing, canoeing, sailing, arts and crafts, drama, dancing, go-carting, riding, swimming, team sports, $450-550; 6 kitchen aides, high school seniors acceptable, $450; 4 cook's assistants/salad makers, college students preferred, $600. Salaries include room, board and laundry. "Only clean-cut, nonsmokers need apply." Apply by May 20 to M. Levine, Camp Pinewood, 1801 Cleveland Rd., Miami Beach FL 33141.

## Pisgah

Located in Asheville. Girl Scout camp for girls ages 6-17. Openings for teachers from June 15 to July 25. Needs assistant director, $650; waterfront director (WSI, CPR), $550; 2 waterfront assistants (WSI, Lifesaving, experienced), $400; riding director (experienced in teaching riding), $450; 2 riding assistants (experienced in teaching riding), $400; head cook (experienced in institutional cooking), $750; 2 cooking assistants, $350; 8 counselors and unit leaders (experienced in camping and working with girls), $350-400; nurse (RN), $550. Cost for room and board is $15/week. Applicant should "enjoy working with girls and camping in the mountains." Send resume or write for application (June 5 deadline) to Barbara A. Dir, Camp Director, 64 King St., Asheville NC 28804; tel. 252-4442.

## Thunderbird

Located 17 miles south of Charlotte, North Carolina. YMCA coed resident camp for ages 7-16. Openings for college students, teachers, and high school seniors from June 8 to August 22. Needs 7 aquatic instructors (WSI), 12 waterskiing, 7 sailing, 5 canoeing (whitewater), 3 campcraft-nature lore, 5 riding, 4 riflery, 7 athletic (soccer, basketball), 3 field hockey. Pays $500 and up/season, commensurate with position, references and age. Apply by May to G. William Climer, Jr., Director, Camp Thunderbird, Route 4, Box 166A, Clover SC 29710; tel. 803/831-2121.

## Windy Wood

Located in Tuxedo. Coed camp for young children. Openings for college students and teachers from June to August 13. Needs instructor in English riding, tennis, crafts; waterfront director; 16 general counselors; specialty counselors for canoeing, boating, sailing, $50/week with additional if ARC certified; nurse (RN). Apply to William Waggoner, Camp Windy Wood, Box 188, Tuxedo NC 28784.

## YMCA Camp Greenville

Located at Cedar Mountain. Christian camp for boys ages 7-16. Needs counselors, program specialists, administrative staff, nurse (RN), van drivers, junior counselors, cooks and dining hall staff. Salaries are $400-1,800/season plus room and board. "We need staff sincerely interested in helping boys grow and develop spiritually, mentally and physically; those who are willing to give them the time and attention needed. The program includes Appalachian Trail backpack trips, Whitewater canoeing, soccer camp, swimming, fishing, riflery, archery, nature lore, crafts, tennis and sports. We are a mountain-top camp with 1,500 acres, waterfalls, lakes and a beautiful chapel on the edge of a cliff at 3000' altitude." Send for application. Apply to Roy W. Tulp, Director, YMCA Camp Greenville, Cedar Mountain NC 28718; tel. 803/836-3291.

# Summer Theaters

## Strike at the Wind!

Located in Pembroke. Summer outdoor theater. Openings from June 10 to

August 25 for college students. Needs 50 actors and actresses, pays up to $1,000/season; 10 actor/technicians, pays up to $1,500/season; and 2 public relations assistants, pays up to $1,500/season. "For those looking for valuable theatre experiences, these jobs are exceptional examples." Send resume. Apply by June 1 to W.H. Thompson, General Manager, Box 1059, Pembroke NC 28372; tel. 919/521-2401.

# North Dakota

## Business and Industry

### Kelly Services, Inc.
More than 450 branches coast to coast, Puerto Rico, Canada, England and France. Temporary work assignments. Offers over 100 job classifications (office, marketing and light industrial assignments) to college students, teachers and other qualified people during summer breaks and year 'round. Kelly Services also has a special referral system that allows you to register at a Kelly office near your school then work near your home during summer recess—or register near your home then work on temporary assignments during the school year. Assignments available include clerks, typists, secretaries, keypunch operators, word processors, bookkeepers and a variety of marketing and light industrial. Offers flexible schedule with "attractive hourly pay rates equal to or higher than the accepted industry standards in most cities." No paycheck deductions except Social Security and income tax. No employment fee for temporary work. See the White Pages for the branch of Kelly Services nearest you. Apply in person or write to: Summer Employment, National Headquarters, Kelly Services, GPO 1179, Detroit MI 48266.

## Resorts, Ranches, Restaurants, Lodging

### Gold Seal Company
Located at Medora. Tourist attraction, resort. Openings for 150 college students, teachers and high school seniors from mid-May to early September. Needs chambermaids, cooks, waitresses, retail clerks, horse guiding-groundsmen, hourly minimum wage; supervisor, $600/month. Apply to Gold Seal Company, Box 198, Medora ND 58645.

## Summer Camps

### Triangle Y
Located on Lake Sakakawea at Garrison. YMCA coed camp for children ages 8-16. Openings for 18 college students and teachers from June 7 to August 16. Needs 12 cabin counselors, $675-800/season; directors: riding, boating, CIT, trips, $800-950/season; nurse, $750-900/season. Room and board provided. Apply to Triangle Y Camp, c/o Minot YMCA, Minot ND 58701.

# Ohio

## Business and Industry

### Davis Associates

Business opportunity in sales management and marketing. Openings for college undergraduates, graduates, teachers, retirees, couples or singles during the summer, year 'round, full time or part time. Needs salespersons for 250 consumer goods (home care, food supplements, household items including smoke alarms, mail order items and cosmetics) with opportunity to develop into area management. No experience necessary. Commission. In Ohio, apply to: R. Teigen, 6648 Michael Dr., Cincinnati OH 45243. Other area coordinators: (Kentucky) Joe Davis, 2449 Williams, Cincinnati OH 45212; (Indiana) C. Magee, Keyway Associates, 3530 Redwood Lane, Anderson IN 46012; (Illinois) J. Nethero, 7162 Juniper View, Cincinnati OH 45243.

### Kelly Services, Inc.

More than 450 branches coast to coast, Puerto Rico, Canada, England and France. Temporary work assignments. Offers over 100 job classifications (office, marketing and light industrial assignments) to college students, teachers and other qualified people during summer breaks and year 'round. Kelly Services also has a special referral system that allows you to register at a Kelly office near your school then work near your home during summer recess—or register near your home then work on temporary assignments during the school year. Assignments available include clerks, typists, secretaries, keypunch operators, word processors, bookkeepers and a variety of marketing and light industrial. Offers flexible schedule with "attractive hourly pay rates equal to or higher than the accepted industry standards in most cities." No paycheck deductions except Social Security and income tax. No employment fee for temporary work. See the White Pages for the branch of Kelly Services nearest you. Apply in person or write to: Summer Employment, National Headquarters, Kelly Services, GPO 1179, Detroit MI 48266.

## Commercial Attractions

### Cedar Point, Inc.

Located in Sandusky. Amusement/theme park, hotel, campgrounds, marina. Openings for 3,300 people from early May to mid-September. Needs ride hosts and hostesses, refreshment hosts and hostesses, sales cashiers, ticket takers, groundskeepers, craftsmen, lifeguards, waiters and waitresses, hotel personnel and many other positions. Salaries are hourly rate plus bonus. Dormitory and apartment style housing available for 1,900 people. Benefits include ride and beach privileges, dances, movies, etc. Send early for application and information to Personnel Department, Cedar Point, Inc., Sandusky OH 44870.

### Clay's Park Resort

Located in Canal Fulton. Campground, swimming lake, picnic grounds. Openings from June to September. Needs 25 lifeguards, college students, high school seniors, local applicants acceptable, $1.20-2/hour; 3 reservation/hosts, teacher or local applicant preferred, $2-3/hour; 1 waterfront director, college student or teacher preferred, $2.50-3.50/hour; 2 grounds and building maintenance, $2-3/hour. Will have need of general manager for water slide now being built; must have knowledge of crowd-control, general organization, money handling (teacher, coach). Apply to Michael Clay, Manager, Clay's Park Resort, Box 182, Canal Fulton OH 44614; tel. 216/854-3961 or 854-2102.

### Fantasy Farm Park & Motel

Located in Middletown. Family amusement park. Openings for college students and teachers from April 25 to September 10. Needs several food stand supervisors, 2 supervisors of ride operators. Pays $2.65-3/hour according to experience and ability. Must have some experience. Apply to Edgar Streifthau, Secretary-Treasurer, Fantasy Farm Park & Motel, Route 1, Middletown OH 45042; tel. 513/539-8864.

### Jungle Larry's African Safari

Located at Cedar Point in Sandusky, Ohio. Zoological park at resort. Openings for college students, ages 18 to 23, from May 1 through mid-September. Needs guides and animal keepers. All employees must be capable of public speaking and have a love for the animal kingdom and people. Room ($5) and board available at employee's expense. Apply by March 1 to Mrs. N.R. Tetzlaff, Dept. SED, Box 7129, Naples FL 33941.

# Resorts, Ranches, Restaurants, Lodging

### Eddie's Grill & Dairy Queen

Located at Geneva-on-the-Lake. Resort restaurant. 30th season. Openings for 24 college students and high school seniors from June 15 through Labor Day; some from May 26. Needs fountain workers, bus boys, waitresses, counter attendants, $100; fry cooks, clean-up help, $115-125. Salaries are weekly plus room and board. Apply by July 10 to Edward Sezon, 247 S. Broadway, Geneva OH 44041.

### The Lakeside Association

Located at Lakeside. Church, education, resort. Openings for college students and teachers from June 1 through Labor Day. Needs desk clerks, maids, gardeners, stage hands, tennis instructors, gatemen, youth director, lifeguards, miniature golf manager, miniature golf helper, playground supervisors, recreation directors, security guards, trailer park superviser. Salaries vary according to experience and position. Apply to The Lakeside Association, 236 Walnut Ave., Lakeside OH 43440.

# Summer Camps

### Campbell Gard

Located in Hamilton. YMCA coed camp. Openings for college students, teachers, high school seniors and foreign students from June 16 to August 2. Needs pool director, 4 swimming instructors, 8 specialty counselors, campcraft instructor, craft counselor, 6 general counselors. Salaries are $275-725. Send for application. Apply early (May deadline) to Larry DeLozier, Camp Director, YMCA Camp

Campbell Gard, Dept. SED, 105 N. 2nd St., Hamilton OH 45011.

## Cheerful

Located in Strongsville. Camp for physically and mentally handicapped children. Openings from late June through late August. Needs 14 counselors, directors: 2 waterfront (WSI), 2 arts and crafts, 2 nature, 2 recreation, $500 and up; nurse (RN), $700 and up. Salaries are for season. Apply to Director, Camp Cheerful, 15000 Cheerful Lane, Strongsville OH 44136.

## Conestoga

Located at Minerva. Coed camp for children ages 7-14. Openings for college students and teachers from June 26 to August 6. Needs 24 counselor-specialists, head counselor, nurse (RN). Salaries are $400-900/season. Send for resume or request application. Apply to James W. Barton, Camp Conestoga, Dept. SED, 1300 Lilly Rd. NW, Minerva OH 44657.

## Courageous

Located at Whitehouse, 12 miles southwest of Toledo. Residential camp for mentally retarded children and adults. Openings for college students, teachers, and high school seniors from June 11 through August 26. Needs 19 counselors, $440-550/season; crafts director, $660/season; nurse (RN), $1,210/season; cook, $990/season; waterfront director (WSI), $880/season; cook's helpers, $220-440/season; maintenance, $495/season; secretary, $495/season. Room and board provided. "We need mature individuals who are interested in doing hard but exciting work." Apply soon to Camp Courageous, 12701 Waterville, Swanton Rd., Whitehouse OH 43571.

## Echoing Hills

Located in Warsaw. Christian residential camp for physically handicapped and mentally retarded persons, ages 7-77. Openings for Christian college students and high school students from June to the end of August. Needs 10 senior counselors, snack shop manager, 10 junior counselors, 6 food service personnel. Room and board provided. Apply by May 1 to David Jarrett, Camp Director, Camp Echoing Hills, Route 2, Warsaw OH 43844.

## Libbey

Located in Defiance. Girl Scout camp for girls ages 7-17. Openings for college students, teachers and foreign students from June 15 to August 16. Needs 7 unit leaders, $600-800/season; 14 unit counselors, $375-550/season; pool director, business manager, $550-700/season; 3 pool assistants, $425-500/season; 5 kitchen staff, $340-1,000/season. Apply to Kathy Hay, Maumee Valley Girl Scout Council, 470 One Stranahan Sq., Toledo OH 43604.

## Riding Service

Locations at camps throughout Ohio. Riding service for camps; serves children ages 7-16. Openings from June 10 to August 20. "We need 20 horseback riding instructors, minimum age 18 or high school graduate, to live in and teach riding at Girl Scout, YMCA, 4H, and Camp Fire Camps in Ohio. You don't have to be expert riders or have past teaching experience to get this job. Some training is available." Salaries are $60-75/week plus room and board. Send for application and information. Apply to Joyce Summers, Program Director, Dept. SED, 38 E. 18th Ave., Columbus OH 43201.

## Ross Trails

Located in Ross. Girl Scout camp for ages 7-17. Openings for mid-August season. Needs counselors (high school graduates), $385 and up; unit leaders (21 years old), $525 and up. Also nurse; WSIs for pool, lake, small crafts; counselors for riding, biking, backpacking and primitive camping. Room and board provided. Eager to hire staff from out-of-state, Girl Scout experience helpful but not necessary. Apply by May 30 to Camp Administrator, Great Rivers Girl Scout Council, Dept. SED, 4930 Cornell Rd., Cincinnati OH 45242.

## Swoneky

Located north of Cincinnati. Salvation Army resident Christian camp. Openings for college students from June 13 through August 26. Needs senior counselors, cooks, nurse (RN), lifeguards-WSI; specialty counselors for crafts, nature, $450-750. Provides food, lodging and laundry services. Apply to Captain Lester L. Baker, Jr., The Salvation Army, 114 E. Central Pkwy., Cincinnati OH 45210.

## Valley Vista Sports Camp

Located in Bainbridge. Summer sports camp for boys ages 8-18; facilities include 5 baseball diamonds (3 lighted), 5 basketball courts, 3 lighted tennis courts, 4 dormitories and mess hall. Openings starting June 1 for 8 college athletes to serve as counselors in the areas of baseball and basketball, $800-1,200/season plus room and board. Applicants will be "enforcing strict set of discipline rules, and must be understanding and able to work with younger kids." Send resume or application request. Apply by May 1 to Valley Vista Corp., c/o James Dunkle, Director, Box 524, Bainbridge OH 45612; tel. 614/634-2233.

## Wakatomika

Located in Fallsburg. Girl Scout camp for ages 6-17. Openings for college students and teachers from June 10 to August 5. Needs 5 unit leaders, 15 assistant unit leaders, 3 waterfront assistants, 2 dietitians, nurse. Apply by April 15 to Director, Camp Wakatomika, 1215 Newark Rd., Zanesville OH 43701.

## Whip-Poor-Will Hills

Located in Morrow. Girl Scout camp. Openings for college students, teachers, high school seniors and foreign students from June 15 to August 17. Needs 20 counselors, $450-750/season; 5 waterfront staff (WSI), $500-750/season; nature and arts program specialist, $450-750/season; 5 cooks and kitchen staff, $60-100/week. Send resume or application request. Apply to Camp Director, Buckeye Trails Girl Scout Council, Dept. SED, 184 Salem Ave., Dayton OH 45406.

## Alfred L. Willson

Located in Bellefontaine. YMCA coed camp. Openings for college students, teachers and high school seniors from June 8 to August 9. Needs 16 resident-program-general counselors, 10 special program counselors (canoe, bicycling, minibike, tripping, horsemanship), $45-80/week; special area directors for arts and crafts, nature, swimming, boating, horsemanship, $45-80/week; 10 kitchen and maintenance workers—cooks, dishwashers, general maintenance skills,

$20-80/week. Room and board provided. Work-study students welcome. Apply by April to Bruce Boyer, Dept. SED, 40 W. Long St., Columbus OH 43215.

### Wyandot
Located at Rockbridge. Resident Camp Fire Girls camp for ages 6-18. Openings mid-June through mid-August. Needs business manager, college student or teacher preferred, $500-850/season; nurse (RN), $500-700/season; 3 waterfront staff (WSI), college students, teachers, high school seniors, foreign students, local applicants; 20 specialty counselors, $300-475/season; 2 cooks $650-800/season. Send request for application. Apply by March 31 to Brooke Ketner, Camping Specialist, Columbus Area Council of Camp Fire Girls, Inc., 718 S. High St., Columbus OH 43206; tel. 614/443-9713.

# Oklahoma

## Business and Industry

### Kelly Services, Inc.
More than 450 branches coast to coast, Puerto Rico, Canada, England and France. Temporary work assignments. Offers over 100 job classifications (office, marketing and light industrial assignments) to college students, teachers and other qualified people during summer breaks and year 'round. Kelly Services also has a special referral system that allows you to register at a Kelly office near your school then work near your home during summer recess—or register near your home then work on temporary assignments during the school year. Assignments available include clerks, typists, secretaries, keypunch operators, word processors, bookkeepers and a variety of marketing and light industrial. Offers flexible schedule with "attractive hourly pay rates equal to or higher than the accepted industry standards in most cities." No paycheck deductions except Social Security and income tax. No employment fee for temporary work. See the White Pages for the branch of Kelly Services nearest you. Apply in person or write to: Summer Employment, National Headquarters, Kelly Services, GPO 1179, Detroit MI 48266.

### Temp Force
Temporary office personnel contractor. Openings for college students, teachers and high school seniors during vacations and holidays. Needs secretaries, typists, stenographers, clericals and accountants. Salaries based upon experience. Apply to Temp Force, 4801 Classen Blvd., Suite 137, Oklahoma City OK 73118, tel. 405/843-9496; 5700 E. 61st St., Tulsa OK 74136, tel. 918/494-3618.

## Summer Camps

### Cimarron
Located in Oklahoma City. Camp Fire camp for girls, grades 2-12. Openings from early-June to late-July. Needs CIT director, 3 riding instructors, waterfront director, 2 waterfront counselors and 10 general cabin counselors for archery, riflery, sports and games, crafts and nature. Send resume or request application. Apply by early

March to Meredith E. Maddux, Camp Director, Camp Cimarron, 717 NE 21st St., Oklahoma City OK 73105; tel. 405/524-2255.

### Tiawah Hills Guest Ranch
Located in Claremore. Coed camp for ages 8-14. Openings for college students and teachers from approximately June 1 to August 10. Needs cabin/riding counselors; specialty counselor for music, WSI, games; kitchen helper. Salaries are $350-800 plus room and board. Apply by April 15 to Barbara Wells Turnbull, Tiawah Hills Ranch, RFD 7, Box 225, Claremore OK 74017; tel. 918/341-3364.

# Oregon

## Business and Industry

### Kelly Services, Inc.
More than 450 branches coast to coast, Puerto Rico, Canada, England and France. Temporary work assignments. Offers over 100 job classifications (office, marketing and light industrial assignments) to college students, teachers and other qualified people during summer breaks and year 'round. Kelly Services also has a special referral system that allows you to register at a Kelly office near your school then work near your home during summer recess—or register near your home then work on temporary assignments during the school year. Assignments available include clerks, typists, secretaries, keypunch operators, word processors, bookkeepers and a variety of marketing and light industrial. Offers flexible schedule with "attractive hourly pay rates equal to or higher than the accepted industry standards in most cities." No paycheck deductions except Social Security and income tax. No employment fee for temporary work. See the White Pages for the branch of Kelly Services nearest you. Apply in person or write to: Summer Employment, National Headquarters, Kelly Services, GPO 1179, Detroit MI 48266.

## Resorts, Ranches, Restaurants, Lodging

### Oregon Caves
Located 50 miles from Grants Pass. Family resort, national monument. Openings for college students, from May 1 or June 25 to September 10. Needs 20 cave guides, 3 bell hops, 3 desk clerks, 9 kitchen help, 9 buffet help, 7 gift store help, 3 child care persons, 9 coffee shop help, waiters and waitresses. Pays federal minimum wage. Apply by May to Chuck Quigley, Manager, Oregon Caves Chateau, Box 151, Grants Pass OR 97526.

### Singing Springs
Located at Agness. Summer resort. Openings for college students from May through September. Needs waiters, bus boys, kitchen helpers, $195 plus tips; 2 cook's helpers, $300. Salaries are monthly plus room and board, travel allowance

west of the Mississippi. Include stamped return envelope. Apply to Rudy Valente, Singing Springs Resort, Agness OR 97406.

### Sunriver Properties, Inc.

Located in Sunriver. Family resort. Resort is open year-round, busiest season is summer. Positions start early May to mid-June and extend through September and October. Needs cooks ($150-250/week), pantry helpers ($140/week), buspersons ($120 plus tips/week), tennis courts/monitors ($130/week), golf course/cart rental/marshall ($120/week), maids ($120/week), laundry attendants ($130/week), housemen ($120/week), janitors ($130/week), local applicants, college students, teachers, high school seniors all acceptable; cashiers/hostesses ($130/week), waiters/waitresses ($120 plus tips/week), cocktail waitresses ($120 plus tips/week), bartenders ($160 plus tips/week), clerks/cashiers ($140-200/week), bell persons ($120 plus tips/week), PBX operators ($130/week), reservations clerks ($150/week), night auditors ($180/week), grounds maintenance ($150/week), golf course maintenance ($170/week), stables/trail guides ($130/week), swimming pool/guards-instructors ($130/week), marina/boatmen ($130/week), airport/linemen ($130/week), nature center/ naturalist assistant ($130/week), local applicants, college students, teachers all acceptable. Wages quoted are averages and are not to be construed as actual wages. "A personal interview is a prerequisite for employment. Applicants should submit resumes by January, with a request for an interview date. Employee housing is available in surrounding area, and in Bend, Oregon, 15 miles north of Sunriver. Applicants should have a reliable means of transportation. Transportation is supplied, at no charge, for housekeeping employees *only.* Applicants with past resort experience are preferred; however, persons with public contact experience are favorably considered." Apply to Personnel Manager, Sunriver Properties, Inc., Sunriver OR 97701; tel. 503/593-1221, ext. 288.

### Timberline Lodge

Located in Government Camp. Resort. Needs 6-8 room attendants, $3/hour minimum wage plus gratuities; 6 bus persons (dining room), $2.65/hour plus meals and gratuities. Work any time in May, earliest possible in June until *after* Labor Day. "Lodge does not provide living quarters for staff. Our employees (80% students) live in village of Government Camp (6 miles from lodge) or other villages down the road. Company bus transportation provided from and to Government Camp." Apply to Pamela Ashland, Personnel Supervisor, Timberline Lodge, Government Camp OR 97028; tel. 503/231-5400.

# Summer Camps

### Cleawox

Located in Florence, on a fresh water lake, one mile from the Pacific Ocean in the Dunes Recreational Area. Girl Scout camp for ages 8-15. Openings from mid-June to mid-August. Needs assistant director, waterfront director, waterfront assistant, unit leaders, unit assistants, assistant cook, nurse, kitchen aides. Minimum age 18 or high school graduate. Salary range $250-700. Apply by March 1 to Karin L. Carlson, Western Rivers Girl Scout Council, 2055 Patterson, Room A, Eugene OR 97405.

## Collins
Located in Portland. YMCA coed recreational camp for children, ages 8-12. Openings July and August. Needs 4 unit directors, 1 waterfront, 1 craft specialist, college students preferred, $100-125/week; 16 cabin counselors, local applicants, college students, foreign students, $75/week. Room and board provided. Apply by April 30 to Robert L. Smith, Camp Administrator, YMCA Camp Collins, 2831 SW Barbur Blvd., Portland OR 97201; tel. 503/223-9622.

## Kilowan
Located in Salem, 27 miles west in Coast Range foothills. Camp Fire Girls camp. Openings for 40 college students, teachers and foreign students from June 9 to August 16. Needs cabin counselors, unit directors, waterfront director, horse director, nurse (RN). Salaries are $300-900. Apply by May 1 to Missy Tangeman, Camp Director, Camp Kilowan, Willamette Council of Camp Fire Girls, Box 2352, Salem OR 97308.

## Namanu
Located in Sandy. Camp Fire Girl camp. Openings for 70 college students and teachers from approximately June 15 to August 25. Needs cabin counselors; directors: unit, activity, CIT, assistant camp; instructors for riding, archery; waterfront staff, cooks, $450-1,200. Room and board provided. Apply to Camp Namanu, 718 W. Burnside, Suite 410, Portland OR 97209.

## Tyee
Located at Oakland. Camp Fire Girls camp. Openings from late June to early August. Needs 8 cabin counselors, $250-300; naturalist, $300; waterfront director (WSI), $400; assistant waterfront, $270; nurse, cook, $600. Salaries are seasonal and are subject to change. Apply early to Camp Director, Umpqua Council Camp Fire Girls, 2035 NE Stephens, Roseburg OR 97470.

## Westwind
Located in Otis. YWCA camp for girls and coeds, ages 8-17; family, all ages, mother-child and single parent-child, ages 3 and up. Openings for college students, teachers and foreign students. Needs riding and waterfront staff, other specialists and kitchen staff from early June to late August; cabin counselors from mid-June to late August. Needs 9 cabin counselors; instructors: riding, 3 riding assistants, 2 waterfront (familiar with motor boats and tides), small craft; directors: seasonal director, assistant camp; specialty counselors: nature (with emphasis on marine biology), archery, CIT, arts and crafts; head cook, 2 assistants, nurse. Apply to Camp Administrator, YWCA, 1111 SW 10th St., Portland OR 97205.

# Pennsylvania

## Business and Industry

### Kelly Services, Inc.
More than 450 branches coast to coast, Puerto Rico, Canada, England and France. Temporary work assignments. Offers over 100 job classifications (office,

marketing and light industrial assignments) to college students, teachers and other qualified people during summer breaks and year 'round. Kelly Services also has a special referral system that allows you to register at a Kelly office near your school then work near your home during summer recess—or register near your home then work on temporary assignments during the school year. Assignments available include clerks, typists, secretaries, keypunch operators, word processors, bookkeepers and a variety of marketing and light industrial. Offers flexible schedule with "attractive hourly pay rates equal to or higher than the accepted industry standards in most cities." No paycheck deductions except Social Security and income tax. No employment fee for temporary work. See the White Pages for the branch of Kelly Services nearest you. Apply in person or write to: Summer Employment, National Headquarters, Kelly Services, GPO 1179, Detroit MI 48266.

**Mature Temps Inc.**
Located in Philadelphia. National temporary employment service. Openings for college students, teachers, high school seniors, local applicants and foreign students from May to September or year-round. Needs secretaries, clerks, typists, bookkeepers, stenographers, accountants, demonstrators and marketing research persons. High hourly rates based on skills. Apply to Mature Temps Inc., 1700 Market St., Suite 1920, Philadelphia PA 19103, tel. 215/665-1150; One Plymouth Meeting Mall, Suite 10, Plymouth Meeting PA 19462, tel. 215/825-4400; GSB Building, Suite 617, Bala Cynwyd PA 19004, tel. 215/667-1565; #48 Great Valley Center, 81 Lancaster Ave., Malvern PA 19355, tel. 215/644-5860.

**Temp Force**
Temporary office personnel contractor. Openings for college students, teachers and high school seniors during vacations and holidays. Needs secretaries, typists, stenographers, clericals and accountants. Salaries based upon experience. Apply to Temp Force: 1 Bala Cynwyd Plaza, Bala Cynwyd PA 19004, tel. 215/667-3023; 1520 Market St., Camp Hill PA 17011, tel. 717/761-8096; 200 York St., Hanover PA 17331, tel. 717/632-5400; Fox Pavilion, Suite 737, Jenkintown PA 19046, tel. 215/885-4336; 729 DeKalb Pike, King of Prussia PA 19406, tel. 215/265-4844; 227 N. Duke St., Lancaster PA 17602, tel. 717/394-7180; 815 Cumberland St., Lebanon PA 17042, tel. 717/273-8813; 130 N. 5th St., Reading PA 19601, tel. 215/374-3120; 428 Market St., Williamsport PA 17701, tel. 717/323-9443; 1632 E. Market St., York PA 17331, tel. 717/843-0031.

**Temporaries, Inc.**
Located in Pittsburgh. Office positions. Secretaries, typists, receptionists, clerks, $3.00-4.50/hour, 1 year office experience required. Positions open year 'round. Apply to Temporaries, Inc., 23rd Floor, Pittsburgh National Bank Bldg., 5th Wood St., Pittsburgh PA 15222.

# Commercial Attractions

**Conneaut Lake Park, Inc.**
**Fairyland Forest**
Resort and amusement park, children's theme park. Openings for college students, teachers and high school seniors from Memorial Day weekend to Labor Day. Needs 50 ride operators, 50 game operators, 5 lifeguards, 50 waiters and

waitresses, 40 kitchen help, 35 clerks, 20 cashiers, 50 concession workers, 20 hotel helpers and others. Free room, beach privileges and ride tickets to all employees. Apply to Personnel Manager, Conneaut Lake Park, Inc., Conneaut Lake Park PA 16316.

# Expeditions, Guide Trips

## Mountain Streams and Trails Outfitters

Located in Ohiopyle. Whitewater rafting. Openings from April to September. Needs several river guides (minimum age 18) for trips on the Youghogheny, Cheat, and Gauley Rivers, $150-250/week. Red Cross cards for advanced lifesaving, first aid and CPR required. "We want competent kayakers and rafters who enjoy working with people. Room and kitchen facilities provided." Apply to John Lichter, Personnel Manager, Box 106, Ohiopyle PA 15470; 412/329-4730.

## Wilderness Voyageurs, Inc.

Located in Ohiopyle, in Ohiopyle State Park. Guided river trips; whitewater rafting. Openings for college students, teachers, high school seniors, foreign students and local applicants from May 1 to October 1. Needs 16 guides, $110-175/week plus room; 3 secretaries, $110-140/week plus room. Raft and kayak guides must be 18 years of age or older, have Red Cross Advanced First Aid training or equivalent; Red Cross Advanced Lifesaving training or equivalent; and previous experience in working with people. Whitewater and/or flatwater paddling experience preferred but not necessary. Training program provided. Apply by June 1 to Personnel Manager, Wilderness Voyageurs, Inc., Box 97, Ohiopyle PA 15470; tel. 412/329-5517.

# Resorts, Ranches, Restaurants, Lodging

## Lake Mount Farm

Located at Saylorsburg. Guest, farm resort. Openings from June 30 to September 5. Needs lifeguard, chambermaid, $70; 3 waitresses, $65. Apply to Mrs. Russell Young, Dept. SED, Lake Mount Farm, Box 66, Saylorsburg PA 18353.

# Summer Camps

## Akiba

Located in Reeders, near Stroudsburg. Private brother-sister camp for children ages 5-16. Openings for college students and teachers from approximately June 25 to August 21. Needs 50 cabin counselors; specialty counselors for riflery, dramatics, overnight, waterskiing, archery, arts and crafts, tennis, assistant director, athletic assistant, waterfront assistant; nurses, kitchen manager. Includes room and board. Apply to Director, Camp Akiba, Box 400, Dept. SED, Bala-Cynwyd PA 19004.

## Association of Independent Camps

Located throughout Pennsylvania. Openings at 100 children's (ages 6-16) summer camps located in New England and Middle Atlantic States. Needs head counselors, group leaders, general and all specialty counselors. Includes room and board. Apply by July to Association of Independent Camps, Dept. SED, 55 W. 42nd St., New York NY 10036; tel. 212/695-2656.

## Beacon Lodge Camp For The Blind

Located in Mt. Union. Children (ages 6-18) and adults (18-senior citizens). Openings for 25 college students and teachers during the summer. Needs assistant camp director, unit director for adult camp, unit director for children's camp, general counselors; specialty counselors for waterfront (WSI), music, arts and crafts, ceramics, nature; secretary, nurse (RN); canteen operators, supervisors: 2 cleaning, 2 dining room. Salaries based on age, experience and education. Includes room and board. Apply by April 15 to Carl Shoemaker, Coordinator, Beacon Lodge Camp for the Blind, Dept. SED, Box 428, Lewistown PA 17044.

## Blue Mountain Camp

Located in Hamburg. YWCA residential camp for girls. Openings for college students and teachers from June 15 to August 23. Needs 1 horseback riding instructor and 1 waterfront director, $700/season; 1 program director, $650/season; 1 business manager, $500/season; 16 general counselors, $100-450/season; 1 CIT director, $500/season. Apply by April 1980 to Camp Director, YWCA, 8th and Washington St., Reading PA 19601; tel. 215/376-7317.

## Blue Ridge
## Equinunk

Located in Equinunk, Pennsylvania. Member ACA. Openings for college students and teachers from July 1 to August 26. Needs instructors: 10 water safety (ARC), 4 smallcraft (ARC), 10 tennis, 2 golf, 10 physical education, 2 music, 2 dramatics, gymnastics, 2 arts and crafts, photography, science, pioneering, riding; 4 nurses (RN). Salaries are $400 and up. Apply April 1 to Martin Gelobter, 20 Burton Ave., Woodmere NY 11598.

## Brandywine Valley YMCA Camps

Located in Downingtown. Camp Lookout is a traditional resident camp for children ages 7-12; Circle-Y Ranch is a Western style horseback riding camp for children ages 10-16; Camp Dwight is a teenage camp featuring out-trips in canoeing, backpacking, caving and rock climbing. "Clientele is generally from Philadelphia area, both urban and suburban, ages 7-16. There are 4 2-week sessions campers may choose from." Openings from June 23 through August 23. Needs 15 cabin counselors/instructors (experienced with horses for Circle-Y, practical experience in activities listed above for Camp Dwight), college students preferred, $450-600/season; 10 assistant counselors/instructors, high school students preferred, $270/season. Room and board provided. "We generally hire staff first on their ability to relate to the campers they will be working with." Send for application to Jack Prior, Executive Director, Dept. SED, Box 205, Rt. 322, Downingtown PA 19335; tel. 215/269-0787.

## Bryn Mawr Lake Camp

Located in Honesdale. Girls camp for ages 6-16; family weekends in June; 59th year. Openings for men and women, college students and teachers, in all activity areas applicable to summer camp programming, including land and water sports;

music and drama; jewelry, ceramics, leather; the arts; nature; camping; sailing; waterskiing; English riding; specializing in tennis and gymnastics. Minimum age 19 years. Salaries are $400-1,500 plus room and board. "Insurance policy costs $20." Apply by April 1 to Herb Kutzen, 81 Falmouth St., Short Hills NJ 07078; tel. 201/467-3518.

## Bucoco—Scout Camp

Located in Slippery Rock. Openings for college students and teachers with Boy Scout background, from late June to mid-August. Needs specialists for aquatics, archery, camping and outdoor skills, canoeing, ecology, and conservation, field sports, handicrafts and riflery. Also needs qualified first aid personnel (EMTs, RNs, Advanced Red Cross First Aider), camp directors, program director, provisional scoutmasters, cooks, dishwashers, and clerks. Salaries are $300-1,000/season depending on position and experience. Room and board provided. Apply to Program Director, Moraine Trails Council, Boy Scouts of America, 830 Morton Ave. Ext., Butler PA 16001.

## Chase Tennis Center

Located in Westtown. Private coed tennis camp; the country's oldest. Openings for college students, teachers and foreign students from early to mid-June to late August. Needs 3 tennis instructors (all proficient instructor/counselors), $400-800; assistant camp director, nurse, up to $1,000. Apply early to Neil Chase, Box 1446, Manchester MA 01944.

## Choconut

Located in Friendsville, 17 miles south of Binghamton, New York, on a private, natural lake. Boys camp for ages 9-14; 8-week camp, 9-week camp season (June 25 to August 25). Openings for 10-15 college students and teachers, minimum age 19. Needs counselors for 50-60 campers; supervise basic outdoor activities to help boys help themselves gain self-reliance. High salaries for the right persons and extra pay for additional work before and/or after camp. Especially needed are those with carpentry skills and work-project ability and waterfront (WSI); also natural science, farm animal care, campcraft, nurse (RN), and general counselors. "Most jobs are filled by April, but I sometimes need male personnel all the way until late June." To apply write S. Hamill Horne, Box 33D, Gladwyne PA 19035.

## College Settlement

Located in Horsham. Agency/environmental studies camp for coeds, ages 7-12. Openings from June 27 to August 24. Needs 10 cabin counselors, college students preferred, $650 base/season; 2 unit leaders, teachers preferred, $1,000 base/season; 2 waterfront (WSI), 2 environmentalists, college students and teachers preferred, $800/season; 1 registered nurse, $1,500/season. Full job

**All employers listed in *SED* agreed to be in the book providing that they would be contacted in exactly the way they specify. Read carefully all details in each listing on how to apply.**

descriptions available upon request. "Applications are available upon request and should be returned no later than April 1, if possible. 130 campers, total staff 47 persons, 57 years in operation. Camp is a twelve months operation." Apply to Leonard C. Ferguson, Executive Director, College Settlement Camps, 600 Witmer Rd., Horsham PA 19044; tel. 214/542-7974.

## Conshatawba

Located in Summerhill on 300 wooded acres. Girl Scout resident camp for girls ages 6-10; facility includes platform tents and pool. Openings for college students, teachers and high school graduates from mid-June to mid-August. Needs camp director, $1,000-1,700; business manager, $500-800; 6 troop leaders, $400-750; 15 troop assistants, $300-500; waterfront director (WSI), $500-750; 5 waterfront assistants (SLS), $250-400; nurse (RN or LPN), $400-800; food supervisor, $500-800; cook, $300-700; 3 kitchen aides (high school students), $200-350. Room and board provided. Special program areas generally include backpacking, cycling and horse ranch. Apply by May 15 to Talus Rock Girl Scout Council, Dept. SED, 111 Walnut St., Johnstown PA 15901.

## Echo Trail, Furnace Hills

Located in southcentral Pennsylvania. Girl Scout camp. Openings for 90 students and teachers, minimum age 18, from mid-June to mid-August. Needs program directors, business manager, waterfront directors and assistants, unit leaders and assistants; program specialists in the performing arts, folk arts, nature, canoeing and sailing, backpacking, primitive camping, aquatics, English riding; nurses, head and assistant cooks. Salaries are $450-1,000/season. An equal opportunity employer. Apply by April 1 to Educational Services Director, Penn Laurel Girl Scout Council, Inc., 1600 Mt. Zion Rd., York PA 17402.

## Freedom Valley Girl Scout Council

Located in Valley Forge, 30 miles from Philadelphia in Montgomery County. 3 Girl Scout resident camps; 8-week season for girls ages 6-17. Openings for college students, teachers, local applicants and high school seniors (for horseback riding only) from mid-June to mid-August. Needs 3 program/assistant directors, age 23 or older, to assist and supervise younger staff members, creative programs, $700-900/season; 15 waterfront/boating/WSI instructors to instruct in swimming lessons, diving, row boats, canoes, and other pool activities, $450-800/season; 6 riding director/instructors for English riding program, $450-900/season; 50 counselors/trip leaders for 4 or 8 weeks, $400-800/season (backpacking, cycle and canoe leaders must be 21); 3 business managers, 21 or older, with driver's license, $700-900/season; 3 nurses, 21 or older, RN, graduating RN student or LPN, $900-1,100/season. "Apply as early as possible for best selection for for pre-camp planning. Request application, arrange for interview and negotiate for position and salary." Apply to Agnes M. Hepler, Director of Camping, Freedom Valley Girl Scout Council, Dept. SED, Valley Forge PA 19482; tel. 215/666-6141.

## Girl Scouts of Southwestern Pennsylvania

Located near Pittsburgh. Camps Henry Kaufmann, near Ligonier; Redwing, near Butler; Youghahela, near McKeesport. Openings for college students, teachers and high school students from June 15 to August 17. Needs 50 unit assistants, $300-400; 15 unit leaders, $440-600; 9 waterfront assistants and directors (WSI & SLS), $360-560; 4 assistant directors and program directors, $850-950; 4

maintenance assistants, $280-400; 1 food program director, $1,000-1,400; 2 kitchen managers, $630-720; 10 cooks, $495-585; 10 program specialists, $320-480; 4 CIT instructors and assistants, $360-700; 2 nurses (RN, LPN), $560-640. Send for application. Apply by May to Camping Director, Girl Scouts of Southwestern Pennsylvania, Dept. SED, 327 5th Ave., Pittsburgh PA 15222.

## Helping Hands Inc. Day Camp
Located in Palm. Day camp with one week residential, for mentally, physically and emotionally handicapped persons, ages 5-35, of nearby communities. Openings from June to August. Needs 8 senior counselors (college students, teachers), $95/week; 2 activity coordinators to plan arts, crafts and music activities (college students, teachers), $95/week; 8 junior counselors (college students, high school students), $75/week; secretary (college students, teacher, local applicant), $100/week. "Staff can room for 8 weeks at camp at minimal fee. Applicant must be willing to work hard and care for campers." Send for application or call. Apply by May 10 to Beverly Farkas, Executive Director, or Janis Weldon, Program Director, Dept. SED, Ziegler Road, Palm PA 18070; tel. 215/679-8885.

## Hidden Valley
Located in Equinunk. Girl Scout camp for girls ages 6-17. Openings from June 20 to August 17. Needs 1 waterfront director (WSI), 3 waterfront assistants (senior life), 10 unit leaders, 20 unit assistants, 3 kitchen aides, college students and teachers preferred. Platform tents with cots provided. "Camp is located on 1,200 acres in Pocono Mountains. Camp skills, backpacking, canoeing and horseback riding are part of the program. Counselors are housed in platform tents." Apply by June to Kay Coriell, Camping Services Manager, Hidden Valley Camp, Rolling Hills Girl Scout Council, Bridgewater NJ 08807; tel. 201/725-1226.

## Hugh Beaver
Located at Bushkill, Pennsylvania, in the Pocono Mountains. Coed camp, ages 6 to 12. Openings for college students and teachers. Needs instructors in riflery, arts and crafts, Indian lore, camp craft, athletics, archery, waterfront, $50-80; assistant camp director, $75-120. Apply to Director, Dept. SED, Camp Hugh Beaver, YMCA, 109 N. 3rd St., Easton PA 18042.

## Ken-Crest
Located in Mont Clare. Coed camp for mentally retarded children and adults, ages 8 and up. Openings for college students and teachers from end of June through mid-August, for 7 weeks. Needs camp coordinator, salary open; camp nurse, $85-100; 15 tent counselors, $75-85; specialty counselors for arts and crafts, music, swimming (WSI), recreation, $80-90; swimming (SLS), $75-85. Salaries are weekly. Counselors sleep either in tents or cabins on bunks. Campers sleep in same area as counselors. Tents are placed on platforms off the ground. Apply by May 1 to Camp Director, Ken-Crest Camp, Dept. SED, Route 29, Mont Clare PA 19453.

## Laughing Waters
## Indian Run
Laughing Waters located in Gilbertsville and Indian Run located in Glenmoore. Girl Scout camps for girls, ages 7-17. Openings for college students, teachers and foreign students, minimum age 18, from approximately June 20 to August 20.

Needs general counselors, WSI, SCI, specialists (arts, sports, environmental education), tripping staff (bike, canoe, backpacking). Salaries are $500-850/season. Nurses (RN) and administration staff salaries higher. "Racially and economically integrated urban camper population. Live in tents." Apply by March 30 to Camping Services Director, Girl Scouts of Greater Philadelphia, 1411 Walnut St., Philadelphia PA 19102.

## Lee Mar
Located in Lackawaxen. Camp for educable mentally retarded and neurologically impaired. Openings for college students, teachers and foreign students from June 25 to August 26. Needs 6 teacher-counselors, 8 general counselors; specialty counselors; 3 arts and crafts, 2 music, 2 nature; 6 speech therapists, 4 waterfront instructors; 4 nurses (RN). Salaries are commensurate with experience and maturity, includes room and board. Apply by May to Mrs. Lee Morrone, 985 E. 24th St., Brooklyn NY 11210.

## Log-N-Twig
Located in Dingmans Ferry. Coed Jewish camp. Openings for college students from June 22 to August 22. Needs counselors: 25 general, 4 swimming (WSI), 12 sports, 2 arts and crafts; 2 nurses (RN). Salaries commensurate with experience and maturity. Apply to Dr. Morton "Moe" Tener, 7700 Doe Lane, Laverock PA 19118; tel. 215/887-9367.

## Mosey Wood
## Wood Haven
Mosey Wood is located in White Haven; Wood Haven located in Pine Grove. Girl Scout resident camps, ages 6-17. Openings for college students and teachers from June 15 to August 17. Needs 12 unit leaders, $540-900/season; 30 unit counselors, $400-600/season; 2 waterfront directors (WSI), $630-1,000/season; 5 waterfront assistants (WSI), $450-600; 1 sailing instructor, $450-650/season; 2 canoeing instructors, $450-650/season; and 4 riding instructors, $500-1,000/season. Salaries include room and board. Apply by May 30 to Camp Administrator, Great Valley Girl Scout Council, 2633 Moravian Ave., Allentown PA 18103; tel. 215/791-2411.

## Mount Lake
Located in Fannettsburg. Coed camp for ages 6-16. Openings for college students, teachers and foreign students from June 19 to August 16. Needs 10 general counselors, $700/season; 2 WSI $800/season; 2 cooks, $150/week; nurse (RN), $120/week. Salaries include room and board. Apply by May 1 to James M. Close, Mt. Lake Camp, Box 208, Enola PA 17025.

## Oneka
Located in Tafton, in the Pocono Mountains. Private camp for girls ages 7-16. Openings for college students from June 26 to August 18. Needs specialty counselors: 6 swimming, 6 boating, 8 land sports, $400-600; 4 crafts, $300-500. Salaries include room and board. Apply by June to Director, Camp Oneka, 2508 Highland Ave., Broomall PA 19008.

**William Penn**

Located in East Stroudsburg. Resident camp sponsored by the Philadelphia Department of Recreation. Openings for college students, teachers, high school seniors and foreign students from June 19 to August 19. Needs 16 junior counselors, $200/season; 26 counselors, $300/season; 13 senior counselors, $400/season, 13 unit leaders, $800/season; 10 specialists for crafts, nature, waterfront, pioneering, $700-1,000/season; 2 nurses (RN or LPN), $950/season; 8 food service workers, $600/season; third cook, $1,000/season. Salaries include room and board. Apply by March 15 to Henry E. Windish, Director, Camp William Penn, 1450 Municipal Services Bldg., Philadelphia PA 19107.

**Pine Forest, Coed**
**Timber Tops, Girls**
**Lake Owego, Boys**

Three private camps in northeastern Pennsylvania, in the Poconos. Good food, clean air, nice people. Openings from June 25 to August 22. Needs specialty counselors (minimum age 19) for canoe tripping, athletics, archery rock climbing, riflery, nature, waterfront (WSI), scouting, tennis, drama; kitchen staff. Apply by June 1 to Marvin N. Black, 110-A Benson, East Jenkintown PA 19046.

**Pocono Highland Camps**

Located in Marshalls Creek. Coed camp. Openings for college students, teachers and foreign students from June 25 to August 22. Needs specialty counselors for all land sports, water safety (ARC), smallcraft, sailing, waterskiing, golf, arts and crafts, dramatics, dancing, riflery, riding, tennis, ham radio, pioneering, archery, canoeing, nature, music, song leading, basketball, baseball, soccer, karate, judo, bowling, fencing, photography, wrestling; unit leaders; doctor; nurse (RN). Excellent salaries. Apply to Louis Weinberg, Pocono Highland Camp, 6528 Castor Ave., Philadelphia PA 19149.

**Pocono Ridge**

Located in South Sterling, Pennsylvania. Coed camp for ages 7-16. Openings for college students or teachers, male or female from June 25 to August 25. Needs 12 general counselors with specialty such as WSI, sailing, NRA instructor, waterskiing, arts and crafts, drama, team sports, horseback riding, golf and outdoor camping. "Prefer nonsmokers—should have driver's license." Salaries are $350-800. Apply by March 1 to T. Santay, Director, Pocono Ridge, RD 2, Box 458, Jamesburg NJ 08831.

**Rock Creek Farm**

Located in the Blue Ridge Mountains. Camp for children, ages 6-17, with learning disabilities or emotional problems. Openings for college students and teachers from June 20 to August 20. Needs specialty counselors: music, construction, arts and crafts, forestry, auto mechanics, swimming, nature, woodworking. Also needs group counselors and nurse. Excellent salaries; includes room and board. Apply by May to Bernard Wray, Rock Creek Farm, RD 1, Thompson PA 18465; tel. 717/756-2706.

**Sun Mountain**

Located in Shawnee-On-Delaware. Camp for retarded and physically handicapped people, ages 6-adult. Openings for college students and teachers from the end of June to the end of August. Needs 80 counselors, $300 and up/season; 3 nurses, $600 and up/season. Salaries include room and board. Apply to Camp Sun Mountain, Box 175, Dept. SED, Bala-Cynwyd PA 19004.

## Susquehannock

Located in Brackney, in Susquehanna County, 15 miles south of Binghamton, New York. Private boys camp. Openings for college students and teachers from approximately June 21 to August 24. Needs athletic counselors for basketball, baseball, soccer, football, track, lacrosse, wrestling; instructors for waterfront-canoeing, waterfront-sailing, lacrosse; specialty counselors: tennis, waterfront (WSI), campcraft and tripping, arts and crafts, $500-800; English riding assistant, $450-650; nurse (RN), $900. Apply to E.H. Shafer, Director, Camp Susquehannock, Box 71, Brackney PA 18812; tel. 717/967-2323.

## Swago
## Swatonah

Located in Damascus. Swago: camp for boys, ages 6-16; Swatonah: camp for girls, ages 6-16. Openings for college students, minimum sophomore, from June 27 to August 26. Needs counselors for waterfront (WSI), gymnastics, ceramics, nature, waterskiing, dance, all sports, archery, riflery, fencing, photography, ham radio; 4 RNs, doctor (MD). Salaries depend on experience, ability and education. Apply to David Blumstein, 1410 E. 42nd St., Brooklyn NY 11210.

## Tegawitha

Located in Tobyhanna. Camp for girls, ages 6-16. Openings for college students and teachers from June 25 to August 12. Needs 10 waterfront counselors, $500-700/season; 10 athletic counselors, $450-675/season; 2 campcraft counselors, 2 arts and crafts counselors, 2 drama counselors, 2 dance counselors, $450-650/season. Apply to Mrs. Robert R. Miller, Director, Camp Tegawitha, Tobyhanna PA 18466; tel. 717/839-9413.

## Towanda

Located in Honesdale. Camp for boys and girls, ages 7-16. Openings for college students and teachers. Needs coaches; general counselors; specialty counselors for tennis, golf, baseball, basketball, WSI, canoeing, sailing, waterskiing, stage scenery, arts and crafts, nature, pioneering, riflery; nurse (RN). Salaries depend on age and experience. Enclose return stamped envelope. Apply to Lynne S. Nordan, 316 Lynncroft Rd., New Rochelle NY 10804.

## Watonka

Located in Hawley, Pennsylvania. Private camp for boys, ages 8-15, interested in science. Openings for college students, teachers and foreign students from June 20 to August 22. Needs 6 cabin counselors, $500-600; riflery instructor, $500-700; minibike riding instructor, $600-800; directors for arts and crafts, $600-800; waterfront (ARC), $900-1,100; program director, $900-1,500; 6 science instructors for chemistry, photography, biology, electronics, astronomy, $700-1,200. Salaries include room and board. Apply by June 1 to Donald G. Wacker, Dept. SED, 43 Franklin St., Cedar Grove NJ 07009.

**Wayne**
Located in Preston Park, Pennsylvania. Private camp for coeds. Openings for teachers, high school and college coaches and college students from June 23 to August 22. "Specializes in people first; fine professional staff recruited from throughout US and abroad. Many fun, creative activities." Needs head counselors and assistant; waterfront director; athletic director; group leaders; specialists in tennis, camping, nature, golf, sailing, canoeing, waterskiing, swimming (WSI), soccer, basketball, baseball, ceramics, batik, macrame, yoga, guitar, ham radio, art, shop, archery. Salaries are $350-1,500 depending on age, skill and experience. Also needs nurses (RN), $650-750; doctor; and assistant director. Apply to Camp Wayne, 12 Allevard St., Lido Beach NY 11561.

## Summer Theaters

### Allenberry Playhouse
Located in Boiling Springs, Pennsylvania. Openings from March 20 to November 12. Needs costume designer (college student), $90/week; property person (college student), $75/week; 4 apprentices (college students, local applicants), $40/week plus room; assistant costumer (college student, local applicant), $40/week plus room. Send resume and letter by January. Apply to Nelson Sheeley, Managing Director, 433 W. 21st #6-D, New York City NY 10011; tel. 212/675-3884.

### Cresson Lake Playhouse
Located in Spangler. Openings for college students and teachers from mid-May to the end of August. Needs technical assistants for construction, art, sewing, props, electrician, choreography. Salaries quoted upon receipt of resume; lowcost housing available. Apply by April 15 to K.L. Resinski, Artistic Director, Cresson Lake Playhouse, 38 College Heights, Loretto PA 15940.

### The Pennsylvania Festival Theatre
Located at University Park. Equity U/RTA. Openings from early June through mid-August. Needs apprentice and journeyman actors, technicians, management aides, $85-115/week; staff positions for designers and management, salaries negotiable. Send resume. Apply by February 29 to John R. Bayless, General Manager, Dept. SED, The Pennsylvania Festival Theatre, 137 Arts II Bldg., University Park PA 16802.

### Prather Productions
Located in Shamokin Dam. Operator of 4 non-equity theaters. Openings for 15 college students and teachers from June to September, or longer. Needs actors, actresses, singers, dancers, technical staff, costumers, lighting. Salaries are $50-150/week plus board or room for candidates with previous professional dinner theater experience. Openings for college students only as staff assistants who act, $50/week stipend plus room. Apply by May 1 to T.R. Prather, Prather Productions, Shamokin Dam PA 17876.

# Rhode Island

## Business and Industry

### Kelly Services, Inc.
More than 450 branches coast to coast, Puerto Rico, Canada, England and France. Temporary work assignments. Offers over 100 job classifications (office, marketing and light industrial assignments) to college students, teachers and other qualified people during summer breaks and year 'round. Kelly Services also has a special referral system that allows you to register at a Kelly office near your school then work near your home during summer recess—or register near your home then work on temporary assignments during the school year. Assignments available include clerks, typists, secretaries, keypunch operators, word processors, bookkeepers and a variety of marketing and light industrial. Offers flexible schedule with "attractive hourly pay rates equal to or higher than the accepted industry standards in most cities." No paycheck deductions except Social Security and income tax. No employment fee for temporary work. See the White Pages for the branch of Kelly Services nearest you. Apply in person or write to: Summer Employment, National Headquarters, Kelly Services, GPO 1179, Detroit MI 48266.

## Resorts, Ranches, Restaurants, Lodging

### Ballard's Inn and Champlin's Marina
Located at Block Island. Resort. Openings for 100 college students, teachers and high school seniors from June 25 through Labor Day. Needs waiters, waitresses, bus boys, dock attendants, lifeguards, kitchen help, cooks, maids, porters, bartenders, snack shop attendants, cashiers, groundskeepers. Salaries are $25-200/week plus board. Send resume with stamped, self-addressed envelope to Paul A. Filippi, Ballard's Farm, Great Road, Lincoln RI 02865.

## Summer Camps

### Wohelo
Located in Bradford. Camp Fire Girls resident camp for girls ages 7-16. Openings for college students, teachers and high school seniors. Needs 12 cabin counselors with skills in campcraft, arts and crafts, archery, canoeing, sailing, horseback riding or waterfront. Salaries are up to $500/season. Apply to Camp Fire Girls Office, 345 Blackstone Blvd., Providence RI 02906.

# South Carolina

## Business and Industry

### Kelly Services, Inc.
More than 450 branches coast to coast, Puerto Rico, Canada, England and France. Temporary work assignments. Offers over 100 job classifications (office, marketing and light industrial assignments) to college students, teachers and other qualified people during summer breaks and year 'round. Kelly Services also has a special referral system that allows you to register at a Kelly office near your school then work near your home during summer recess—or register near your home then work on temporary assignments during the school year. Assignments available include clerks, typists, secretaries, keypunch operators, word processors, bookkeepers and a variety of marketing and light industrial. Offers flexible schedule with "attractive hourly pay rates equal to or higher than the accepted industry standards in most cities." No paycheck deductions except Social Security and income tax. No employment fee for temporary work. See the White Pages for the branch of Kelly Services nearest you. Apply in person or write to: Summer Employment, National Headquarters, Kelly Services, GPO 1179, Detroit MI 48266.

### Temp Force
Temporary office personnel contractor. Openings for college students, teachers and high school seniors during vacations and holidays. Needs secretaries, typists, stenographers, clericals and accountants. Salaries based upon experience. Apply to Temp Force, 2611 Forest Dr., Richland Building, Suite 201, Columbia SC 29204; tel. 803/254-0594.

## Summer Camps

### Hope
Located in Clemson. Agency camp for mentally retarded persons, ages 8 and older. Openings for college students and teachers from early June to mid August. Needs 12 group counselors, 2 unit leaders, 3 waterfront instructors, 3 camping specialists, 2 program directors, camp nurse, crafts instructor. Salaries are biweekly plus room and board. Apply by March 15 to C.R. White, Camp Hope, RPA, Dept. SED, Clemson University, Clemson SC 29631.

### Pla-Mor, Inc.
Located in North Myrtle Beach. Camp serving church-related and other groups, consisting mostly of junior and senior high students. "Camp Pla-Mor was organized and operates for the benefit of young people who care for the better life." Openings for college students (some high school students for kitchen help) from June 1 to August 31 (manager couple needed year-round). Needs 4 kitchen helpers, $750-1,000/season; cleaner/laundress, $750-1,000/season; 11 life guards (1 pool guard, 10 beach guards), $750-1,000/season; manager team (husband and wife to manage and do odd jobs), negotiated salary plus housing, meals in summer months, utilities. All salaries include room and meals. "We have air conditioned rooms for workers and have a modern cafeteria where all employees eat. Applicant

must work 6, 7 or 8 hours a day with one day off a week. Girls room in motel type rooms, boys in individual rooms that sleep three, all air conditioned." Send for application. Apply to Virgil Yow, President, Box 2189, North Myrtle Beach SC 29582; tel. 803/272-6649 or 272-8216.

# South Dakota

## Resorts, Ranches, Restaurants, Lodging

### Blue Bell Lodge & Resort
Located in Custer State Park. State Park concessionaire; rustic secluded resort. Openings from middle May to September. Needs 4 housekeepers/laundry persons, minimum $2.75/hour, plus bonus; 6 waitresses/waiters, minimum $1.95/hour, plus bonus and tips; 4 cooks and cook's helpers (cooking experience preferred), minimum $2.75/hour, plus bonus; 4 cashiers and clerks, minimum $2.75/hour, plus bonus. "Salaries are open. We charge $5/day for room and board. Applicants must be interested in working first and playing later." Send resume or application request; including self addressed stamped envelope. Apply by April 1 to Phil Lampert, Manager, Dept. SED, Blue Bell Lodge & Resort, Box 63, Custer State Park, Custer SD 57730; tel. 605/255-4531.

### Cactus Cafe and Lounge
Located in Wall. Openings for college students, teachers, high school seniors and foreign students from June to August. Needs 20 waiters/waitresses (minimum age 21), $12.50/shift plus room and board; 12 dishwashers-kitchen help, $75/week plus room and board; 4 fry cooks, $15-20/shift plus room and board; 3 bartenders (minimum age 21), $20/shift plus room; 2 hostess-cashiers, $18/shift plus room. "We cannot help foreign students get visas." Apply to Myron L. Beach, Jr., Cactus Cafe and Lounge, Main St., Wall SD 57790.

### State Game Lodge
Located in Custer State Park. Resort. Openings for college students from May 20 to October 1. Needs 12 motel-cottage housekeepers, 3 salad makers, 10 kitchen workers, 2 registration desk clerks, 8 sales clerks, 4 service station attendant-lawn worker-maintenance, 2 bartenders, 3 fry cooks, salary open; 15 waitresses/waiters, salary plus tips. Salaries start at minimum wage; dormitory accommodations Enclose stamped return envelope for application form. Apply by April 1 to State Game Lodge, Dept. SED, Custer State Park, Custer SD 57730.

## Summer Camps

### Jaycee Camp for Handicapped Children
Located on Big Sioux River near Baltic. Coed camp for handicapped persons age 4 through adult. Openings for college students, teachers and high school seniors

from the second week in June to the first week in August. Needs 2 directors (special education majors), $1,100 and up/session, depending on experience; 24 counselors (some special education majors preferred in music, swimming, nature study, arts), $225/session plus 3.6 credit hours of college work in special education; 10 assistant counselors; nurse (RN), cook, $1,000 and up/session, depending on experience. Apply early (March 1 deadline) to Jaycee Camp President, Box 1763, Sioux Falls SD 57101.

### Sioux Indian YMCAs
Located in Dupree. Openings for 12 college students, teachers and foreign students from June 20 to August 20. Needs counselors, kitchen supervisor, staff coordinator, nurse, waterfront director and community organizers to work in cooperation with local Sioux leaders. Room and board, no salary. Apply by May 1 to Dwight W. Call, Sioux Indian YMCAs, Box 218, Dupree SD 57623.

# Tennessee

## Business and Industry

### Kelly Services, Inc.
More than 450 branches coast to coast, Puerto Rico, Canada, England and France. Temporary work assignments. Offers over 100 job classifications (office, marketing and light industrial assignments) to college students, teachers and other qualified people during summer breaks and year 'round. Kelly Services also has a special referral system that allows you to register at a Kelly office near your school then work near your home during summer recess—or register near your home then work on temporary assignments during the school year. Assignments available include clerks, typists, secretaries, keypunch operators, word processors, bookkeepers and a variety of marketing and light industrial. Offers flexible schedule with "attractive hourly pay rates equal to or higher than the accepted industry standards in most cities." No paycheck deductions except Social Security and income tax. No employment fee for temporary work. See the White Pages for the branch of Kelly Services nearest you. Apply in person or write to: Summer Employment, National Headquarters, Kelly Services, GPO 1179, Detroit MI 48266.

### Southwestern Company
Located in Franklin. Publishers and booksellers of educational and religious books. Summer program for college students, direct selling. No experience needed. Average gross profit per month per student over past 5 years is $1,100. Apply to Spencer Hays, The Southwestern Company, Box 820, Nashville TN 37202.

## Commercial Attractions

### Silver Dollar City
Located in Pigeon Forge. Theme park. Openings for approximately 350 college students, high school seniors and senior citizens from May to October. Needs entertainers; actors and actresses; ticket sellers; retail sales workers; food and

beverage concession workers; attractions operators; parking attendants; grounds keepers; and crafts demonstrators (to demonstrate wagonmaking, dollmaking, glasscutting, blacksmithing, woodcarving, broommaking, basket weaving, candle making, candy making, weaving, lye soap making, gun smithing and knife smithing). "Silver Dollar City gives a 50% discount to employees on food purchases at the park, and will assist employees in finding housing." Apply in person in February. Personal interview required; entertainers must audition with their own musical selection; musical accompaniment will be provided. Write for application (April 1 deadline) to Manager, Silver Dollar City, Dept. SED, Box 928, Pigeon Forge TN 37863; tel. 615/453-4615.

## Resorts, Ranches, Restaurants, Lodging

### Bonanza Sirloin Pit
Located in Gatlinburg. Restaurant. Openings for 30 persons from April to October. Needs broiler cook, counter help, dishwashers, buspersons and cashiers. Pays $3.10-3.75/hour. Personal interview preferred. Apply to Bill Garst, Manager, Bonanza Sirloin Pit, Dept. SED, Box 49, Airport Rd., Gatlinburg TN 37738.

### Lums
Located in Gatlinburg. Restaurant. Openings for college students, teachers, high school seniors, foreign students and local applicants from April to October. Needs 15 short order cooks, 30 waitresses and waiters, 6 dishwashers, 4 busboys, and 4 cashier/hostesses, minimum wage and up. Send application 2-3 weeks before date available for work. Apply to Rick Kyker, Manager, Lums Restaurant, Box 409, Airport Rd., Gatlinburg TN 37738; telephone (615)436-7383.

## Summer Camps

### Hazelwood
Located in Springville, on Kentucky Lake. Girl Scout camp for girls, ages 8-18. ACA accredited. Openings from June 8 to August 1. Needs 8 assistant leaders, $250-400; waterfront staff (WSI), 5 leaders (minimum age 21), $400-550; nurse (RN), $400-500. Provides room, board and health insurance, plus ACA campcrafter training. $3 fee charged to register as a Girl Scout. Apply by April or May to Dottie Carey, Camp Director, Reelfoot Girl Scout Council, Old Humboldt Rd., Jackson TN 38301.

### Sycamore Hills
Located in Ashland City. Girl Scout camp. Openings from mid-June to mid-August. Needs 1 operations director, 3 high adventure trip staffers, 4 unit leaders and 1 waterfront director (college students or teachers); 6 assistant unit leaders, 2 small craft instructors, 2 arts and crafts staffers and 3 waterfront assistants (college students, teachers or high school seniors preferred); and 3 horseback staffers (college students, teachers, or high school seniors preferred). Foreign students welcome to apply. Apply to Jim Weimer, Director of Camping Services and Properties, Box 40466, 830 Kirkwood Lane, Nashville TN 37204; tel. 615/383-0490.

**Tall Pine**
Located in Coker Creek, Tennessee. Camp for trainable and educable retarded people. Openings for college students and teachers from June 23 to August 4, 6-week season. Needs 6 cottage counselors for male campers. Apply by March to Fred C. Slater, Owner, Tall Pine Camp, Dept. SED, 6221 NW 17th St., Ft. Lauderdale FL 33313; tel. 305/735-0727.

# Texas

## Business and Industry

### CDI Temporary Service
Located in Dallas, Ft. Worth, Houston. Office, marketing, light industrial personnel. Offers college students, teachers, high school students and other qualified people interesting temporary work at a variety of companies in diversified industries during summer vacation, semester breaks and year-round. Work 1-5 days, 2 weeks at a time, a month, or for entire summer. Top hourly pay according to skills on a weekly basis. Never a fee. Needs all office, marketing, and light industrial skills, e.g., receptionists, typists, secretaries, transcribers, word processors, keypunch operators, figure clerks, bookkeepers, switchboard operators, sorters, stuffers, inventory workers, product demonstrators, market researchers, machine operators, factory workers, assemblers and many others. Suggest contacting office prior to availability. Apply to CDI Temporary Service, 4255 LBJ Freeway, Suite 194, Dallas TX 75234, tel. 214/233-0046; 705 Ridglea Bank Building, Fort Worth TX 76116, tel. 817/731-9411; 8989 Westheimer, Houston TX 77063, tel. 713/780-2240.

### Kelly Services, Inc.
More than 450 branches coast to coast, Puerto Rico, Canada, England and France. Temporary work assignments. Offers over 100 job classifications (office, marketing and light industrial assignments) to college students, teachers and other qualified people during summer breaks and year 'round. Kelly Services also has a special referral system that allows you to register at a Kelly office near your school then work near your home during summer recess—or register near your home then work on temporary assignments during the school year. Assignments available include clerks, typists, secretaries, keypunch operators, word processors, bookkeepers and a variety of marketing and light industrial. Offers flexible schedule with "attractive hourly pay rates equal to or higher than the accepted industry standards in most cities." No paycheck deductions except Social Security and income tax. No employment fee for temporary work. See the White Pages for the branch of Kelly Services nearest you. Apply in person or write to: Summer Employment, National Headquarters, Kelly Services, GPO 1179, Detroit MI 48266.

### Mature Temps Inc.
Located in Dallas. National temporary employment service. Openings for college students, teachers, high school seniors, local applicants and foreign students from May to September or year-round. Needs secretaries, clerks, typists, bookkeepers, stenographers, accountants, demonstrators and marketing research persons. High hourly rates based on skills. Apply to Mature Temps Inc., One Dallas Centre, Suite

1665, 350 N. St. Paul St., Dallas TX 75201, tel. 214/651-9321; 3701 W. Alabama, Suite 396, Houston TX 77027, tel. 713/961-3136.

### Temp Staff

Temporary personnel contractor. Openings for college students, teachers, high school seniors during vacations and holidays. Needs secretaries, typists, stenographers, clericals and accountants. Salaries based upon experience. Apply to Temp Staff, 307 University Tower, Dallas TX 75206; tel. 214/369-8181.

## Commercial Attractions

### Alamo Village Vacation and Movie Land

Located in Brackettville. Tourist attraction—where movies are made in Texas. Needs sales/cashiers, 2 for Indian Store, 3 for Trading Post, 2 for General; career country western musicians, 1 lead guitar/vocal, 1 rhythm guitar/vocal, 1 bass, 1 drums, 1 piano/vocal; cantina-restaurant, 4 waitress/vocalist. Pays $350/month plus room and utilities, college students preferred. Work May 1 through Labor Day; rehearsals begin May 20. All employees trusted to handle money. "Know what you want. If you do not like people then do not work for a tourist attraction. Be loyal, honest and able to carry out orders. Gentlemen knowledge of horses, livestock and ground maintenance helpful." Written applications after January 1; send resume and photograph; live auditions/interviews scheduled thereafter. Apply to Happy Shahan, President, Alamo Village Vacation and Movie Land, Box 528, Brackettville TX 78832; tel. 512/563-2580.

### AstroWorld—A member of the Six Flags Family

Located in Houston, next to the AstroDome. Family theme park with 75 acres. Openings for college students, teachers, high school students and local applicants from the last week in May through Labor Day. Needs 1,900 ride operators, food service personnel, merchandising personnel, parking lot attendants, game operators, groundskeepers, security officers, $140/week. "AstroWorld has made arrangements with a large apartment complex near the park to provide a 3-month lease to AstroWorld employees. We also have a large special events program which includes such activities as softball and volleyball leagues, trips to Six Flags parks, movie nights, and host and hostess parties." Send for application. Apply to Mike Glennan, Personnel Manager, 9001 Kirby Dr., Houston TX 77054; tel. 713/748-1234.

### Six Flags Over Texas

Located in Arlington. Amusement park. Openings for 2,000 persons from the last week in May through Labor Day, six days per week. Needs ride operators, food service, gifts and souvenirs, parking lot attendants, game operators, groundskeepers, security officers. Salaries are $1,600/season. Room and board not provided; apartments and school dormitories available in the area. Apply to Six Flags Over Texas, Dept. SED, Box 191, Arlington TX 76010.

# Resorts, Ranches, Restaurants, Lodging

### Mayan Dude Ranch
Located in Bandera. Needs housekeepers, assistant cooks, dining room waiters/waitresses. Must be 18 years of age and *have musical talent*. Salary is $200/month plus room, board and a bonus of $500-1,000 at end of season. Employment as soon as possible until end of August or Labor Day. "Employees must be musically talented as we have several shows during the week at which they must entertain. Must also give work references in their application—not personal." Apply to Judy Hicks, Manager, Mayan Dude Ranch, Box 577, Dept. SED, Bandera TX 78003; tel. 512/796-3312.

## Summer Camps

### Amon Carter
Located in Ft. Worth. YMCA summer youth camp, ages 8-15. Offers wilderness trip camping for teenagers. Openings for college students and teachers from June 18 to August 18; camp runs 8 weeks for boys and 2 weeks for girls. Needs 13 senior counselors, $15-100/week; 1 aquatics director, $90-130/week; and 1 crafts director, $75-110/week. Backgrounds needed in sailing, crafts, riflery, nature and canoeing. Room and board provided. Apply by May 15 to Tim Smith, Assistant Director, 6200 Sand Springs Rd., Ft. Worth TX 76114; tel. 817/738-9241.

### Cullen
Located in Trinity. YMCA of Greater Houston Area; resident camp for children ages 9-14. Openings for college students, teachers and foreign students from: summer, approximately May 20 to August 20; fall-spring, approximately September 18 to May 19. Needs 25 summer-cabin counselors, $60-90/week; 8 summer-activities assistants, $30-50/week; 4 summer-program area coordinators, $80-100/week; 20 fall-spring cabin and activity counselors for school outdoor education program, $100-125/week. Room and board provided. "Apply in February. Send complete resume with references. Make attempt for a personal visit. Obtain various certifications in off season, i.e. WSI, canoeing instructor, etc." Apply to Thomas P. O'Connor, Director, YMCA Camp Cullen, Rt. 2, Box 135-D, Trinity TX 75862; tel. 713/659-2733 or 594-2274.

### Ellowi
### T Bar C Camp Wilderness
Located in Dallas. Two resident Camp Fire Girls camps with programs for girls ages 6-17, and boys ages 7-11. Openings for college students and teachers during June and July. Prior resident camping experience and experience working with youth and camp related skills desired. Needs camp directors, program directors, business managers, counselors, unit leaders, WSIs, nurses, horsemanship director. Salaries for the 8-week season range from $450 for counselors to $1,400 for directors. Room and board provided. Apply by May 15 to Director of Camping Services, Camp Fire Girls, Lone Star Council, 5415 Maple, Suite 308, Dept. SED, Dallas TX 75235; tel. 214/638-2240.

### Heart 'o the Hills Camp for Girls
Located in Hunt, on Guadalupe River in Texas hill country. Private camp for girls ages 6-16. Openings for teachers and college students from June 1 to August 15. Needs counselors and instructors in swimming, field sports, canoeing, camp crafts, tennis, golf, archery, riflery, horseback riding, dance, drama, choir, arts, gymnastics, trampoline and photography. Also needs secretarial and kitchen help. Base pay is $500/summer for beginning staff. "Please write for application form and have references available. Counselors must find joy in working with children and teens." Apply to Mr. or Mrs. Whayne Moore, Owners/Directors, Dept. SED, Heart 'o the Hills, Hunt TX 78024; tel. 512/238-4650.

### Manison
Located at Friendswood in Galveston County, 5 miles from NASA between Houston and Galveston. Private coed camp for ages 6-16. Openings for college students, teachers and foreign students year 'round—minimum of 1 month to a maximum of 12 months. Needs 30 general counselors, $200-260/month; 10 specialty counselors for waterfront (WSI), wrangler (Western), arts and crafts, tennis, golf, tumbling-gymnastics, archery, riflery, campcraft, nature, $240-300/month. Room, board and uniforms provided. Apply to Camp Manison, Box 148, Friendswood TX 77546.

### Permian Basin Girl Scout Camps
Located in Alpine and Bakersfield. Openings for college students, teachers, high school graduating seniors and foreign students from early June to mid-August. Needs 25 general counselors, 4 waterfront staff, 4 riding staff, business manager, 7 kitchen personnel. Apply to Permian Basin Girl Scout Camps, Box 1046, Odessa TX 79760.

### Stewart for Boys
Located in Hunt, in the hill country. Private camp for children ages 6-16. Openings for 75 college students and teachers from May 28 to August 16. Needs general counselors with skills in Western horsemanship, waterfront (swimming, diving, sailing, skiing, canoeing), music, arts and crafts, drama, ecology, Indian lore, all land sports, archery, hunting and target shooting, riflery (NRA), tennis, photography, sketching; nurses; cook. Employs 2 counselors per cabin of 16 boys. Salaries are $400-1,000/season. "Room and board included; family style meals." Apply by April 30 to Mrs. Silas B. Ragsdale, Jr., Camp Stewart for Boys, Hunt TX 78024.

### Tejas Girl Scout Council Inc.
Located in Dallas. Camp for girls ages 6-17. Openings from June 1 to August 12. Needs 2 assistant camp directors (college students or teachers preferred); 2 business managers and 2 program specialists (college students or teachers preferred); 2 health supervisors (first aider or nurse preferred); 2 waterfront directors (college students or teachers preferred); 6 waterfront instructors and 6 unit leaders (college students, teachers or high school seniors preferred); 4 wranglers (college students, teachers or high school seniors preferred); and 22 assistant unit leaders (college students, teachers or high school seniors preferred). Room and board provided. "Apply early, February on" (May 1 deadline) to Scottie Hubbard, Director of Camping Services, Dept. SED, 4411 Skillman, Dallas TX 75206; tel. 214/823-1342.

**Texas Lions Camp**
Located in Kerrville. Private nonprofit 504-acre camp (run by Lions Club of Texas) with complete recreational program; sessions are for deaf, blind, and orthopedically handicapped children ages 7-16; also sessions for diabetic children ages 6-16. Openings for college students, teachers, local applicants from May 29 to August 9. Needs 36 unit counselors, 8 arts and crafts counselors, 3 camp craft counselors (to teach nature skills and outdoor living), 4 recreation/athletics counselors, $625/season; 8 Red Cross WSIs, $687.50/season. Salaries include room, board, laundry and bed linens. "Applicants must be able to meet the physical demands of lifting, running, pushing and pulling in a long work day. Those with majors in education, music, drama, and recreation and special education may find the work rewarding, a good on-job-training experience. Only those with a sincere interest in helping others should apply." Send for application. Apply by March 15 to Al Fehrenbach, Public Relations Director, Box 247, Kerrville TX 78028; tel. 512/896-8500.

**Wood Lake**
Located on Lake Brownwood. Girl Scout camp for girls ages 6-17. Openings from June 3 to July 20. Needs 4 unit leaders ($60-80/week), 12 unit counselors ($40-60/week), 1 waterfront director ($60-100/week), 2 waterfront assistants ($50-75/week), college students, teachers, foreign students all acceptable; 1 CIT ($60-80/week), college student or teacher preferred; 1 business manager ($60-75/week), college student or teacher preferred. "Indicate current Red Cross certifications (WSI, etc.) and other pertinent training, age, background, and experience." Room and board provided. Apply by February 15 to Zola Moon, Camp Director, Heart of Texas Girl Scout Council, 700 E. Baker, Brownwood TX 76801; tel. 915/646-1516.

**YMCA of The Greater Houston Area**
Located in Houston. Recreation, informal education, etc. Openings approximately from May 15 to August 15. Needs 10-20 day camp directors ($4.00-4.50/hour), 12-25 pool managers ($150/week), 50-75 swim instructors ($130/week), college students and teachers preferred; 50-75 life guards ($120/week), college students and high school seniors preferred; 25 senior counselors for resident camp ($75-110/week plus room and board), college students and teachers preferred. Also needs 50-100 day camp counselors, college students, teachers and high school seniors preferred. Apply to Betsy Rose, Personnel Coordinator, YMCA of the Greater Houston Area, Dept. SED, 1600 Louisiana, Houston TX 77002; tel. 713/659-5442.

# Utah

## Business and Industry

### Kelly Services, Inc.
More than 450 branches coast to coast, Puerto Rico, Canada, England and France. Temporary work assignments. Offers over 100 job classifications (office, marketing and light industrial assignments) to college students, teachers and other

qualified people during summer breaks and year 'round. Kelly Services also has a special referral system that allows you to register at a Kelly office near your school then work near your home during summer recess—or register near your home then work on temporary assignments during the school year. Assignments available include clerks, typists, secretaries, keypunch operators, word processors, bookkeepers and a variety of marketing and light industrial. Offers flexible schedule with "attractive hourly pay rates equal to or higher than the accepted industry standards in most cities." No paycheck deductions except Social Security and income tax. No employment fee for temporary work. See the White Pages for the branch of Kelly Services nearest you. Apply in person or write to: Summer Employment, National Headquarters, Kelly Services, GPO 1179, Detroit MI 48266.

# National Parks

### Bryce Canyon Lodge
### Zion Lodge
### Grand Canyon Lodge
Located in Utah (Bryce Canyon Lodge and Zion Lodge); North Rim, Arizona (Grand Canyon Lodge). Openings for college students, teachers and high school seniors from May to October. Needs management and nonmanagement personnel in the following operations: lodging, restaurant, souvenirs, camper store, service stations, accounting; security; registered nursing. Give dates available for work. Applicatons in by February 15 given first consideration. Send applicaton request to Personnel Manager, Dept. SED, TWA Services Inc. Box 400, Cedar City UT 84720.

# Resorts, Ranches, Restaurants, Lodging

### Bullfrog Resort & Marina, Inc.
### Hite Resort & Marina, Inc.
### Hall's Crossing Resort & Marina, Inc.
Located in the Glen Canyon National Recreational Area in southern Utah/ northern Arizona on Lake Powell (180-mile-long lake with 1,900 miles of shoreline). Resorts with boat rentals, boat tours, campgrounds, fishing charters, lodging, restaurants, service stations and boat and car repair shops. "Our primary season runs from Easter through mid-October although open year-round, presenting a continuous need for qualified employees." Needs marina mechanics, boat pilots, dockhands, housekeepers, cashiers, food servers, cooks, accounting clerks, office clerks, maintenance people, service station attendents and houseboat maids and instructors. "Employees are housed primarily in mobile homes. Housing for married couples is limited and available only when both partners are willing to accept shift work and work Sundays and holidays. We encourage semi-retired people to work for short periods in spring, summer and/or fall. Living in this beautiful, but remote, desert area provides the opportunity to take advantage of all the water and outdoor activities. Please specify beginning and ending dates of availability." Equal opportunity employer. Send resume to Personnel Office, Del Webb Recreational Properties, Inc., Box 29040, Phoenix AZ 85038.

### Flaming Gorge Lodge
Located in Dutch John. Resort. Openings for college students from April 1 to

October 31. Needs waitresses, $3/hour; 4 store clerks, $3.20/hour; chambermaids, $3.50/hour. Rooms available for $20/month. Apply by May 1 to Craig W. Collett, Flaming Gorge Lodge, Dutch John UT 84023.

### Snowbird Ski and Summer Resort
Located in Snowbird. Skiing and summer resort. Openings for college students, teachers, high school seniors and local applicants from May 1 to November 15 (earlier release may be arranged). Non-US citizen must have permanent resident visa or applicable work permit. Many jobs are year-round positions if desired. Needs 4 office clerks, $130-160/week; 60 housekeepers, $115-130/week; 20 dishwashers, $120-140/week; 15 food preparers, $130-175/week; 15 cooks, $140-200/week, 10 waitpersons, $75/week plus tips; 10 buspersons, $90/week plus tips; 12 janitors, $120-140/week; 8 convention set-up, $120-140/week. An equal opportunity employer. Apply to Dave Hilbig, Dept. SED, Director of Personnel, Snowbird Ski and Summer Resort, Snowbird UT 84070; telephone (801)742-2222 or 521-6040.

## Summer Camps

### Utah Girl Scout Council Camps
Openings in 3 camps for 50 college students and teachers from June 1 to August 20, depending on camp. Needs specialty counselors for riding, swimming (WSI), smallcraft, handcraft; instructors; consultants; unit leaders; assistant unit leaders; health supervisors; maintenance persons; cooks. Salaries are $375-1,200, plus room and board. Apply by May 1 to Camp Employer, Dept. CLC, Utah Girl Scout Council Camps, 2386 E. 2760 S., Salt Lake City UT 84109.

# Vermont

## Business and Industry

### Kelly Services, Inc.
More than 450 branches coast to coast, Puerto Rico, Canada, England and France. Temporary work assignments. Offers over 100 job classifications (office, marketing and light industrial assignments) to college students, teachers and other qualified people during summer breaks and year 'round. Kelly Services also has a special referral system that allows you to register at a Kelly office near your school then work near your home during summer recess—or register near your home then work on temporary assignments during the school year. Assignments available include clerks, typists, secretaries, keypunch operators, word processors, bookkeepers and a variety of marketing and light industrial. Offers flexible schedule with "attractive hourly pay rates equal to or higher than the accepted industry standards in most cities." No paycheck deductions except Social Security and income tax. No employment fee for temporary work. See the White Pages for the branch of Kelly Services nearest you. Apply in person or write to: Summer Employment, National Headquarters, Kelly Services, GPO 1179, Detroit MI 48266.

# Resorts, Ranches, Restaurants, Lodging

### North Hero House
Located in North Hero on Lake Champlain. Country inn, resort. Openings for college students from June 19 to the day after Labor Day. Needs chambermaids, waitresses, combination dock attendant-dishwashers (alternating days), assistant front desk manager, assistant cooks. Salaries are $800 and up/season plus room and board. US residents only. Apply to North Hero House, Champlain Islands, North Hero VT 05474.

## Summer Camps

### Abnaki
Located in North Hero on Lake Champlain. Vermont State YMCA resident camp for children, ages 7-15. Openings from June 19 to August 21. Needs 5 male senior counselors ($450 and up/season), 1 male hike master ($600/season), college students, teachers, foreign students all acceptable; 1 male village leader ($600/season), college student or teacher preferred; 1 male or female waterfront director ($850 and up/season), teacher or high school graduate preferred. Room and board provided. Apply by April 1 to Norman F. van Gulden, Director, Camp Abnaki, Box 806, Burlington VT 05402; tel. 802/862-8981.

### Dunmore
Located in Salisbury. Private camp. Openings for college students and teachers from June 24 to August 24. Needs specialty counselors (minimum age 20) for athletics, tennis, arts and crafts, drama, dance, music (pianist), pioneering, hiking, tripping, nature, gymnastics, swimming (WSI) ($450-650), canoeing, sailing nurse (RN). Apply to Mrs. George Ross, Camp Dunmore, 400 E. 85th St., New York NY 10028; tel. 212/861-2120.

### Farnsworth
Located in Thetford. Girl Scout camp for girls ages 6-17. Openings for college students, teachers and high school graduates from mid-June to August. Needs unit leaders; assistant unit leaders; waterfront staff; specialists in arts and crafts, riding, canoeing, backpacking, sports, bicycling; cooks; nurse. "Experience with children in groups is a prerequisite." Salaries are $700-800 for unit leaders, $450-550 for unit assistants. Apply to Martha Netsch, Swift Water Girl Scout Council, Box NF, 325 Merrill St., Manchester NH 03103.

### Hochelaga
Located in South Hero. YWCA overnight camp for girls ages 8-15. Openings from June 24 to August 24. Needs 8 waterfront counselors (WSI), $350-700/season; 2 drama counselors, 3 landsport counselors, 7 arts and craft counselors, 3 nature counselors, $350-600/season; 3 line leaders, $450-700/season. College students and teachers preferred. Also needs 4 kitchen helpers, $350-600/season. Apply to Paul C. Simpson, Director, Camp Hochelaga, 61 Terrace St., Montpelier VT 05602.

## Keewaydin Camps

Located on Lake Dunmore, Salisbury, Vermont. Private camp for boys. Openings for college students and teachers from June 20 to August 25. Needs 2 general counselors; specialty counselors: 2 nature, 2 sailing, wrestling. Salaries are $325-500. Apply by March 15 to A.G. Hare, Jr., 113 Anton Rd., Box N, Wynnewood PA 19096.

## Lochearn

Located at Lake Fairlee, Ely. Girls camp for ages 6-15. Openings for college students and teachers from June 23 to August 24. Needs riding director, $1,000-1,200/season; riding instructors, $500-700/season; trip director, $450-600/season; stable workers, kitchen/maintenance workers, $450-600/season; instructors: scuba, water safety, gymnastics, sailing, ceramics, trampoline, archery, drama, tennis, arts and crafts, $425-600/season; bookkeeper, secretary, $500-750/season. Apply to Peter and Mary Shays, Lochearn, Ely VT 05044.

## Marycrest

Located in Grand Isle. Camp for girls ages 6-16. Openings for college students and teachers from late June to late August. Needs specialty counselors for tennis, golf, sports, arts and crafts, archery, drama, dancing, waterfront (sailing, canoeing, swimming), $400 and up. Room and board provided. Apply by April 30 to Sr. Virginia Cain, 100 Mansfield Ave., Burlington VT 05401.

## New England Camping Association, Inc. (ACA)

Located in Vermont. Camp counselor referral service. Openings for college students and teachers, minimum age 19, for 8 weeks. Needs specialty counselors for advanced lifesaving, archery, arts and crafts, bicycling, boating, campcraft, canoeing, drama, golf, guitar, gymnastics, horseback riding, land sports, music, nature-ecology, photography, piano, radio-electronics, riflery, sailing (SCI), scuba, tennis, waterskiing, WSI; trip leader, unit leader, administrative, chef, baker, kitchen workers, clerical, maintenance, doctors, nurses (RN). Salaries start at $400 and are commensurate with age, education, camp experience and type of position. $2 application fee. Enclose stamped return envelope. Apply to New England Camping Association, Inc., Room 410, 29 Commonwealth Ave., Boston MA 02116.

---

**Want to write about your summer job experience?** *SED* **pays for short evaluations of your summer experience with employers listed here. See page 14 for details.**

**Passumpsic**
Located in Ely, Vermont. Private camp for boys ages 6-15. Openings for college undergraduates, graduate students and teachers of all faiths, races and nationalities (minimum age 18) from mid-June through the end of August. Needs chef, chef's helper, head counselor, unit leaders; directors: CIT, program, waterfront, land sports; trip leader and trip counselors; specialty counselors for riflery, archery, tennis, soccer, baseball, basketball, street hockey, swimming (WSI preferred), waterskiing, sailing, scuba diving, boating, canoeing, music, photography, dramatics, arts and crafts, woodworking, nature, campcraft, fishing, fly tying; kitchen workers, maintenance workers. "Room and board is part of our contracts; additional FICA tax must be deducted from paychecks according to Vermont state valuation of room and board." Apply by June 1 to Mr. and Mrs. Garth Nelson, Dept. SED, 45 Woodland Dr., Hanover MA 02339.

**Thorpe**
Located at Brandon. Camp for physically handicapped, mentally retarded adults and children (ages 6-14) with adjustment problems. Openings for college students and teachers from mid-June to mid-August. Needs 12 general counselors, $500 and up; 12 specialty counselors, $600 and up; nurse (RN or LPN), $100/week. Apply by February 1 (but will consider later applicants) to Mrs. Benjamin W. Heath, Director, Dept. SED, RFD 3, Brandon VT 05733.

**Wapanacki**
Located in Hardwick. Summer camp for visually handicapped youth ages 7-21, "primarily from New York Metropolitan area but also from many states of the eastern USA; campers are mobile, communicative, some totally blind, some partially sighted, and some additional handicaps such as mental retardation, learning difficulties or mild physical handicaps." Openings for college students, teachers and high school students from late June to late August. Needs counselors and activity leaders, $300 and up/season; RN, salary dependent upon experience. Room and board provided. "An active program of outdoor recreational activities including swimming, boating, athletics, nature and trips such as 3-day mountain trail hikes, lake canoe trips and local overnights. Staff is expected to assist campers with activities of daily living as well as with recreational activities. They should expect to spend their time and attention with all aspects of a camper's life at Camp Wapanacki—recreational, emotional and social. There is only a minimum of staff free time. We are looking for staff who are experienced or seeking experience with the recreational and living needs of handicapped youth. Send resume or application request between January and April to Joe V. Ingram, Camp Director, Camp Wapanacki, Dept. SED, Hardwick VT 05843; tel. 802/472-6612 (9 a.m. to 12 noon).

# Virginia

## Business and Industry

**Kelly Services, Inc.**
More than 450 branches coast to coast, Puerto Rico, Canada, England and France. Temporary work assignments. Offers over 100 job classifications (office,

marketing and light industrial assignments) to college students, teachers and other qualified people during summer breaks and year 'round. Kelly Services also has a special referral system that allows you to register at a Kelly office near your school then work near your home during summer recess—or register near your home then work on temporary assignments during the school year. Assignments available include clerks, typists, secretaries, keypunch operators, word processors, bookkeepers and a variety of marketing and light industrial. Offers flexible schedule with "attractive hourly pay rates equal to or higher than the accepted industry standards in most cities." No paycheck deductions except Social Security and income tax. No employment fee for temporary work. See the White Pages for the branch of Kelly Services nearest you. Apply in person or write to: Summer Employment, National Headquarters, Kelly Services, GPO 1179, Detroit MI 48266.

**Temp Force**
Temporary office personnel contractor. Openings for college students, teachers, high school seniors during vacations and holidays. Needs secretaries, typists, stenographers, clericals, accountants. Salaries based upon experience. Apply to Temp Force, Box 205, Norlyn Building, Madison Heights VA 24572, tel. 804/528-0796; 4 Koger Executive Center, Suite 100, Norfolk VA 23502, tel. 804/461-6900.

# Resorts, Ranches, Restaurants, Lodging

### Mountain Lake Hotel
Located at Mountain Lake. Resort. Openings for college students, college graduates and teachers from May 1 to September 30. Needs 4 front office helpers, 7 waiters, hostess, 3 hall boys, 7 maids, 2 bellmen, dock attendant, yard attendant, horse handler, 2 cooks, 8 kitchen helpers. Salary information upon application. Room and board provided. Apply to Dept. SED, Mountain Lake Hotel, Mountain Lake VA 24136.

# Summer Camps

### Easter Seal
Located in New Castle. Camp for handicapped people, ages 8 and up. Openings for college students, teachers and foreign students from early June to mid-August. Needs 35 counselors, 12 program staff and 2 nurses. Apply to Director, Camp Easter Seal, Box 5496, Roanoke VA 24012; tel. 703/362-1656.

### May Flather
### Potomac Woods
Located in Virginia. Resident Girl Scout camps. Openings for 115 females and males, minimum age 18, from mid-June through mid-August. Needs camp director, assistant director (program), unit managers and assistants, counselors, waterfront, kitchen and maintenance staff. Salaries are $350-1,200/season plus meals, lodging, health and accident insurance. Write to Resident Camping Administrator, Girl Scout Council of the Nation's Capital, 2133 Wisconsin Ave. NW, Washington DC 20007.

## Friendship

Located in Palmyra. Private coed camp for children ages 6-15. Looking for energetic young men and women interested in working with boys and girls from mid-June to mid- or late August. Needs counselors (minimum age 18) with skills in teaching, riding, swimming, sports, tennis, gymnastics, and other skills. Also needs kitchen workers, program director and waterfront director. "Room and board provided. Extra costs include weekly laundry and linen, staff shirt, providing own transportation for days off. Prefer to receive applications by January 31, but will accept them later." Apply to Director, Camp Friendship, Palmyra VA 22963.

## Hanover

Located in Mechanicsville. Coed church camp for children, ages 9-17. Openings from June 4 to August 17 for male and female college students completing sophomore year (minimum age 19), college graduates and teachers. Needs 3 lifeguard-waterfront (ARC-WSI), smallcraft (ARC); 30 general counselors who lead varied trip and resident program. Apply by April 1 to John E. Ensign, Director, Dept. SED, 1205 Palmyra Ave., Richmond VA 23227.

## Happyland

Located in Virginia, 75 miles south of Washington, DC. Coed resident camp for children, ages 7-17; coed day camp for senior citizen. Openings for college students from June to August. Needs counselors, lifeguards, craft instructor, nurse. Apply by April to The Salvation Army—D.Y.S., 503 E St. N.W., Washington DC 20001.

## Holiday Trails

Located in Charlottesville. Residential camp for children and youth with medical and health impairments, such as diabetes, cystic fibrosis, hearing and speech impairment, hemophilia, cancer. Openings for college aged and older persons from mid-June to mid-August. Needs counselors, $500-800; directors of waterfront (WSI), arts and crafts, nature, athletics, pool (WSI), nutrition and teenage program. Also needs physical therapists aides. Personal interviews preferred. Apply early to Camp Holiday Trails, Box 5806, Charlottesville VA 22903.

## Mawavi

Located at Prince William Forest Park, Triangle, Virginia. Resident camp for boys ages 6-11, and girls ages 6-18. ACA accredited. Openings for college students, teachers and others from mid-June to late August. Needs cabin counselors and waterfront assistants (minimum age 19), $325-425; waterfront director (minimum age 21, Red Cross WSI), $500-700; unit directors (minimum age 21), $500-600; nurse (RN or LPN), $650-750; driver/maintenance chief (minimum age 21), $600-700; maintenance/kitchen helpers (minimum age 16), $300-350. Room and board provided. Apply to Maude T. Katzenbach, Executive Director, Camp Fire Potomac Area Council, 1761 R St. NW, Washington DC 20009.

## Pleasant
## Goodwill
## Moss Hollow

Located in Virginia. Agency camp for children ages 8-15. Openings for college students, teachers and high school seniors from June 16 to August 30. Needs 4 waterfront directors, $130/week; 12 specialists, $70-100/week; 15 counselors, $65/week; 4 drivers, $100/week; 4 nurses (RN), $150/week; 4 cooks, $130/week. Apply by the end of May to Camps Pleasant, Goodwill, Moss Hollow, Dept. SED, 929 L St. NW, Washington DC 20001.

### Shenandoah

Located 14 miles from Winchester, Virginia. Residential camp for mentally retarded children and young adults, ages 9 to late 20s. Openings for 43 college and high school students, and teachers from June 15 to August 24. Needs 20 general counselors, 2 maintenance counselors (teachers and college students preferred), $550-700/season; 8 program specialists in swimming (WSI), canoeing, riding, crafts, gymnastics, camping (teachers and college students preferred), $600-800/season; 12 CITs (high school juniors and seniors), room, board and spending money; nurse (RN or LPN), $650-1,050/season. Apply to Staff Office, Rolf H. Mielzarek, Camp Shenandoah, Concord, Yellow Spring WV 26865.

### Skimino—Heritage Girl Scout Council of Virginia

Located in Newport News. Camp for girls ages 6-18. Openings for college students and teachers from mid-June to August. Needs waterfront director, minimum age 21 (WSI), $105-125/week; 2 waterfront assistants, minimum age 18 (ALS or WSI), $70-90/week; 3 unit leaders, minimum age 21 (Girl Scout background preferred), $90-110/week; 6 unit assistants, minimum age 18, $55-75/week. Salaries include room and board. "Applicant must enjoy working in the out-of-doors, sleeping in tents and most important, enjoy working with children." Send for application. Apply by April to Nancy Wagner, Supervisor of Camping, Heritage Girl Scout Council of Virginia, 5 Greenwood Rd. VA 23601; tel. 804-595-9802.

# —————— Washington ——————

## Business and Industry

### Kelly Services, Inc.

More than 450 branches coast to coast, Puerto Rico, Canada, England and France. Temporary work assignments. Offers over 100 job classifications (office, marketing and light industrial assignments) to college students, teachers and other qualified people during summer breaks and year 'round. Kelly Services also has a special referral system that allows you to register at a Kelly office near your school then work near your home during summer recess—or register near your home then work on temporary assignments during the school year. Assignments available include clerks, typists, secretaries, keypunch operators, word processors, bookkeepers and a variety of marketing and light industrial. Offers flexible schedule with "attractive hourly pay rates equal to or higher than the accepted industry standards in most cities." No paycheck deductions except Social Security and income tax. No employment fee for temporary work. See the White Pages for the branch of Kelly Services nearest you. Apply in person or write to: Summer Employment, National Headquarters, Kelly Services, GPO 1179, Detroit MI 48266.

# Resorts, Ranches, Restaurants, Lodging

### Lake Quinault Lodge
### Kalaloch Lodge
Located in Quinault, Washington. Openings from June through September 12. "Must finish the season through September 12." Positions available for reservation and front desks persons, dining room and kitchen, yard and maintenance and housekeeping. Salaries are $2.90/hour starting and up, according to job, experience and performance. "Housing in Quinault is very scarce. We are building some employee housing at Kalaloch Lodge." Apply to Fran Still, Manager, Lake Quinault Lodge, Quinault WA 98575; tel. 206/288-2571.

# Summer Camps

### Bishop
Located at Lost Lake in Elma. YMCA camp for children ages 6-15. Openings for college students for 1 week of staff training and 6-7 weeks of camp from late June to mid-August. Needs 5 male and 5 female counselors, and 1 waterfront director (WSI), $100/week; and 1 cook, $100-140/week. Apply to Glenn Madden, Camp Director, Aberdeen YMCA, 320 W. Market, Aberdeen WA 98520; tel. 206/533-3881.

### Four Winds * Westward Ho
Located on Orcas Island of the San Juan Island group. Openings for college students and teachers from mid-June to late August. Needs 16 group counselor/activity leaders, $200-300/month; 2 head counselors, $400-600/month; 2 sailing trip leaders, $300-400/month; canoe program leader, $350-450/month; and 3 activity specialists, $300-350/month. Apply by February 1 to Michael Douglas, Director, Dept. SED, Four Winds * Westward Ho, Box B, Deep Harbor WA 98243; tel. 206/376-2277.

### Hidden Valley
Located at Granite Falls, in the Cascade Mountain Foothills. Coed camp for ages 8-16, serving the Greater Seattle area. Openings for college students, teachers and foreign students from June 15 to August 29. Needs 2 pool counselors (WSI); 15 group counselors; sailing (WSI); canoeing (WSI); dramatics. Salaries are $45-55/week. Apply to Bob McKinlay, Dept. SED, Hidden Valley Camp, 8053-132 Ave. NE, Kirkland WA 98033; tel. 206/883-0449.

### Nor'wester
Located on Lopez Island. Coed camp for boys and girls ages 9-16. Openings for college students and teachers from June 23 to August 23. Needs 12 assistant unit leaders, $60/week; 12 unit leaders, $75/week; activity directors: riding, arts and crafts, canoeing, sailing, swimming, mountaineering, riflery, archery, $70-80/week; 5 dishwashers, 3 pantry girls, $50/week; 2 cooks, kitchen manager, $80-120/week; nurse (RN), $100-120/week. Apply by March 30 to John B. Helsell, 4601 91st Place NE, Bellevue WA 98004.

## Pacific Peaks Girl Scout Council

Located in Olympia. Camp for girls ages 6-17. Openings for 50 college students, teachers, high school seniors and foreign students, minimum age 18, from mid-June to mid-August. Needs unit leaders, unit counselors, backpacking and canoe trip leaders, horseback counselors, waterfront director, waterfront assistants, assistant camp directors, business managers, head cooks, assistant cooks, food packers, nurses. Salaries are $275-1,200. An equal opportunity employer. Apply by March or April to Karen J. Stay, Camping Administrator, Dept. SED, Pacific Peaks Girl Scout Council, Box 4, Olympia WA 98507.

## Sealth

Lcoated at Vashon Island. Camp Fire Girls camp for grades 2-12. Openings for college students, teachers and foreign students from mid-June through late August. Needs unit counselors, program counselors, unit leaders, waterfront staff (WSI), office staff, cooks and assistants, assistant camp directors, nurses (RN). Salaries are $300-1,100/season plus room and board. Apply to Camp Sealth Director, 8511 15th Ave. NE, Seattle WA 98115.

## Volasuca

Located in Sultan. Coed christian camp for ages 8 and up, normal children and adults, mentally retarded and physically handicapped. Openings for college students, teachers, high school seniors and foreign students from mid-June to the end of August. Needs 8 counselors; 1 craftperson, $250 and up; 2 WSI, $600 and up; nurse (RN or LPN), negotiable; cook. Special education background is helpful. Send resume or letter of introduction to Major Gilbert A. Saparto, Dept. SED, The Volunteers of America, 2801 Lombard Ave. Everett WA 98201.

## Zanika-Lache

Located at Lake Wenatchee. Camp Fire Girls camp. Openings for college students and teachers from mid-June to mid-August. Needs cabin counselors, unit coordinators, archery supervisor, CIT director, smallcraft (WSI), swimming (WSI), cook, assistant cook, business manager, maintenance, nurse, assistant director, food pack-out. Salaries are $300-800. Apply to Rhonda Hutton, North Central Washington Council of Camp Fire Girls, Box 1734, Wenatchee WA 98801.

# West Virginia

## Business and Industry

### Kelly Services, Inc.

More than 450 branches coast to coast, Puerto Rico, Canada, England and France. Temporary work assignments. Offers over 100 job classifications (office, marketing and light industrial assignments) to college students, teachers and other qualified people during summer breaks and year 'round. Kelly Services also has a special referral system that allows you to register at a Kelly office near your school then work near your home during summer recess—or register near your home then work on temporary assignments during the school year. Assignments available include clerks, typists, secretaries, keypunch operators, word processors, bookkeepers and a variety of marketing and light industrial. Offers flexible schedule with "attractive hourly pay rates equal to or higher than the accepted industry standards in most cities." No paycheck deductions except Social Security and income tax. No employment fee for temporary work. See the White Pages for the branch of Kelly Services nearest you. Apply in person or write to: Summer Employment, National Headquarters, Kelly Services, GPO 1179, Detroit MI 48266.

# Expeditions, Guide Trips

### Wildwater Expeditions Unlimited, Inc.
Located in Thurmond. Openings for 40 persons May through September a must; year-round positions available. Needs river guides. Will train but must have multimedia first aid; training sessions to be held in March. Job includes camp chores such as kitchen, carpentry, masonry, maintenance. All hiring is completed by February. Salary plus room and board, 6 days a week. Apply to Personnel Director, Dept. SED, Wildwater Unlimited, Box 55, Thurmond WV 25936.

# Summer Camps

### Bronco Junction
Located in Red House. 176-acre coed summer camp for children with bronchial asthma. Openings for 50 persons from June 8 to August 12. Employs area directors and counselors (minimum age 18 or 1 year college) in waterfront (must be WSI, minimum age for director is 21), nature, sports, gymnastics, arts and crafts, campcraft, music, dance, and drama; also hires medical student and student nurse counselors, registered nurses, dietician kitchen helpers, grounds/maintenance personnel. Salary is negotiable. Also provides room, board and insurance. Excellent work and learning opportunity for those in recreation, health, or education-related fields. College credit can be arranged. Write to Bronco Junction, 506 Medical Arts Building, Charleston WV 25301; tel. 304/373-5427.

### Emma Kaufmann
Located 8 miles north of Morgantown, West Virginia. Jewish Community Center; coed camp for children, ages 9-16. Openings from June 20 to August 27. Needs 40 counselors, 20 specialists, $300-600/season; 6 unit heads, $800-1,000/season; 6 head specialists, $700-1,000/season. Apply to Bill Laden, Camp Emma Kaufmann, 315 S. Bellefield, Pittsburgh PA 15213.

### Rim Rock
Located in Yellow Spring, West Virginia. Resident camp for girls, ages 7-15. Openings for college students from mid-June to late August. Needs 7 swimming instructors (WSI), 5 riding instructors, 12 unit counselors, 1 archery instructor, 2 crafts instructors, 2 tennis instructors, 2 canoeing instructors, 1 campcraft instructor. Salaries are $500-800 plus room and board. Apply by May to James L. Matheson, Director, Box 882, Winchester VA 22601; tel. 703/662-4650.

### Timber Ridge Camping Reservation
Located in High View, West Virginia, 20 miles west of Winchester, Virginia. Coed summer recreational camp for children 6-16. Openings for college students or

teachers from June 23 to August 20. Needs 20 general counselors, 6 tennis counselors, 6 arts and crafts counselors, 6 riding counselors, 6 athletics counselors, 6 swimming counselors, and 6 nature and camping counselors. Pays $250-500/season plus room, board and free laundry service. "We are looking for young men and women who would like to work with children and who are interested in spending the summer in a rural, pollution-free area. We are 90 miles from Washington, D.C." Apply by April to Jerry Smith, Director, Timber Ridge Camping Reservation, Dept. SED, 11615 Fulham St., Silver Spring MD 20902; tel. 301/649-5577.

# Wisconsin

## Business and Industry

### Kelly Services, Inc.
More than 450 branches coast to coast, Puerto Rico, Canada, England and France. Temporary work assignments. Offers over 100 job classifications (office, marketing and light industrial assignments) to college students, teachers and other qualified people during summer breaks and year 'round. Kelly Services also has a special referral system that allows you to register at a Kelly office near your school then work near your home during summer recess—or register near your home then work on temporary assignments during the school year. Assignments available include clerks, typists, secretaries, keypunch operators, word processors, bookkeepers and a variety of marketing and light industrial. Offers flexible schedule with "attractive hourly pay rates equal to or higher than the accepted industry standards in most cities." No paycheck deductions except Social Security and income tax. No employment fee for temporary work. See the White Pages for the branch of Kelly Services nearest you. Apply in person or write to: Summer Employment, National Headquarters, Kelly Services, GPO 1179, Detroit MI 48266.

## Commercial Attractions

### Mini Bike Trail Rides Inc.
Located in Wis Dells. Needs 15 ride operators for mini bikes, Dune Cats, Bashmobiles and Grand-Prixs, 5 ticket booth girls, 5 people to sell Grand-Prix tickets, minimum age 16. "Applicant must be willing to work any hours, be neat and clean, and be good with people." Apply in person by May 20. Apply to Jonathon Holtz, President, Box 392, Wis Dells WI 53965; tel. 608/254-2123.

## Resorts, Ranches, Restaurants, Lodging

### Boyd's Mason Lake Resort
Located in Fifield. Family-oriented summer resort. Openings for quality high school seniors and college students able to work from late May to October 20. Needs 5 laundress-cabin maids, 7 waitresses, 3 dishwashers, 2 outside maintenance people, boat dock attendant and a night watchman. From June 1 to September 1 needs a qualified horse wrangler. Salary plus room and board with 2 days off per week for

waitresses, dishwashers, and laundress-cabin maids. Off-duty activities include swimming, boating, and horseback riding. For an application and personal response to your questions, please send a stamped, addressed envelope after January 1 to Dick Simon, Boyd's Mason Lake Resort, Dept. SED, Fifield WI 54524.

## Chanticleer Inn
Located in Eagle River. Resort, motel, condominiums. Openings from June 15 through Labor Day, longer if possible. Needs 10 waitresses, salary plus tips, less room and board; 3 bartenders; 4 yardmen/waterfront men; 10 chambermaids; 4 kitchen helpers; 2 cooks, salary but must find own room and board. Apply to Jack Alward, Chanticleer Inn, RFD 3, Eagle River WI 54521.

## Deer Park Lodge
Located in Manitowish Waters. Summer resort. Openings for college students, teachers and high school seniors (minimum age 18) from the first week in June to Labor Day. Needs 14 waiter/bus boys, 14 chambermaid/laundry personnel, 2 desk clerk/receptionists, 2 play school teachers, lifeguard/pool attendant, boat dock attendant, 2 stable attendants, waterskiing instructor/driver, cocktail waitress, 5 dishwasher/kitchen help, 4-piece dance band. Salaries are $1,200-2,400/season plus room and board; dance band, salary open. Apply to Deer Park Lodge, Manitowish Waters WI 54545.

## Dillman's Sand Lake Lodge
Located at Lac du Flambeau. Resort. Openings for college students, teachers, high school seniors and foreign students from June through September. Needs 10 waitresses, 4 cabin maids, 2 recreation directors, dock attendant, 3 dishwashers. Salaries are less room and board. Needs staff that can stay into September. Apply to Dillman's Sand Lake Lodge, Lac du Flambeau WI 54538.

## Eagle Knob Lodge
Located in Cable. Resort. Openings for college students, teachers and high school seniors from late May through Labor Day. Needs 3 waitresses, 2 kitchen help, 2 general workmen, dishwasher, maids. Salaries are $325-650/month plus room and board and laundry. Enclose stamped return envelope. Letter of application should include references, former employers, earliest starting and terminating dates. Apply by April 1 to Don Milne, Eagle Knob Lodge, Dept. SED, Lake Owen, Cable WI 54821.

## Eagle Waters Resort
Located in Eagle River. Openings for college students, teachers, high school seniors and foreign students with proper visas from mid-May to mid-September, minimum age 18. Needs waitresses, waiters, bus boys, cabin maids, laundry assistants, boat and dock attendants, yard workers, bartenders, student cooks, kitchen workers, play school teachers, pool attendants, office assistants, cocktail waitress, bellhops. Earn from $800-2,000 or more, depending on position. Room and board provided. Also need 3- or 4-piece dance band, social director and/or entertainment group. Salaries are open and include room and board. State available working dates in application. Include stamped return envelope. Apply by May 1 to Eagle Waters Resort, Room 100 N.D., 6536 N. Maplewood Ave., Chicago IL 60645.

## Hazen's Long Lake Lodge, Inc.
Located in Phelps. Resort. Openings for college students, teachers and high school seniors from early June to Labor Day. Needs 5 waitress-cabin maids, $60/week plus tips; 2 dishwashers, laundress, chore boy/girl, kitchen helper, pastry cook, $350-400/month plus tips. Room and board provided. Apply by May 15 to N.H. Meyer, Manager, Hazen's Long Lake Lodge, Inc., Dept. SED, Phelps WI 54554.

## Lake Lawn Lodge
Located in Delavan, 11 miles from Lake Geneva. Resort. Openings from May to end of September. Needs help for food service, recreation, pool/health club; maids, lifeguards, general maintenance, front desk clerk, bartenders, cocktail waitresses. Hourly salaries, housing not available at resort. Apply to Personnel Department, Lake Lawn Lodge, Delavan WI 53115.

## Little Swiss Village
Located in Minocqua. Resort, restaurant and gift shops. Openings for college students, teachers and high school seniors from May through September. Needs waitresses, shop people, hostess, cabin help, dishwasher, pantry help, student cook, cook's helper. "We have rooms available at $14.50 per week." Send references and give earliest starting and latest departure dates. Apply by May to Harold Hines, Little Swiss Village, RFD 2, Box 338, Dept. SED, Minocqua WI 54548.

## Nippersink Resort
Located in Genoa City. Hotel. Openings for college students, teachers, high school seniors and foreign students from May 1 to October 1. Needs 8 governesses, 25 waitresses, 15 pool attendants, 25 waiters, 8 cooks, 20 bus boys, 20 general kitchen workers, 12 bellhops, 5 clerks, 10 porters, 4 bartenders, 30 maids, 10 children's counselors, 16 social staff workers, 8 snack shop workers, 4 bar boys. Room and board provided. State any musical talents. Apply by May to Jim Powers, Nippersink Manor Resort, Genoa City WI 53128.

## Schwartz Resort Hotel
Located at Elkhart Lake. Openings for college students, teachers and high school seniors from approximately May 28 to September 15. Needs 25 waitresses, 8 bus boys, 8 cooks, 8 bellhops, 4 beach guards and 4 pool guards (LSC required), 3 bartenders, 2 yardmen-maintenance, 3 secretaries (shorthand required), 3 desk clerks (typing required), 2 desk clerks with bookkeeping experience, 20 maids, 8 general counselors (specialties helpful), head counselor for day camp program for guests' children; 2 social directors for adults to organize tournaments, games, and other activities (guitar or other talent helpful); 2 social directors to organize and plan activities for teens and tweens. Room, board and tips provided. Apply to Ralph Lawrence, Manager, Schwartz Resort Hotel, Elkhart Lake WI 53020.

## Telemark Lodge
Located in Cable. Hotel and recreation area. Openings for college students, teachers and high school seniors from May through August or full time. Needs waiters/waitresses, $1.90/hour plus tips; bartenders, kitchen help, cooks, maids, $3.10/hour and up; bellmen, bus persons, $2.15/hour plus tips. Room and board not included; "limited rental housing available." Personal interview required. Apply to Telemark Lodge, Dept. SED, Cable WI 54821.

# Summer Camps

### Agawak

Located in Minocqua. Private girls camp, ages 8-16. Openings for 30 college students, teachers and foreign students from June 15 to August 16. Need specialty counselors for diving, life saving, sailing, small craft, water ballet, waterskiing, swimming (all with WSI); archery, arts and crafts, campcraft, dance, dramatics, golf, riflery, trampoline, tennis, fencing, baton, gymnastics, riding. Also needs tripping director, doctor, nurse, secretary, cook, second cook, baker, kitchen workers, assistant caretaker. Salaries are $450 and up. Room and board, transportation allowance, laundry, workmen's compensation and profit sharing plan provided. Apply to Oscar Siegel, Dept. SED, 6704 N. Talman, Chicago IL 60645; tel. 312/761-1838.

### Algonquin

Located in Rhinelander. Recreational, educational reading clinic for ages 7-17. Openings for college students and teachers from June 24 to August 11. Needs for camp recreation program: 15 male-cabin counselors, $500-800/season; 2 cooks, $1,000/season. Room and board provided. Apply by May 15 to James G. Doran, Camp Algonquin, Dept. SED, Route 3, Rhinelander WI 54501; tel. 715/369-1277.

### American Camping Association/Illinois Section

Located in Illinois and surrounding states including Wisconsin, Indiana, Michigan and Minnesota. The American Camping Association/Illinois Section is an association of persons involved with camps operated by social agencies, and private camp owners. More than 100 camps in Associaton. Openings for college students, teachers, foreign students and local applicants from late June to late August. Needs persons over 18 years of age who possess a variety of camp leadership skills for positions such as counselors, cooks, waterfront staff, camping and athletic skills teachers, nurses and program directors. Salaries are $500-1,000 for eight weeks or more. Room and board provided. Apply by writing or calling the American Camping Association/Illinois Section, 19 S. LaSalle St., Room 1024, Chicago IL 60603; tel. 312/332-0833.

### Anokijig

Located in Plymouth. YMCA coed resident camp with 285 acres, for children ages 8-15. Christian living in a democratic environment. Needs 2 cooks (experienced in mass feeding, dietetics and food management), May 4 to August 31, $70-120/week; program director (teacher with previous camp experience and experience in program administration), June 15 to August 24, $120-140/week; ranch director (teacher or person with advanced training in equestrian programs, including Western style riding, experience in administration and management of staff and horses), June 15 to August 24, $80-100/week; maintenance director (college senior with experience using tractors and light truck, good skills in carpentry, plumbing and electricity), June 15 to August 10, $70-90/week; camp nurse (RN licensed by State of Wisconsin, hospital experience working in pediatrics), June 29 to August 10, $90-100/week; at least 2 senior counselors/program specialists (college students) in the areas of smallcraft, sailing, waterskiing, swimming, landgames, horsemanship, campcrafts, nature, archery, Indian lore, arts and crafts, June 15 to August 10, $70-90/week. Room and board is included as a fringe benefit and is added to each employees total reported earnings. "We are a youth-oriented camp, designed to help youngsters improve their interpersonal relationships, have fun and learn new skills in a Christian environment. All staff are expected to serve as part of the workcrew and in a total team effort. Only people with an interest in working with children and who enjoy working in a rustic outdoor setting should apply for these positions." Send resume or write for application by March 1 to David C. Himes, Camp Executive Director, Dept. SED, Racine YMCA, 725 Lake Ave, Racine WI 53043; tel. 414/634-1994.

## Campo Fiesta

Located at Boulder Junction in northern Wisconsin on Trout Lake. Private girls camp. Openings for college students, teachers and foreign students, minimum age 19, from June 20 to August 13. Needs 20 cabin counselors skilled and experenced to teach one of the following activities: tripping, waterskiing, sailing, scuba, diving, swimming, riding (hunt seat—show experience preferred), gymnastics, arts and crafts, drama, tennis, archery, riflery, $475-800 depending on skill and experience plus room and board; office manager, kitchen helpers, housekeeping/laundry, $500-1,000. Apply early (April deadline) to Mr. and Mrs. N.D. Frisbie, 420 E. Tropical Way, Plantation FL 33317.

## Chippewa Bay

Located 40 miles north of Eau Claire, Wisconsin. Girl Scout camp. Openings for college students, teachers, high school seniors and foreign students from June 10 to August 20. Needs camp director, assistant director, unit leaders, $660-760; unit counselors, $560-640; arts and crafts specialists, naturalist, $560-700; waterfront director, $660-800; business manager, $600-750; 2 cooks, $900-1,600; nurse (RN, GRN), $850-1,000; approximate salaries. Unit programs include canoeing, sailing, backpacking, creative arts, primitive, and a special unit for EMR children. Philosophy of girl planning with adult guidance. Apply early to Camp Director, Girl Scouts of DuPage County Council, 8 S. 021, Route 53, Naperville IL 60540; tel. 312/963-6050.

## Deerhorn

Located in Rhinelander, Wisconsin. Private boys camp for ages 7-15. Openings for college students and teachers. Needs 22 general counselors to instruct archery, crafts, tennis, team sports, swimming, sailing, waterskiing, riding, riflery, golf, soccer, $700-1,000/season plus room, board and transportation; 2 cooks, $1,100-1,400/season. Apply by April to Don C. Broadbridge, Owner/Director, Camp Deerhorn, 2863 Shannon Ct., Northbrook IL 60062; tel. 312/272-6080.

## Edwards

Located in East Troy on Lake Beulah. YMCA resident camp. Openings from June 10 or 17 to August 18 or 25. Needs 16 counselors for coed youth camp, $75-125/week, college students preferred; 2 trip leaders, $75-125/week, college students preferred; 1 waterfront director, $115-140/week, teacher preferred; 1 assistant waterfront director, $90-125/week; 1 nature director, $75-90/week; 1 crafts director, $75-90/week; 1-2 assistant cooks, $2.65-3.00/hour, college students and teachers preferred. Room and board provided. Apply by March 1 to Merrill G. Oleson, Camp Director, Camp Edwards YMCA, 1275 Army Lake Rd., East Troy WI 53120; tel. 414/642-7466.

### Harand Camp of the Theatre Arts

Located at Elkhart Lake, Wisconsin. General coed camp for pre-teen and teenage children plus theater activities. Openings for college students and teachers from June 22 through the end of August. Needs counselors, specialists for water and sports, 6 accompanists, and dining room help. All salaries $500 and up plus room and board, linen and insurance. Staff lives in cabins that are heated. Apply by May to Byron Friedman, Director, 708 Church St., Evanston, IL 60201; tel. 312/864-1500.

### Hilltop

Located in Spring Green. Private girls camp, ages 9-16. Openings for college students, teachers and foreign students from June 15 to August 15. Needs specialty counselors: 2 WSI, dance, dramatics, general, 2 riding, music, $600/season; cooks, assistant cooks, $400-800/season. Room and board are provided Apply by May to Mrs. Jan Fritz, Hilltop Summer Camp for Girls, Dept. SED, Spring Green WI 53588.

### Holiday Home Camp

Located on Lake Geneva at Williams Bay, Wisconsin. Coed camp for disadvantaged and diabetic children, ages 8-12. Openings from mid-June to mid-August. Needs 2 waterfront directors (WSI), 2 unit directors, laundry worker, $600-700/season; crafts director, college students preferred. 12 counselors, college students and high school seniors preferred. Send resume. Apply to James Myers, Director, Dept. SED, 916 Hollywood Dr., Monroe MI 48161.

### Horseshoe, Inc.

Located at Horseshoe Lake, Minong. Private boys camp, ages 9-17. Openings for college students and teachers from June 15 to August 15, 8-week session plus week of precamp training. Needs cabin/specialty counselors: 4 swimming instructors (WSI), 4 boating-canoe-sailing (SCI), 3 tennis, 2 riflery-skeet, 2 craft (wood, leather), 3 athletics, 4 canoe and backpack, 2 fishing, archery, ecology. Salaries are $400 and up/season. Room and board provided. Apply by April 1 to Camp Horseshoe, Inc., Box 218, Shell Lake WI 54871.

### Jackpine

Located in Wascott. Small modern camp with free choice program; for boys ages 8-16. Openings for applicants (minimum age 19 or one year of college), from June 18 to August 18. Needs 4 senior cabin counselors, $400/season; 2 waterfront directors (WSI), $450/season; 1 specialist each in the areas of archery, riflery, tennis, and tripping, $400/season. Salaries include room and board, and costs to and from camp. "We want counselors who like to work with kids outdoors." Send for application. Apply to Stewart F. Buhai, Director, 1988 Green Bay Rd. #3, Highland Park IL 60035; tel. 312/432-8854.

### Kawaga

Located in Minocqua, Wisconsin. Private boys camp for ages 8-16. Openings for college students, teachers and high school seniors from mid-June to mid-August. Needs specialty counselors for scuba, sailing, waterfront (WSI), waterskiing, tennis, Indian lore, tripping, small craft (rowing, canoeing), arts and crafts, piano, dramatics, photography, archery, riflery, $400 and up; 4 kitchen staff, $60/week;

cook; baker; nurse. Some housing available for married staff. Room and board are provided. Apply by April 1 to Ron Silverstein, Director, 2235 Grandview Pl., Glenview IL 60025.

## Rodney Kroehler YMCA Camp

Located in Hayward. Coed summer camp for children ages 9-15. Openings from the second week in June to late August. "We are seeking qualified, experienced and mature college age and older persons who understand and have the patience to work with affluent children on a 24 hour per day basis for two-week periods," Needs 15 cabin counselors-instructors, college students and teachers preferred, $700/season; 1 RN/Camp Nurse, $1,300/season; 1 waterfront director, 21 or older, $1,000 up/season. "Can teach programs such as sailing, leathercraft at all levels, backpacking and outdoor living, waterskiing, and have motivation and originality to adapt. Applicants must be prepared to accept the role of educators, surrogate parents, and friends in the development of character and leadership in our campers. Staff members have an equal opportunity to learn and develop under excellent working conditions. An equal opportunity employer." Apply by March 1 to R.J. Mernitz, Executive Director CCD, Rodney Kroehler YMCA Camp, Route 6, Box 395, Hayward WI 54843; tel. 715/634-2484.

## Ma-Ka-Ja-Wan Scout Reservation

Located in Pearson. Boy Scout Camp for boys ages 10-15; high adventure base offering backpacking and river raft trips; ranch camp with related program. Openings from approximately June 15 to August 15. Needs aquatics director (WSI), 6 aquatics counselors, 2 program directors, rifle range director, provisional scoutmaster, maintenance director, backpacking director, nurse (RN), ranch foreman, chaplain, minimum age 21; 2 archery directors, 6 camp commissioners, 3 maintenance and vehicle drivers, 2 ecology/conservation directors, 2 dining lodge directors, 2 wranglers, minimum age 18. Also needs 2 handicraft counselors, trading post operators, kitchen personnel, craft specialists. Salaries are $400-1,200/season depending on position and experience plus room and board. "The positions of aquatics director, program director, rifle range officer and ecology-conservation director must be BSA Camp School certified or be willing to attend camp school during the first part of June. Applicant should have scouting background but it's not necessary. We have housing accommodations for families." Send for application. Apply by February 1 to Robert G. King, Administrator, Ma-Ka-Ja-Wan Scout Reservation, Pearson WI 54462; tel. 715/484-2346.

## Marimeta

Located in Eagle River, Wisconsin. Private girls camp for ages 8-15. Openings for college students and teachers, minimum age 19, from June 15 to August 15. Need specialty counselors for gymnastics, swimming (WSI), sailing, canoeing, waterskiing, tennis, riflery, arts and crafts, golf, archery, $500-700 plus room and board and transportation to and from Chicago area. Counselors must also assume cabin responsibilities. Apply by May 1 to Mrs. Marshall Rabovsky, 645 Lavergne Ave., Wilmette IL 60091.

## Minne Wonka Lodge

Located in Three Lakes, Wisconsin. Private camp for girls. Openings for 25 college students (at least sophomore) and teachers from approximately June 16 to August 15. Needs specialty counselors for arts and crafts, campcraft, tripping, canoeing, sailing, waterskiing, nature, riding, swimming, archery; typist; and bookkeeper. Salaries are $400-800. Room, board and laundry service provided. Live in cabins with campers. Apply to Mr. and Mrs. C.R. Hanna, Minne Wonka Lodge, 235 Sterncrest Dr., Chagrin Falls OH 44022; tel. 216/248-7207.

## Nebagamon for Boys

Located in Lake Nebagamon, Wisconsin. Private camp for children ages 10-15. Openings for 13 college students and teachers from June 15 to August 14. Needs 8 senior counselors; specialty counselors: crafts, photography, nature, wilderness tripping (canoe, backpacking, cycling); food service manager; and RN. Salaries are appropriate to positions. Apply by March 1 to Bernard Stein, Camp Nebagamon, 7433 Cromwell Dr., Clayton MO 63105.

## Nicolet for Girls, Inc.

Located in Eagle River. Private camp for girls ages 8-15. Openings for college students and teachers, minimum age 18 or one year college completed, from June 16 to August 16. Needs specialty counselors: swimming (WSI), small craft (SCI or ARC), waterskiing, tennis, arts and crafts, English riding (dressage, jumping) and gymnastics. Salaries are $550-1,000 depending on age, qualifications and position. Room, board and laundry provided. Nursing, kitchen and stable staff also needed. Apply by March 1 to Dr. Jeff Starz, Associate Director, Camp Nicolet for Girls, Inc., Eagle River WI 54521.

## Nokomis, Inc.

Located in Mercer, Wisconsin. Private camp for girls ages 8-16. Openings for college students, teachers and foreign students from approximately June 18 to August 14. Needs instructors for archery, crafts, music, all water sports (swimming, sailing, canoeing, boating, waterskiing), tennis, riflery, English riding, drama, gymnastics (minimum age 19); nurse (RN). Salaries based upon experience and skill. Room, board, laundry and travel allowance provided. Apply by April to Charlotte L. Mendes, Director, Camp Nokomis, Inc., Dept. SED, 3180 Lake Shore Dr., Chicago IL 60657.

## Northwoods

Located in northern Wisconsin near Ashland. Girl Scout camp serving girls ages 10-17; specialty programs in horseback riding, backpacking, canoeing, primitive camping, waterfront activities and arts exploration. Openings for college students, teachers and high school seniors from mid-June to Mid-August. Needs assistant camp director (must have car, camp experience, knowledge of Girl Scout program and valid driver's license), $880-1,200/season; 6 unit leaders (experienced in working with groups of children, and preferably in camp counseling or Girl Scouting, and Red Cross Lifesaving and/or First Aid), $720-960/season; 12 assistant unit leaders (experienced in working with groups of children, and preferably in camp counseling or Girl Scouting, and Red Cross Lifesaving and/or First Aid), $640-880/season; waterfront director (WSI, experienced in canoeing, and preferably in camping), $760-1,040; 2 waterfront assistants (ALS, prefers camp experience), $680-840/season; health supervisor (RN, LPN, EMT, prefers First Aid training), $800-1,200/season; food superviser (experienced in quantity cooking, prefers training in food management), $880-1,360/season; 2 cook's assistants (prefers experience in cooking), $800-1,000/season; packout person (physical stamina and basic math skills required), $640-760/season; business manager (chauffer's driving license required), $720-1,000/season; bus driver (school bus driver's license required), $640-840/season; horseback riding specialist, $640-840/season. Room and board provided. Equal opportunity/affirmative Girl Scout Council of St. Croix Valley, 400 S. Robert, St. Paul MN 55107; tel. 612/227 8835.

## Osoha

Located in Boulder Junction, Wisconsin, 14 miles north of Minocqua. Camp for teenage girls. Openings for college students and teachers from June 14 to August 18; secretaries earlier and later. Needs cabin counselors-instructors for swimming, diving, waterskiing, water ballet, canoeing, sailing, English riding, campcraft, vocal music, modern dance, sketching, arts and crafts, archery, badminton, tennis; secretaries; nurse; cook; and kitchen helpers. Room, board and laundry provided. State age and qualifications in letter of application. Apply to Linda Porter, Dept. SED, 854 Prospect Ave., Winnetka IL 60093.

## Red Pine

Located in Minocqua. Private camp for girls ages 6-16. ACA accredited, 43rd season. Openings for college students and teachers from June 17 to August 17 including 5 days precamp training. Needs specialty counselors (minimum age 19): canoeing (WSI or SCS), tripping, campcraft, English riding (dressage and jumping), sailing (SCS), swimming (WSI), waterskiing (WSI or SCS), karate, photography, crafts, gymnastics, tennis; nurse (RN), kitchen assistants; and cook. Salaries are $500 and up depending on age and qualifications plus room and board. Apply by April 30 to Irene Boudreaux, Associate Director, Red Pine Camp for Girls, Inc., Minocqua WI 54548.

## Shewahmegon

Located at Lake Owen, Drummond, Wisconsin. Private camp for boys ages 8-14. Openings for college students and teachers from June 15 to August 15. Needs 14 instructors for crafts, rock polishing, woodshop, riflery (NRA), trampoline, power mechanics, ecology, scuba diving, ARC instructors in sailing-canoeing-power boating, tennis, golf, 3 canoe and campout trip leaders, $500-900/season; medical doctor, RN or LPN, $700-1,000/season; 2 camp maintenance, $500-900/season; assistant cooks, kitchen helpers and kitchen maintenance, minimum wage or more. Room and board provided. Apply to William T. Will, Camp Shewahmegon, 1208 E. Miner St., Arlington Heights IL 60004; tel. 312/255-9710.

## Tiwaushara

Located in Redgranite. Girl Scout camp for girls ages 9-14. Openings from June 15 to August 16 or 26. Needs 10 counselors, $390-475; 3 unit leaders, $430-675; 1 business manager, $390-$475; 1 waterfront director, 2 cooks, $735-950; 2 waterfront assistants (one with boating), $590-675; health supervisor, $735-900, program director $735-950. Apply to Kris Martin, Camp Director, Camp Tiwaushara, 307 N. Main St., Fond du Lac WI 54935; tel. 414/921-8540.

## Towering Pines
## Woodland

Located at Eagle River, Wisconsin. Camp for boys (Towering Pines), camp for girls (Woodland). Openings for men, women and married staff in an unusually varied program, for a single 7½ week season from June 20 to August 19. Needs specialists in tripping, nature lore, tennis, sailing, all land and water sports, crafts, riding, marksmanship, performing arts. Also needs man capable of sailing a 34-foot sloop on Lake Superior; department directors; nurse; and cooks. Starting salaries are $400-700 plus room and board, laundry and travel allowance. Apply to John M. Jordan, Dept. SED, 242 Bristol St., Northfield IL 60093.

## Union League Boys' Clubs

Located in Salem, Wisconsin. Resident camp for children ages 6-14; 7 weeks of boys and 1 week of girls. Openings for college students, teachers and foreign students from June 14 to August 18 (dates of employment depend on school schedules). Needs 16 cottage counselors, assistant cook, nurse. Starting salary is $600 per season plus room and board. Two days off every two weeks. "Good experience with inner city youngsters from the Chicago area. Dedicated workers needed." Swimming, fishing, boating, sailing, sports, and camping activities offered. Apply to Frank J. Matkovich, Camp Director, Union League Boys' Clubs Camp, 2157 W. 19th St., Chicago IL 60608; tel. 312/829-6840.

## Waupaca For Boys, Inc.

Located in Waupaca, Wisconsin. Camp for children ages 9-14. ACA accredited, 30th year. Openings for college students and teachers, minimum age 19, from mid-June to mid-August. Needs instructors in swimming (WSI); specialists in waterskiing, tennis, golf, riflery (NRA), archery, crafts (woodworking), photography, horseback riding, baseball, wrestling, nature; swimming director (WSI); nurse (RN); and caretaker. Salaries are open. Room (cabins with washrooms and showers attached), board, laundry, medical insurance and travel allowance provided. Cabins with washrooms and showers available; board provided. Apply by February to Camp Waupaca for Boys, Inc., 6850 N. Crawford Ave., Lincolnwood IL 60646; tel. 312/676-0911.

## Windego

Located in Wild Rose, Wisconsin. Girl Scout camp for girls ages 9-17. Openings for 28 college students, teachers and foreign students from mid-June to mid-August. Needs unit leaders, counselors, specialty counselors for arts and crafts, training campcraft, sailing, canoeing, natural science, sports, swimming instructors (WSI), cooks, nurses. Salaries are $630-1,200. Apply by June 30 to Illinois Shore Girl Scout Council, Inc., Box 544, Dept. SED, Wilmette IL 60091.

## Wisconsin Girl Scout Resident Camp Association

Located throughout Wisconsin. Six residential camps for girls ages 7-17; also special programs for emotionally and physically handicapped children, families, and adult women. Openings for college students, teachers, high school students, foreign students and local applicants from approximately June 15 to August 18. Will employ over 225 people. Needs assistant camp directors (minimum age 21), $85-135/week; nurses (minimum age 21), $75-125/week; business managers (minimum age 21), $68-100/week; head cooks (minimum age 21), $85-150/week; assistant cooks (minimum age 18), $70-108/week; waterfront directors (minimum age 21), $75-100/week; small craft directors (minimum age 21), $70-94/week; waterfront assistants (minimum age 18), $63-85/week; unit leaders (minimum age 21), $68-100/week; assistant unit leaders (minimum age 18), $63-85/week; program consultants in the areas of arts & crafts, sports, environment, riding (minimum age 19), $63-88/week; tripping leaders in the areas of backpacking, canoeing, bicycling, horseback riding (minimum age 21), $70-100/week; CIT directors (minimum age 21), $84-100. "Staff lives with other staff in platform tents or small cabins which are supplied with beds and mattresses. Lodging on the trail consists of trail equipment such as lightweight tents, which are supplied. All meals are provided either on cookouts, in a dining hall, or on the trail. Women and men who apply for our jobs should be prepared to help children live comfortably in the out-of-doors, as well as help them learn the skills of living in a group of about 24 girls. The job will require you to be healthy, sensitive to children's needs, able to make changes easily, and concerned with the natural environment." Send resume or send for application. Applications accepted January 1 through June. Apply to Linda Huffmon, Resident Camp Coordinator, Dept. SED, 225 N. Grand Ave., Box 1227, Waukesha WI 53187; tel. 414/542-4491.

# Wyoming

## Business and Industry

### Kelly Services, Inc.
More than 450 branches coast to coast, Puerto Rico, Canada, England and France. Temporary work assignments. Offers over 100 job classifications (office, marketing and light industrial assignments) to college students, teachers and other qualified people during summer breaks and year 'round. Kelly Services also has a special referral system that allows you to register at a Kelly office near your school then work near your home during summer recess—or register near your home then work on temporary assignments during the school year. Assignments available include clerks, typists, secretaries, keypunch operators, word processors, bookkeepers and a variety of marketing and light industrial. Offers flexible schedule with "attractive hourly pay rates equal to or higher than the accepted industry standards in most cities." No paycheck deductions except Social Security and income tax. No employment fee for temporary work. See the White Pages for the branch of Kelly Services nearest you. Apply in person or write to: Summer Employment, National Headquarters, Kelly Services, GPO 1179, Detroit MI 48266.

## National Parks

### Hamilton Stores, Inc.
Located in Yellowstone National Park, Wyoming. General merchandising. Openings for 500-600 college students, teachers and high school seniors, minimum age 18, from late May through mid-September. Needs sales clerks, fountain clerks, dishwashers, grocery stock clerks, maintenance workers, kitchen helpers, housekeepers, cashiers and security guards. Federal minimum wage. Also needs cooks (for employees' dining rooms), office workers, construction workers; salaries based on experience. Write for application and descriptive brochure. Apply by July 15 to Personnel Department, Hamilton Stores, Inc., Box 2700, Dept. SED, Santa Barbara CA 93120.

## Yellowstone Park Company

Located at Yellowstone National Park. Concessionaire. "We have over 2,000 openings from late April to October in food service, lodging, reservations, accounting, vending, gift shops and transportation." Minimum age 18. Employment information sent with application. Equal opportunity/Affirmative Action employer. Please write to Yellowstone Park Company, Personnel Office, Yellowstone National Park WY 82190.

## Yellowstone Park Service Stations

Located in Yellowstone National Park, Wyoming. Concessionaire. Openings for college students and teachers (US citizens only, minimum age 18) from May 1 to October 31; minimum period June 10 to Labor Day. Need 85 male or female gasoline service station attendants, 10 service station cashiers, 6 warehouse/office/clerical help, 8 journeyman automobile mechanics, 8 mechanic helpers. Wages for all positions are based on hourly rates, with none being less than the federal minimum wage. Apply by May 1 to Employment Department, Box 11, Dept. SED, Gardiner MT 59030.

# Resorts, Ranches, Restaurants, Lodging

## Blackwater Lodge

Located in Cody, 15 miles from east entrance of Yellowstone Park. Resort. Openings from April 25 to October 15. Needs 2 food-cocktail waitresses, $125/month plus tips; cabin maids, kitchen help, $225/month; breakfast cook (will train), dinner cook (will train), salary open. Room, board and use of horses provided. Send resume and dates available for employment. Apply to Mrs. Thomas Ivanoff, Blackwater Lodge, Box 1162, Cody WY 82414.

## Bill Cody's Ranch Inn

Located in Cody. Dude ranch. Openings for college students and teachers. Must be available to work for a 3-month period between May 1 and October 1. Needs cook's assistants, office assistants, cabin maid/waitresses, cabin maid/laundry workers, $110-200/month, depending on experience and ability. Horse wranglers must have basic horse care knowledge and Western and mountain riding experience, horse shoeing ability helpful, $125-200/month depending on experience and ability. Salaries include room and board (plus tips), riding privileges, and end of season/contract bonuses; bed and bath linen not provided but laundry service is available. Openings for winter resort program, December 10-March 20. Needs cabin maids, waitresses, cooks. Salaries and details upon request. Please specify which season you are applying for and dates you are available to work. Please include resume, photo and references. Apply by March 15 (summer program) and November 15 (winter program) to Mrs. William Cody, Bill Cody's Ranch Inn, Box 1390, Cody WY 82414.

## Deer Creek Ranch

Located in Cody. Small dude ranch. Openings for college students from June 20 to approximately October 10. Needs cabin maid-waitress. Salary is $200/month. Salary includes room and board. Apply to Hope W. Read, 125 E. 72nd St., New York NY 10021.

## Flagg Ranch Resort
Located in Moran, south entrance to Yellowstone Park. Openings for college students, teachers and high school seniors from May 1 to October 1. Needs cabin maids, bus boys, fountain clerks, store clerks, waitresses, service station attendants, dishwashers, cooks, maintenance personnel, general workers. Salaries are $250/month plus room and board. Enclose stamped return envelope. Apply by March to Leo Dentino, Flagg Ranch, Box 187, Moran WY 83013.

## Flying L Skytel
Located on the Cody Road to Yellowstone National Park in Cody. Western guest ranch/resort with private airstrip, elevation 5,670 feet. Openings from May 1 to December 1. Needs 2 cooks, 4 cabin maids, 5 waitresses, 3 wranglers, 1 yard man and 2 out-of-door steak cookout men. Salary open depending on ability and honesty. Meals, room, uniforms, utilities along with recreational activities, i.e., horseback riding, heated pool, tennis, fishing, all furnished classified as reimbursed wages plus a cash stipend. "We send a mimeographed list of company policies for the consideration of all personnel. Living facilities at the ranch are excellent." Apply to Cecil A. Legg, Box 1136, Cody WY 82414.

## Goff Creek Lodge Motel
Located in Cody. Resort. Openings for high school or college students from May 15 to October 15. Needs 8 waitresses or waiters (prefers waitresses), 8 cabin maids, 8 kitchen help, 4 assistant cooks (will train), 4 wranglers (must have some knowledge of horses), 2 chore and yard persons (male or female). Salaries are $150-250/month plus room and board, tips and use of horses. Send resume, recent photo, and dates of employment. Will hire some to start work in July. "Work in the mountains for the summer." Apply by February 15 to Gloria T. Schmitt, Manager, Goff Creek Lodge, Box 167, Cody WY 82414.

## Hatchet Motel and Restaurant
Located in Moran, near Grand Teton National Park. Openings for college students, teachers and high school students from mid-May to early September, June 1 to August 31 minimum. Needs 3 waitresses, $250/month plus tips; 2 kitchen helpers, 2 relief persons, 3 maids, 2 desk clerks, 2 station attendants, $425/month; 3 cooks, $500/month. Room and board, $125/month. Send stamped, self-addressed envelope with inquiry. Apply by March 1 to Leland J. Luther, 1415 Jackson St., Great Bend KS 67530.

## H F Bar Ranch
Located in Saddlestring. Dude ranch. Openings for college students, teachers and high school seniors from June 1 through September 10 or later. Needs waiters/waitresses, room attendants, kitchen helpers, hay hands. Must stay entire

**Commercial attractions usually offer the most job openings in each state; and often the best pay. But while they may be more lucrative, few of them offer housing. Check these listings carefully for full details.**

season. Apply to H. S. Horton, President, H F Bar Ranch, Saddlestring WY 82840; tel. 307/684-2487.

## Medicine Bow Lodge and Guest Ranch
Located in Saratoga. Dude ranch in the mountains of Medicine Bow National Forest. Needs 2 housekeepers, 1 kitchen helper/waitress, 3 wranglers (must ride well), 1 kiddie wrangler (must ride well). Salaries are $200/month, plus room, board and tips, college students and high school seniors preferred; 1 cook, mimimum $450/month, room, board and tips, college student or teacher preferred; 1 cook's helper, minimum $200/month, room, board and tips, college student, high school senior or teacher preferred. Needs some employees as early as May 15, others first week in June. All needed through week of Labor Day. Open year round. Occasionally will have fall and winter openings. Knowledge of snowmobiling and/or cross country skiing required. Apply by May 15 to Mr. and Mrs. John F. Owens, Managers, Medicine Bow Lodge and Guest Ranch, Box 752 P, Saratoga WY 82331.

## One Bar Eleven Ranch
Located in Saratoga. Ranch. Openings for college students and high school students from June 1 to September 1. Needs 3 ranch hands to drive tractor, repair fence and ride cattle, $400-600/month plus room and board. "Travel expense to and from ranch will be refunded to applicant at end of season if employee stays full season and has proven satisfactory." Send resume. Apply by March 1 to J.E. Rouse, Box 646, Saratoga WY 82331; tel. 307/327-5571.

## Pahaska Tepee
Located 50 miles west of Cody, Wyoming, at the east entrance to Yellowstone National Park. Resort, hotel, ranch, restaurant. Buffalo Bill's original hunting lodge. Openings for 50, between May 1 and September 30. Needs waitresses, $125/month plus tips; station attendants, gift shop clerks, cabin maids, yard crew people, kitchen help, $200/month; cooks, salary open. Salaries include room and board. Apply early to Ronald K. Lynde, Pahaska Tepee, Box 491, Cody WY 82414.

## Siggins Triangle X Ranch
Located in Cody. Openings for qualified teachers, college students and high school seniors during summer season (June 1 to September 1) and fall season (September 1 to November 20). Needs cabin maid/waitress, cook, assistant cook, kitchen assistant, lawn/maintenance, chore boy, floater, youth program counselor, horse wrangler, housekeeper. Salaries vary according to position and sincerity of purpose. Beginning salary is $150/month plus room, board, tips, use of ranch recreational facilities (horses, swimming pool, tennis court, and recreation lodge). Include a stamped, self-addressed envelope with your letter of application. Apply by November 1 to Mrs. Stanley D. Siggins, Siggins Triangle X Guest Ranch, Dept. SED, Cody WY 82414.

## South Fork Ranches, Inc.
Located in Cody. Dude ranch. Openings for college students, high school seniors and local applicants from May 16 to November 16. Needs 1 ranch wrangler and 1 mountain trips wrangler, $380-680/month depending on experience; 1 cook,

about $550/month; 1 baby sitter and 3 cabin girls, about $200/month; 1 or 2 yard workers (grounds and pools), about $200-300/month; and 1 irrigator, about $500/month. Salaries include room, board and tips. "Enthusiasm, ability to diversify and good attitude are essential!" Apply by March/April to Allison M. Tilden, Vice President, RR 2, Box 3700, Cody WY 82414; tel. 307/587-2076.

**UXU Lodge**
Located in Wapiti. Motel, restaurant. Openings from June 15 to August 30. Needs 1 cabin maid and 1 kitchen helper, $200 plus room and board. Apply to William D. Paschke, Owner, UXU Lodge, Wapiti WY 82450; tel. 307/587-2143.

**Valley Ranch, Inc.**
Located in Cody. Openings for 15 persons, minimum age 19, from June 1 to October 31. Needs cook, assistant cook, 2 waiter/waitress, dishwasher, 3 wrangler/guide, laundry worker, head housekeeper, 2 cabin maids, arts and crafts director, gardener, chore person. Salaries are $250-400/month plus room and board. Apply by April 1 to Manager, Valley Ranch, South Fork Star Route, Cody WY 82414.

**Wapiti Valley Inn**
Located in Wapiti, 18 miles west of Cody on the road to Yellowstone Park. Resort. Openings for college students and high school seniors from May 1 through October 15. Needs waitresses, cooks, cabin maids, and maintenance workers. Salaries are $250/month plus room, board and tips. Apply to Christel Bauer, Wapiti Valley Inn, Wapiti WY 82450; tel. 307/587-3961.

# —————— Canada ——————

## Business and Industry

**Kelly Services, Inc.**
More than 450 branches coast to coast, Puerto Rico, Canada, England and France. Temporary work assignments. Offers over 100 job classifications (office, marketing and light industrial assignments) to college students, teachers and other qualified people during summer breaks and year 'round. Kelly Services also has a special referral system that allows you to register at a Kelly office near your school then work near your home during summer recess—or register near your home then work on temporary assignments during the school year. Assignments available include clerks, typists, secretaries, keypunch operators, word processors, bookkeepers and a variety of marketing and light industrial. Offers flexible schedule with "attractive hourly pay rates equal to or higher than the accepted industry standards in most cities." No paycheck deductions except Social Security and income tax. No employment fee for temporary work. See the White Pages for the branch of Kelly Services nearest you. Apply in person or write to: Summer Employment, National Headquarters, Kelly Services, GPO 1179, Detroit MI 48266.

# Summer Camps

### Pine Valley Camp
Located in Ste. Agathe des Monts, Quebec. Private coed camp for children 7-16. Needs "college students and teachers ready for a challenge with bright, exciting young people, in an outdoor environment, with a commitment for full season only." Openings for cabin group counselors (minimum age 20); activity instructors (minimum age 20) for basketball, baseball, football, tennis, archery, swimming, canoeing, waterskiing, arts and crafts, gymnastics and nature lore; unit directors (minimum age 24); waterfront director (minimum age 24); program director (minimum age 26). Experience and references required. Personal interviews will be arranged. Excellent salaries plus transportation, laundry, room and board provided. Apply by May 1 to Mr. R. Lazanik, MSW, Director, Dept. SED, 5165 Sherbrooke St. W., Suite 316, Montreal, Quebec, Canada H4A 1T6; tel. 514/489-8722.

### Stephens
Located at Kenora, Ontario, 7 miles southeast on Copeland Island. Coed YMCA resident and wilderness camp with canoe tripping for ages 8-16. Openings for 11 college students from June 1 to September 15. Needs 5 counselors, $70/week; 6 canoe trippers (male and female), $70/week. Room and board provided. Apply by June 1 to Jim Leggat, YMCA Camp Stephens, 301 Vaughan St., Winnipeg, Manitoba, Canada R3B 2N7.

### Walden
Located in Palmer Rapids, Ontario. Children's summer camp. Needs general camp counselors (male and female) and specialists (male and female) in swimming, sailing, canoe tripping, water skiing, crafts, ceramics, musical theater and tennis, $500-800/season; college students preferred. Also needs unit heads and heads of all specialties listed above, $800-1,200/season, college students or teachers preferred. Apply to Ted Cole, Director, 3995 Bathurst St. #206, Downsview, Ontario Canada M3H 5V3; tel. 416/635-0049.

### White Pine
Located on Lake Placid, Haliburton, Ontario. Private, coed, decentralized, group centered camp for children ages 8-16. Openings for 36 college students (at least juniors) and teachers from June 24 to August 22. Needs 6 section heads (village directors), cabin counselors; activity instructors and head specialists (experienced) for swimming, sailing, waterskiing, canoeing, riding, land tripping, arts and crafts, tennis, woodshop, copper enamel, ceramics, photography. Salaries are $500-1,000 and up. Salary dependent on experience and references. Interviews available: Toronto, Buffalo, Atlanta, New York, Los Angeles, Cincinnati, Pittsburgh, Boston, Detroit. Enclose stamped return envelope. Apply by May to J. Kronick, 8 Rollscourt Dr., Willowdale, Ontario, Canada M2L 1X5.

# Puerto Rico

## Business and Industry

**Kelly Services, Inc.**
More than 450 branches coast to coast, Puerto Rico, Canada, England and France. Temporary work assignments. Offers over 100 job classifications (office, marketing and light industrial assignments) to college students, teachers and other qualified people during summer breaks and year 'round. Kelly Services also has a special referral system that allows you to register at a Kelly office near your school then work near your home during summer recess—or register near your home then work on temporary assignments during the school year. Assignments available include clerks, typists, secretaries, keypunch operators, word processors, bookkeepers and a variety of marketing and light industrial. Offers flexible schedule with "attractive hourly pay rates equal to or higher than the accepted industry standards in most cities." No paycheck deductions except Social Security and income tax. No employment fee for temporary work. See the White Pages for the branch of Kelly Services nearest you. Apply in person or write to: Summer Employment, National Headquarters, Kelly Services, GPO 1179, Detroit MI 48266.

# West Indies

## Summer Camps

**Bahama Sailing**
Located at Antigua in the West Indies. Water sports camp for ages 13-18. Openings for college students and teachers from June 30 for six weeks. Needs specialists in all water activities: sailing, scuba diving, waterskiing, swimming, marine biology; tennis, drama, dance, yoga, karate, guitar. Salaries are $200-600. Apply to Walter Bush, Dept. SED, Bahama Sailing Camp, 480 W. 246th St., Bronx NY 10471.

# U.S.A.

## Business and Industry

**Kelly Services, Inc.**
See individual listings in each state.

## Summer Camps

**Boy Scouts of America**
Staff positions are available to qualified students and teachers in more than 500

local camps throughout the country. A background in Scouting is preferred, but not necessary. Needed are those with backgrounds in conservation, wilderness backpacking, handicrafts, nature, aquatics, archery, commissary, first aid and administration. Salary is based on background and position. Many camps conduct interviews during Christmas holidays, so contact should be made as early as December. See Boy Scouts of America in your local telephone directory.

## Camp Fire, Inc.

Camp Fire councils in all parts of the country employ college students, graduate students, teachers and other mature adults to work on the staffs of resident camps. Positions available for qualified applicants at least 18 years of age include cabin counselors, unit directors, activity directors, cooks, nurses, business managers and maintenance personnel. Camp director and assistant camp director positions are available for those with at least three previous years' experience in an administrative position. Write to Camping Services, Camp Fire National Headquarters, 4601 Madison Ave., Kansas City MO 64112. Give your age, experience, dates available and part of the country in which you prefer to work; you will be referred to councils having job openings in that area. See also many Camp Fire camps listed throughout *Summer Employment Directory*.

## Girl Scouts of the U.S.A.

Nearly 600 camps are operated by Girl Scout councils from coast to coast and offer a chance to enjoy an expense-free summer with full maintenance plus salary, in a relaxed and informal atmosphere. Needs college students in all fields, as well as nurses, dietitians, teachers and graduate students. Write to Recruitment and Referral, Girl Scouts of the U.S.A., 830 3rd Ave., New York NY 10022 for information. A camp directory will be sent if you give the name of the state in which you would like to work. See also many Girl Scout camps listed throughout *Summer Employment Directory*.

## Young Men's Christian Association

Many opportunities for young men and women in the field of camping, both resident camping and day camping. College students are given first consideration. Gain valuable experience in leadership training and in working with children of all ethnic backgrounds. YMCA camps are located from coast to coast. For further information, contact the regional office nearest you, your local YMCA, or the National Council of YMCAs, 291 Broadway, New York NY 10007. See also many YMCA camps listed throughout *Summer Employment Directory*.

## Young Women's Christian Association

There are varied and interesting YWCA summer opportunities throughout the United States for college students. These include positions in resident and day camps and in other program areas such as swimming and informal group activities. Interested persons should write to the Executive Director or Camp Director of the YWCA in the location in which they wish to work. A listing of YWCAs with a resident camping program is available from the Data Center, National Board YWCA, 600 Lexington Ave., New York NY 10022. See also many YWCA camps listed throughout *Summer Employment Directory*.

# Late Arrivals

## Absaroka Mountain Lodge

Located in a small valley at Cody, Wyoming, 12 miles from Yellowstone Park. Rustic mountain lodge, resort and dining room with 13 cabin units serving families. Openings for college and high school students from May 1 to October 1. Needs 2 cooks, $200-300/month; 5 maids/kitchen helpers/waitresses (girls rotate weekly for variety), $150-200/month plus tips. Training, room, board and laundry service provided. "Apply only for the period you *know* you can work. If you fulfill your working agreement by staying the period we agree to and your work and attitude are satisfactory you will receive a bonus at the end of the season. We are a small resort next to a mountain stream and we specialize in quiet and relaxation. Everyone must pull together to make it work for all of us. The ability to get along with others is essential." Send resume including SASE and dates available to work to Mike Rueffert, Manager, Box 7, Cody WY 82414; tel. 307/587-3963.

## Blue Ridge Camp

Located at Mountain City, Georgia, in the Blue Ridge Mountains. Coed residential camp for ages 6-16. "We are an athletic waterfront and cultural camp." Openings from June 18 to August 18 for college students, teachers and high school seniors. Needs 60 cabin counselors, specialists in instructing children in sports activities, waterfront activities, gymnastics, reading, math, riflery, archery, campcrafts, and arts and crafts. Salaries are $250-600/season. Provides room and board. Send for application to Camp Blue Ridge, Box 2888, Miami Beach FL 33140.

## Busch Gardens, The Dark Continent

Located at Tampa, Florida. Family entertainment center/theme park with many rides, shows and animal exhibits. OPENINGS FROM JANUARY THROUGH APRIL for college students (preferably those who are not taking classes during the winter quarter). Needs persons to work in food service, gift shops, rides, games, warehouse and as lifeguards (LSC required). Consideration must be given to the fact that Busch Gardens is open 7 days a week year 'round. You will be required to work a rotating schedule, weekends and holidays included. "Your availability and dependability are key factors in your employment with us. Each individual is responsible for his or her own transportation and accommodations. Room and board is employee's own responsibility, but there are many apartment complexes in the area. Working at the Dark Continent offers you more than just a paycheck. You are eligible for discounts on items in the gift shop and certain food items. Free admissions for yourself and costumes provided for you at no cost. We also offer a variety of company sponsored activities such as happy hours and sports activities." Equal opportunity employer/MF. For information regarding employment call the Personnel/Employment Office at (813)988-5171, ext. 307. When calling, mention SED.

## Cavell YWCA

Located at Lexington, Michigan, on Lake Huron. YWCA camp for girls ages 7-15 offering general and specialized camping program. Openings from June 15 to August 16 for college students and teachers (local applicants also for cabin counselors and instructors). "Staff required to attend one week staff training." Needs 24 cabin counselors/instructors (minimum age 18), $425-700/season; instructors in archery, nature, arts and crafts, dance, sports, waterfront, tennis, gymnastics and campcraft, $425-700/season; directors of sports, nature, arts and crafts, campcraft, performing arts and waterfront (minimum age 21), $600-900/season; 3 unit directors (minimum age 21), $600-900/season. Room and board provided. Send resume or application request. Apply by May 30 to Carol Kubiak, Camp Administrator, YWCA, 2230 Witherell St., Detroit MI 48201; tel. 313/961-9220.

## Claretknoll

Located in Peru, Illinois. Rural summer camp for developmentally disabled (mentally retarded) people ages 5-55 living in suburban Chicago; direct care focus (self help skills, behavior management, normalization) to promote functional and personal development in an outdoor environment. Openings from approximately May 21 to August 17. Needs camp director (minimum age 21), college student, teacher or local applicant preferred, $1,600-1,800/season; nurse (RN, LPN, minimum age 20), $1,400-1,600/season; cook (minimum age 20, experienced), local applicant preferred, $1,200-1,400/season; lifeguard (WSI, Red Cross LSC, minimum age 20), college student preferred, $950-1,000/season; 7 counselors (minimum age 20, experienced), college students and teachers preferred, $950-1,000/season; 7 counselor aides (minimum age 18), college students preferred, $850-900/season. Room and board provided. Apply to Jim Weise, Associate Director, Park Lawn School & Activity Center, Dept. SED, 10833 S. LaPorte, Oaklawn IL 60453; tel. 312/425-3344.

## Farley

Located in Mashpee, Massachusetts. Coed summer 4-H camp for 4-H and non-4-H members ages 10-12; program includes environmental studies, recreation, swimming, boating, arts and crafts, archery and horses. Openings for college students, teachers and high school seniors from April 1 or July 1 to September 1. Needs program director; maintenance person; specialists: 2 recreation/sports, 1 archery, 2 arts and crafts, 2 smallcraft boating, 2 swimming (WSI), 2 horseback riding, 1 environmental studies and 1 theater arts. Salary negotiable. Room and board provided. "In the case of the program director and in a limited number of other staff members, we provide space for the families of these individuals as well as provide the benefit of allowing the children of such staff members to attend the program free of charge. We are interested in creative individuals who are flexible enough to try new things to make the program work. Previous camp experience is a must whether that means as a camper or counselor. Recreation majors and active people interested in getting other people active in all facets of camping life will be highly regarded. Anyone accepting a position with us should bring any resource materials (books, notes) that might help them here to develop their area." Send resume, request application or call. Apply by July 1 to Peter Mackiewicz, Executive Director, Dept. SED, Box 97, Forestdale MA 02644; tel. 617/477-1081.

## Flaming Arrow Scout Reservation

Located on 1,100 acres at Lake Wales, in central Florida. Summer camp for Boy Scouts ages 11-17, with their troops and adult leaders. Openings for college students, teachers, and Florida residents, from June 8 to July 27. Needs program director (minimum age 21), $200-250/week; ecology director (minimum age 21), $125-150/week; 3 camp commissioners for program development (minimum age 18), $75-125/week; aquatics director (minimum age 21), $125-200/week. Room and board provided. "On-camp housing for married staff *not* provided. Applicant should have knowledge and interest of Scout camping and advancement methods. Scout uniform required. All central Florida theme parks and tourist attractions are within ½-1½ hours drive." Send for application (deadline April 15) to Walter J. Saul, Field Director, Box 24077, Tampa FL 33623; tel. 813/872-2691.

## Long Rivers Council, Inc., Boy Scouts of America
Located in Hartford, Connecticut. Boy Scout camp for boys ages 8-16. Openings for 150 college students or teachers with Boy Scout background, or married couples, from mid-June through August. Needs specialists for aquatics, archery, camping and outdoor skills, canoeing, ecology and conservation, field sports, handicrafts, horsemanship, riflery; nurses (RN); doctors; camp directors; program directors; scoutmasters; cooks; and maintenance personnel. Salaries are $400-1,200/season depending on position and experience. Room and board provided. Send "a complete resume of previous experience and a list of people to be contacted for references." Apply by April 1 to J. Moray Roy, Camping Director, Dept. SED, Boy Scouts of America, 70 Forest St., Hartford CT 06105; tel. 203/525-1112.

## Lycogis
Located in central Pennsylvania. Girl Scout Camp for ages 6-17. Openings for college students, teachers and foreign students. Precamp training June 22 to June 28; one- and two-week sessions beginning approximately June 29, concluding approximately August 17; four days postcamp work. Needs staff in the areas of camp director, assistant director, business manager, general counseling, arts and crafts specialists, ecology specialist, English riding director, waterfront staff, health supervisor, cook and kitchen people. Send for application and salary information. Apply to Director of Educational Services, Hemlock Girl Scout Council, Inc., Dept. SED, 350 Hale Ave., Harrisburg PA 17104.

## Maranatha Bible Camp
Located in North Platte. Camp with Christian atmosphere. Openings for college students and teachers from June 1 to August 3. Needs 20 maintenance workers, 5 recreation specialists, 10 kitchen helpers, and 5 lawns and wood crew. Salaries are 300-500/season. Room and board provided plus use of recreation facilities. "For a very rewarding summer in mid-America, consider Maranatha Bible Camp. Nestled in a ceder forest by a 40-acre lake, many recreational opportunities await you during your free time. Upon request, a complete packet of information including application will be sent to you. Apply by March or April to George W. Cheek, Executive Director, Dept. SED, Box 549, North Platte NE 69101; tel. 308/582-4512.

## May-Mac
Located in Tahoma, California, on Lake Tahoe. Camp for underprivileged children ages 9-14 from the San Jose area. Openings for college students from June 10 to August 31. Needs 12 counselors (minimum 1 year of college), waterfront director (minimum 1 year college), 3 arts and craft counselors (teaching pottery, leather, other craft projects); voluntary, no payment. Also needs 2 food service directors (minimum 1 year experience); tips only. Room and board provided. Send resume or application request. Apply by March 31 to Harry Brown, Program Director,

Dept. SED, Box 143, San Jose CA 95103; tel. 408/998-7400.

## Merrowvista
Located in Ossipee, New Hampshire. Christian oriented camp for girls and boys, ages 10-17, in separate sessions. Also operates Camp Miniwanca, Shelby, Michigan. Openings for college students, graduates, teachers and high school seniors for varying periods from mid-June through August. Needs workstaff (high school seniors and above); counselors (minimum age 18) with skills in archery, bicycling, canoeing, crafts, photography, riflery, sailing, sports, swimming; director (upper college and above) for waterfront, tripping, program, workstaff; food service chef/manager; nurse (RN). Salaries are based on age and experience, plus room and board, travel allowance, laundry, insurance. Apply to Ken Bryant, American Youth Foundation, Dept. SED, 3460 Hampton Ave., St. Louis MO 63139.

## Mill Mountain Playhouse
Located at Roanoke, Virginia. Summer stock with plans for fall and winter productions. Openings for college students, teachers and local applicants from June 1 to August 20. Needs 3 technical assistants (advanced or graduate level skills preferred), $80-100/week; 3 costume assistants (basic skills required), $75-90/week; 30 actors, singers and dancers, $90-125/week; technical director (graduate level skills required), $100-125/week. Room provided. "Employees buy their own meals at numerous area restaurants. Absolutely no actors, singers or dancers can be cast without personal audition. Auditions are held in Virginia and New York in March and April." Send resume by March 15 to Jim Ayers, Producer-Director, Dept. SED, Box 505, Roanoke VA 24003; tel. 703/344-2057.

## Parkway Motel
Located in Jackson, Wyoming. Thirty-nine-unit motel located in a destination summer/winter resort area serving families, senior citizens, young couples and business people. "We cater to middle and upper-middle class travelers including many foreign visitors." Openings from May to October for college students, foreign students and local applicants. Needs 4 housekeepers who are neat, clean, well-organized and able to work with others. Salaries are $3.50/hour, 6 days/week, 6 hours/day. Housing is available, board not included. "This is an ideal area for persons interested in the outdoors as we are located near Grand Teton and Yellowstone National parks. Persons applying should be willing to make a firm commitment from May through September and should be the type of individual that takes pride in doing a good job." Send letter requesting application to Tom Robbins, Dept. SED, Box 494, Jackson WY 83001; tel. 307/733-3143.

## Roger
Located in the Uinta Mountains of northern Utah, about 14.5 miles east of Kamas. Resident YMCA summer youth camp for children ages 8-14 with "special weeks, which some staff will stay for, involving diabetic children, blind persons, senior citizens, families and various weekend groups." Program provides "experience in cooperative group living in the out-of-doors, utilizing the resources of the natural surroundings to contribute to mental, physical, social and spiritual growth." Openings for college students from June 6 to August 15. Needs program director (minimum age 18, recreation-related field of study, and 2 summers camp experience, one as head counselor or program director), horse wrangler (minimum

age 13, riding instruction ability, and 2 years experience with horses), nurse (RN, must like children, camp experience preferred), $100-120/week; 15 senior counselors to participate in horseback riding, archery, nature, riflery, arts and crafts, backpacking, swimming, sports, hiking, boating, canoeing and fishing (minimum age 18, recreation-related field of study, plus desire to live and work with youngsters), $60-70/week. Room and board provided; 3 meals/day and cabin lodging situation. "Employee is responsible for own transportation. I suggest that you enjoy working with children, that you have a great love for the out-of-doors and its preservation, and be adaptable enough to live in a cabin with camp facilities at an elevation of 8000' above sea level." Send for application. Apply by May 15 to Ronald G. Mileur, Camp Director, 737 East 200 South, Salt Lake City UT 84102; tel. 801/322-1294.

## Small Valley
Located in central Pennsylvania. Girl Scout camp for ages 6-17. Openings for college students, teachers and foreign students. Precamp training approximately June 22 to June 28; one- and two-week sessions beginning approximately June 29, concluding approximately August 17; four days postcamp work. Needs staff in the areas of camp director, assistant director, business manager, general counseling, arts and crafts specialists, ecology specialist, English riding director, waterfront staff, health supervisor, cook and kitchen people. Send for application and salary information. Apply to Director of Educational Services, Hemlock Girl Scout Council, Inc., Dept. SED, 350 Hale Ave., Harrisburg PA 17104.

## Westchester Scout Camp
## Putnam Scout Camp
Located in various facilities throughout New York. Scout camps for boys ages 8-10 (Cub Scouts), boys ages 11-15 (Boy Scouts) and boys and girls ages 15-19 (Explorers); general, specialized and experimental Scouting programs (day and overnight). Openings from July 1 to August 31. Needs 15 instructors in aquatics, sports, nature, outdoor skills, college students and teachers preferred, $600-1,200/season; 3 nurses, college students, teachers and local applicants preferred, $900-1,200/season; 3 instructors in mountaineering and backpacking, college students, teachers and high school students preferred, $500-1,000/season; 20 counselors with general scouting skills, college students, teachers and high school students preferred, $400-900/season. Room and board provided. Applicant should be "motivated, interested in young people, innovative and creative. Stress on talent and commitment." Send resume or application request. Apply by February 15 to Kenneth C. D'Apice, Director of Camping, 1111 Westchester Ave., White Plains NY 10604; tel. 914/949-6180.

## YMCA of San Diego County—Northwest Branch
Located in La Jolla, California. Day camp for children ages 5-12 with 6 tennis courts, 6 racquetball courts, gym, pool, meeting rooms, weight room, nursery and offices. "The day camp is decentralized in that it uses Y facilities only occasionally. The program is intended to provide the youngster with educational and recreational experiences with their peers." Openings for college students, teachers and local applicants from June 16 to August 22. Needs day camp director (minimum age 21, must have Class 2 license to drive bus), $1,600/season; 8 day camp counselors (minimum age 18), $1,200/season. "Local housing is available in surrounding areas. Prices range from $150-500/month for an apartment.

Apartment and/or house sharing is common. Come prepared for a very full and active summer. Working hours will be spent dealing with the kids. The beach, mountains, baseball, concerts, Las Vegas are all off-hour options which make San Diego an ideal spot to sport a summer." Send resume, write for application or telephone. Apply by May 9 to Keith Ryan, Program Director, 8355 Cliffridge Ave., La Jolla CA 92037; tel. 714/453-3483.

## Teton Valley Ranch Camps

Located in Jackson Hole, Kelly. Summer camp for boys and girls ages 10-17. Separate seasons for boys and girls. Boys' season June 10 to July 23; girls' season July 20 to August 25. Program of horseback riding and backpacking with extensive in-camp program in Jackson Hole. Needs 12 cabin counselors, season only, college students, teachers, high school seniors, foreign students, local applicants, $250-350; 2 dishwashers, local applicants, high school seniors preferred, $350 plus/season; 1 maintenance and clean-up person, college student, high school senior, foreign student, local applicant acceptable, $500/season; laundry person ($450 plus/summer), 1 crafts counselor ($500 plus/summer), local applicants, college students, teachers, foreign students all acceptable; 4 riflery/archery counselors (pay varies with experience), college students and teachers preferred; 1 ham radio operator, pay varies, college students, teachers, local applicants acceptable. Room and board provided. Send resume. Apply by April 1 to Stuart Palmer or Matt Montagne, Directors, Teton Valley Ranch Camps, Dept. SED, Box 8, Kelly WY 83011; tel. 307/733-2958.

# – Internships and Work/Learn –

## Allentown & Sacred Heart Hospital Center

Located in Allentown. Hospital work-study program. Openings for college students from June 2 to August 22. Positions available are in anesthesia, dietary, educational development, engineering, financial services, management engineering, medical library, microbiology, nursing, pastoral care, pharmacy, physical therapy, respiratory therapy, surgery, utilization review, volunteer services. Salaries are $145/week. Room and board provided for out-of-region students. "Students must be actively pursuing a prescribed course of study at a recognized educational institution. Each department defines the minimum level of education and experience required. Because admission to the program is highly competitive, application is recommended only to students who meet all admission criteria. Each applicant must complete the work-study application form, submit a transcript of grades and provide a narrative stating goals and expectations for the program." An equal opportunity employer. Send for application (March 15 deadline) to Susan Gingrich Knapp, Educational Coordinator, Educational Development, Allentown and Sacred Heart Hospital Center, Allentown PA 18105; tel. 215/821-2026.

## Hinton Rural Life Center

Located in Hayesville, North Carolina. Internships offered in volunteer and service training. Teams of two or more interns work in church programs related to cooperative parishes of small membership churches, usually in town and country settings. Applicants must have completed freshman year of college. Internships located in cooperative parishes in the southeastern United States. Work for seven weeks beginning May 30. Intern receives room and board, all expenses related to the program, and a stipend of $500 for the seven-week period. Maximum of 10 interns accepted. Deadline for application: March 1. Request application forms from VAST, Box 27, Hayesville NC 28904.

## The Psychiatric Institute of Washington, DC

Located in Washington DC. Offers summer mental health internships. The program provides psychiatric experience for students interested in a mental health career. Interns spend 40 hours/week in clinical areas and class. The intern's duties most closely resemble those of a psychiatric aide. Interns are expected to participate actively in the treatment program. Internship lasts ten weeks, beginning the first Monday of June. Applicants must be entering the senior year of undergraduate school or be a beginning level graduate student interested in pursuing a mental health career. A course in abnormal psychology is a prerequisite. Students must be able to work both day and evening shifts and alternate weekends. Openings for 10 interns; pays $1,060 for the ten-week period. Deadline for application: March 1. To apply, an application form, which can be obtained from the Psychiatric Institute, must be completed and returned, along with three letters of reference. Applications are accepted beginning January 1.

Apply to: Mark Schneider, RN, MN Coordinator, Summer Mental Health Internship, The Psychiatric Institute of Washington, 4460 MacArthur Blvd. NW, Washington DC 20007.

## Quebec-Labrador Foundation, Inc.,

Located in northern Maine and New Brunswick, Quebec, Newfoundland and Labrador in Canada. Social service and educational programs. Programs in three categories: community workers, environmental education teachers, outdoor leadership teachers. Needs men and women over 17 years of age, both married and single. Community workers: includes community development, recreation skills in social work, adult education, music, art, swimming or physical education. Environmental education teachers: background in natural sciences and/or environmental education. Outdoor leadership teachers: background in outdoor skills, camping, canoeing, swimming, sailing. Some salaried positions for highly qualified candidates in leadership roles. Apply by May 1 to Judy Henderson, Community Workers; Tom Horn, Outdoor Leadership and Environmental Education Teachers, The Quebec-Labrador Foundation, Inc., Mill Rd., Ipswich MA 01938.

## Rhode Island Intern/Volunteer Consortium

Located in Providence, Rhode Island. College work-study and volunteer internship placements. The Consortium is a clearinghouse capable of placing as many as 500 individuals in over 70 career-related areas statewide in Rhode Island. Paid placements are restricted to recipients of college work-study awards which can be earned in Rhode Island. While the program is not restricted to Rhode Island residents the Consortium makes no guarantees regarding housing. Approximate dates of placements are May 1 to September 1. Duration is set by the individual's academic institution and may begin as late as July 1. Salary is variable not only to the position but also the salary scale of the individual's academic institutional work-study pay scale. Range $2.65-$3.75/hour. No official deadline for applications but most placements begin June 1. Application procedures: 1) Write to Consortium requesting application, 2) return application and documentation of work-study award to Consortium, 3) include description of field of interest or type of position desired, 4) contact agencies referred by Consortium, 5) upon return to RI finalize placement with Consortium program planner. Apply to: Charles Totoro, Program Planner, Rhode Island Intern/Volunteer Consortium, 150 Washington St., Providence RI 02903.

## Student Conservation Association

Located in Charlestown, New Hampshire. Internships offered to college-age individuals at a number of national parks, national forests, and private and local land management and natural resource agencies. Also programs for high school-age individuals. These are *volunteer* positions—over 300 for college program, over 300 for high school program. Specific skills vary for college program. General requirements are college attendance or at least one year out of high school. For high school program applicants must be 16 years old or older. Graduating seniors may apply for high school program. Internship location may be at any number of points throughout the United States. Duration of programs: 10-12 weeks, college; 3-4 weeks, high school. Deadline for application for summer programs: March 1. Request information on deadlines for spring and other off-season programs. Contact the Student Conservation Association, Box 550, Charlestown NH 03603.

## Twin City Area Urban Corps

Located in St. Paul. Offers 600 internships (for Minneapolis and St. Paul, Hennepin and Ramsey counties) in all areas of government service such as law, engineering, planning and development, research, school systems, metropolitan council, state government of Minneapolis; about 85 nonprofit agencies. 10 week minimum commitment. The four types of programs available are: work/study, $3.80/hour for undergraduates, $5/hour for graduates; agency funds or special grants; and educational stipend (must be enrolled at least part-time in post-secondary educational institution), $30/week for part-timers, $60/week for full-timers, (applied to amount of credits). Minimum 10 week commitment. Good reasonable housing available; information can be found through University of Minnesota information office. "Out-of-state students should apply early, by the end of March, so they can get in the program. Chances of getting a position that you would prefer is better if you apply early. Send for application and listing of available positions or call. Apply to Ron Guilfoile, Director, Twin City Area Urban Corps, Dept. SED, Room 1430 City Hall Annex, 25 W. 4th St., St. Paul MN 55102; tel. 612/298-4376.

# If You Are Not a U.S. Citizen

If you are not a U.S. citizen, you can still apply for any job in the *Summer Employment Directory* unless the employer states otherwise. Some employers specify in their listings that they would like to hire foreign college and university students. If an employer in the U.S. offers you a job, however, be sure that he is willing to obtain and file the correct forms *before* you come to the U.S. so that you will be able to get a work permit when you arrive to take the job.

The paperwork involved is long and time consuming, but you will not be able to come to the U.S. on a visitor's visa and get authorization to work *after* you arrive. Regulations are enforced strictly, and certification must be shown on your visa, which will be validated upon arrival in the United States, *before* your employer can allow you to begin work for him.

When an employer decides to hire you, he must obtain Form 1-129B (Petition to Classify Nonimmigrant as Temporary Worker or Trainee) and an H-2 Temporary Alien Labor Certification from his local Department of Immigration and Naturalization office. He must also obtain Form MA 7-50B (Job Offer for Alien Employment) from either the same department or the Bureau of State Employment Services.

The H-2 classification is given to an individual coming into the U.S. for a temporary period to perform a service or labor. An individual with exceptional abilities—for example, a professional athlete or entertainer—receives an H-1 classification. Trainees are classified as H-3.

Form MA 7-50B is completed and filed with the Bureau of State Employment Services, to be processed and returned to the employer. When the form is received, he submits it, together with Form 1-129B and the H-2 Temporary Alien Labor Certification, to the U.S. Department of Immigration office having jurisdiction in the area in which you will work. There is a $25 fee for filing a temporary visa petition.

Your employer must have completed and filed these forms before you arrive in the U.S. You have two responsibilities: First, obtain a passport before leaving for the U.S.; second, upon your arrival in the U.S., have Form I-94 (Arrival-Departure Record) endorsed by the immigration officer to show the period of authorized stay. Form I-94 is your work permit; a summer employer cannot hire you legally unless you can show authorization to work stamped or endorsed on this form. The properly validated visa will then also show the H-2 nonimmigrant classification. For more information, contact your nearest U.S. consulate.

If you are Canadian, you will not need a passport to enter the U.S. from a place within the Western Hemisphere. You will, however, need to comply with all other regulations.

These strict regulations are intended to give citizens of the U.S. the first chance at jobs. Therefore, the number of temporary summer workers admitted to the United States from other countries depends a great deal on the level of unemployment in the U.S. at that time. When unemployment is high, there will be few permits to work granted; the policy is relaxed as unemployment decreases. If you write to an employer listed in this book, be certain that the employer also understands the regulations involved and that he is willing to take the time to do the paperwork.

Persons who attend school in the United States but who are citizens of another country would usually be classified F-1 nonimmigrant students. An F-1 nonimmigrant who would like to take a summer job in the U.S. should check with his local Department of Immigration and Naturalization office to find out how to obtain certification for work.

*SED* lists a few jobs in Canada. As in the U.S., foreign workers are permitted to enter Canada to take seasonal jobs only when the jobs cannot be filled by Canadians. The number of aliens given authorization to work varies somewhat from province to province.

A job offer from a Canadian employer must be presented by the employer to the nearest Canada Employment Centre (CEC) office. If the CEC agrees that no qualified Canadian resident is available to fill the job, the Canadian office nearest your home will be notified. That office will contact you and ask you to come in to be interviewed and to apply for Employment Authorization. The interview will determine if you are qualified for the job and if you may enter Canada temporarily under Canada's immigration laws.

If your application is approved, you will receive a visa and an Employment Authorization to cover the particular job for a predetermined amount of time.

The Employment Authorization must be issued before you enter Canada; you will not be allowed to enter Canada to look for a job. In all but a few exceptional cases, persons who have entered Canada already on a visitor's visa will not be able to obtain authorization to work. For more information, contact the nearest Canadian consulate.

British Universities North America Club (BUNAC) administers a student exchange program between Britain and the United States that has been approved by the U.S. Department of State. For details on jobs write to BUNAC, 30/31 Store Street, London WC1E 7BS, England. The telephone number is 01-637-7686.

Camp America, another exchange program recognized by the U.S. Department of State, arranges for European and Australian university students to work as counselors in U.S. summer camps. For more information, write Camp America, 37 Queen's Gate, London SW7 5HR, England, or telephone 01-589-3223.